The LNICST series publishes ICST's conferences, symposia and workshops.
LNICST reports state-of-the-art results in areas related to the scope of the Institute.
The type of material published includes

- Proceedings (published in time for the respective event)
- Other edited monographs (such as project reports or invited volumes)

LNICST topics span the following areas:

- General Computer Science
- E-Economy
- E-Medicine
- Knowledge Management
- Multimedia
- Operations, Management and Policy
- Social Informatics
- Systems

Shancang Li · Shanshan Zhao · Muddesar Iqbal
Editors

Broadband Communications, Networks, and Systems

15th EAI International Conference, BROADNETS 2024
Cardiff, UK, December 14–15, 2024
Proceedings

 Springer

Editors
Shancang Li
Cardiff University
Cardiff, UK

Shanshan Zhao
University of the West of England
Bristol, UK

Muddesar Iqbal
Prince Sultan University
Riyadh, Saudi Arabia

ISSN 1867-8211 ISSN 1867-822X (electronic)
Lecture Notes of the Institute for Computer Sciences, Social Informatics
and Telecommunications Engineering
ISBN 978-3-032-14349-5 ISBN 978-3-032-14350-1 (eBook)
https://doi.org/10.1007/978-3-032-14350-1

Preface

We are pleased to present the proceedings of the 2024 International Conference on Broadband Communications and Networks (BROADNETS 2024). Hosted by Cardiff University, Cardiff, UK, the conference was held from December 14-15, 2024. This conference convened leading experts from across the globe to explore the dynamic landscape of 5G-enabled digital societies, focusing on the theme, "Advancing Wireless Communications for the Internet of Everything."

BROADNETS 2024 featured a robust technical program comprising 10 full and 4 short papers, covering key topics including 5G/6G systems, IoT smart systems, cloud, fog computing, vehicle network, smart city, digital twin, data privacy and integrity, etc. These papers were selected from 36 submissions. Each submission was reviewed following a double-blind process with a minimum of 3 reviews per paper. Beyond the paper presentations, the program included two keynote addresses, one invited talk, and two specialized workshops. Keynote speeches were delivered by Trung Q. Duong, on 6G Digital Twin: A Joint Computing and Communications Design and Muddesar Iqbal from Wireless Network Innovations.

The success of BROADNETS 2024 was made possible by the invaluable contributions of our steering committee, including Shancang Li, Shanshan Zhao, and Muddesar Iqbal. We extend our sincere gratitude for their unwavering support and guidance. The organizing committee, led by our esteemed Technical Program Committee Co-Chairs, Honghao Gao and Xinheng Wang, ensured a rigorous peer-review process and a high-quality program. We also acknowledge the dedication of Conference Managers Timea Madarova and Ly Dao, and express our appreciation to all authors who contributed to the conference.

We are confident that BROADNETS continues to serve as a vital platform for researchers, developers, and practitioners to exchange ideas and advance the field of wireless communications and networking. We anticipate that future editions of BROAD-NETS will build upon the momentum established in 2024, fostering further innovation and collaboration.

Shancang Li
Shanshan Zhao
Muddesar Iqbal

Organization

Steering Committee

Prosanta Gope								University of Sheffield, UK

Organizing Committee

General Chair

Shancang Li								Cardiff University, UK

General Co-Chairs

Xiaohu Li								Xi'an Jiaotong University, China

Program Chairs

Shanshan Zhao							University of the West of England, UK
Muddesar Iqbal							Prince Sultan University, Saudi Arabia

TPC Chair

Honghao Gao								Shanghai University, China

Sponsorship and Exhibit Chair

Muddesar Iqbal							Prince Sultan University, Saudi Arabia

Local Chair

Neetesh Saxena							Cardiff University, UK

Workshops Chair

Thomas Tan   Edinburgh Napier University, UK

Publications Chair

Sarah Bin Hulayyil   Cardiff University, UK

Publicity & Social Media Chair

Yifan Liu   Cardiff University, UK

Web Chair

Shanshan Zhao   UWE Bristol, UK

Posters and PhD Track Chair

Xueyi Wang   Cardiff University, UK

Panels Chair

Qindong Sun   Xi'an Jiaotong University, China

Technical Program Committee

Alessandro Bruni   University of Copenhagen, Denmark
Ashad Kabir   Charles Sturt University, Australia
Chao Shen   Xi'an Jiaotong University, China
Chi Lin   Dalian University of Technology, China
Chiara Pero   University of Salerno, Italy
Chong Yu   University of Nebraska-Lincoln, USA
Ernest Foo   Griffith University, Australia
Fariza Sabrina   Central Queensland University, Australia
Fee Hao   ShaanxiNormal University, China

Guhan Zheng	Lancaster University, UK
Guohui Ding	Shenyang Aerospace University, China
Hafizah Mansor	International Islamic University Malaysia, Malaysia
Hamid Ali Abed Al-Asadi	Iraq University College, Iraq
Han Qi	Shenyang Aerospace University, China
Harald Gjermundrod	University of Nicosia, Cyprus
Hasan Jamil	University of Idaho, USA
Jia Hu	University of Exeter, UK
Jun Shen	University of Wollongong, Australia
Jun Zheng	Huazhong University of Science and Technology, China
Junggab Son	University of Nevada Las Vegas, USA
Li Xu	Old Dominion University, USA
Ling Li	Old Dominion University, USA
Muddesar Iqbal	Prince Sultan University, Saudi Arabia
Qiang Zhang	Dalian University of Technology, China
Qiangsheng Hua	Huazhong University of Science and Technology, China
Raja Naeem Akram	University of Aberdeen, UK
Ramadan Elaiess	University of Benghazi, Libya
Shahid Mumtaz	Nottingham Trent University, UK
Shancang Li	Cardiff University, UK
Thomas Tan	Edinburgh Napier University, UK
Xinheng Wang	Xi'an Jiaotong-Liverpool University, China
Yang Xiao	University of Kentucky, USA
Yifan Liu	Cardiff University, UK

Contents

Probabilistic Packet Scheduler for Multipath Data Transfer in Highly Variable Delay Conditions

Michał Morawski$^{(\boxtimes)}$ and Przemysław Ignaciuk

Lodz University of Technology, Lodz, Poland
{michal.morawski,przemyslaw.ignaciuk}@p.lodz.pl

Abstract. Multipath communication has emerged as a feasible alternative to expensive quality-of-service networking solutions. Despite its numerous advantages, multipath transport protocols suffer from increased protocol delay and jitter, which arise from path heterogeneity. The current algorithms that manage the data distribution across the paths rely on assessing the most recent channel characteristics. Given the time lag between a path allocation decision and the actual effects experienced by the sender, the conventional approaches are susceptible to temporal fluctuations of transmission delays. In this work, it is shown how to apply both historical and current information regarding the receiver's state to establish a more responsive connectivity. In contrast to the standard scheduling logic, the receiver rewards or penalizes the paths irrespective of the channel-specific metrics, creating a competitive environment. As a result, a swift response to the variations in networking conditions is obtained and surges in protocol delay caused by path deterioration and Head-of-Line blocking are alleviated.

Keywords: Multipath Communication · Real-time Applications · Path Scheduling

1 Introduction

A majority of business and entertainment services rely on dependable and efficient networking. In addition to the standard data exchange, modern applications necessitate prompt responses from the peers. This requirement is particularly critical in machine-to-machine communications, where the network needs to accommodate the feedback from a remote agent or in human-interactive processes [1]. Such applications avoid buffering, as it introduces additional delays. To address those challenges, various network-layer approaches have been proposed, such as differentiated [2] and integrated [3] services architectures. While successfully deployed, they come with notable drawbacks, including high costs, limited applicability in public access networks (owing to network neutrality regulations [4]), and susceptibility to the failures in the first and last mile.

As an alternative to enhancing the quality of experience, the simultaneous use of multiple interfaces and transmission paths has been considered. By adopting this approach, the communicating peers can capitalize on the path independence, which reduces

S. Li et al. (Eds.): BROADNETS 2024, LNICST 674, pp. 1–13, 2026.
https://doi.org/10.1007/978-3-032-14350-1_1

the likelihood of simultaneous congestion or failure across all the connections. Historically, it has been regarded as a niche due to the high costs associated with communication hardware. However, recent reductions in the prices of network interfaces—such as Ethernet, WiFi, and cellular technologies—as well as lower provider fees have led to the widespread installation of multiple interfaces in smartphones, laptops, servers, and Internet of Things (IoT) devices by default.

Incorporating additional interfaces, by itself, neither enhances data rates nor resolves issues related to communication quality. Default settings of the leading operating systems disallow multiple interfaces for the same application to be used simultaneously. Even if this restriction is relaxed, the design of the existing network protocols precludes bonding interfaces at the transport layer because peers are identified by the tuple (protocol, address, port). For these reasons, new protocols that support multipath transmission have been developed [5]. The initial implementations of these protocols faced challenges in public networks originating from insufficient application support and ubiquitous firewall incompatibilities. However, the current solutions can be readily implemented without such constraints. Among these, the most prominent protocols include Multipath TCP (MPTCP) [6, 7], which is embedded in modern Linux kernels, and Multipath QUIC (MPQUIC) [8], which is implemented at the application layer, i.e., without operating system restrictions.

This paper proposes a new strategy for sending a data stream simultaneously via multiple paths. The approach is implemented in the path scheduler module, which, contrary to solutions developed so far, neglects path properties. Instead, it relies on the information embedded in acknowledgments, typically used by congestion controllers. Thus, no receiver-side changes in the protocol stack are required. The scheduler itself distributes packets randomly based on probabilities computed thanks to these acknowledgments. The presented solution is general and can be applied to any multipath protocol, particularly in MPTCP and MPQUIC. It performs similarly to the standard solution in nominal conditions, yet it responds faster when a path deteriorates. The strategy is implemented and tested using public networks. Hence, the presented results should be considered credible.

2 Multipath Protocol Architectures

Both MPTCP and MPQUIC protocols share a similar design, consisting of three modules in MPQUIC and two in MPTCP, each serving distinct purposes and modes of operation (Fig. 1). Although these protocol stack components were developed independently, they interact in a complex way. The network, as well as the sender and receiver applications, also influence the data transfer process.

The protocols function as follows: after establishing the first channel between the peers through an arbitrarily chosen pair of interfaces, the path manager creates or tears down additional paths. Its activity is only loosely connected to the actual data transfer. The application threads insert data into sender-side buffers. In MPQUIC, the stream scheduler aggregates the application-defined substreams into a single data transmission pipe. In contrast, MPTCP is designed to handle a single stream transfer, rendering a stream scheduler unnecessary. The congestion controller then determines the data transmission rate. In MPQUIC, a single congestion controller governs the rate for the assembled stream. When multiple paths are available, the path scheduler selects the most appropriate path for transmitting a specific data segment. In MPTCP, the congestion controller manages both stream pacing and path congestion. Thus, the underlying path scheduling algorithm plays a critical role in determining transmission quality in multipath scenarios.

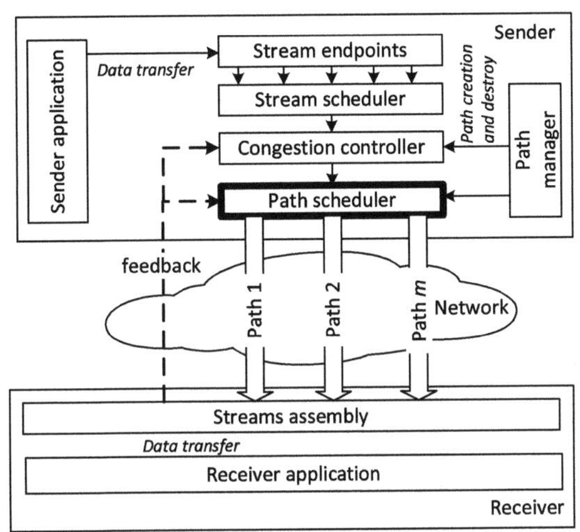

Fig. 1. MPQUIC and MPTCP architecture with the path scheduling module emphasized. The stream scheduler is exclusive to the MPQUIC suite.

3   Delay Analysis

The delay perceived by the communicating peers (at the application level) encompasses the following sources:

1. Application-related delay, which is the time the application spends preparing or processing the data. During this time, the transferred data is temporarily stored in buffers. This time depends only on the algorithms' implementation in the application, ciphering methods, etc., and is outside of the interest of the communication protocol design.
2. Path delay, also known as SRTT (Smoothed Round Trip Time), which is a sum of propagation and transmission delays along the links within each path. The path delay grows if the routers must queue packets to avoid drops. The instantaneous value of path delay depends on the activity of multiple users on the Internet.
3. Retransmission time, which is necessary to correct errors induced by packet loss and is responsible for spikes in the protocol delay.

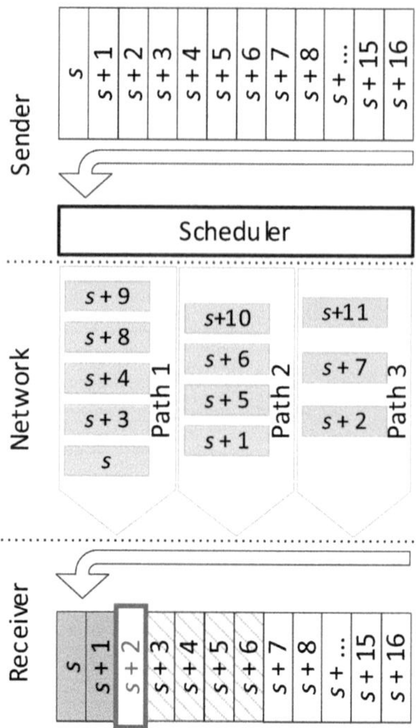

Fig. 2. HoL blocking phenomenon in a three-channel transmission. Solid rectangles at the receiver – data ready for retrieval by the application (acknowledged both at the path and transport level), slanted rectangles – data acknowledged only at the path level, hollow rectangles – inflight data. HoL blocking: missing segment $s + 2$ prevents stream reconstruction, even though the subsequent segments $s + 3, \ldots, s + 6$ have already been delivered to the receiver.

4. Head-of-line (HoL) blocking, concerning the situation when an application requires the data to be received precisely in the same order as they are sent, as commonly required in contemporary networking. The HoL blocking phenomenon [9, 10] is illustrated in Fig. 2. When a transmission through a path experiences intensity degradation (Path 3 in Fig. 2), newly arriving segments are not allowed into the receiver application endpoint to preserve the coherence of the application stream. Instead, they are kept in the buffer (slanted segments) until the missing data (the red packet) arrives. HoL blocking thus aggravates the delay variability observed by the application. The increase of SRTT on a single path intensifies the HoL blocking. The peer buffer temporarily absorbs the growing queue, increasing the application's latency. HoL blocking time can be even one order of magnitude larger than SRTT [10].

4   Path Schedulers – State of the Art

The default scheduler in MPTCP and MPQUIC forces data to be sent using the shortest SRTT path until this path is not blocked by *cwnd* exhaustion. The default scheduler maximizes throughput, but by design, it leads to an increase in HoL blocking. Thus, other algorithms need to be developed for time-sensitive applications. Most of the research concerning algorithms of data allocation on the paths concentrates on popular MPTCP protocol [6, 7]. However, it turns out that the design principles of MPQUIC [8], like multistream support or retransmission using arbitrary paths, make it better suited to industry-related real-time applications. As in the case of congestion controllers, path schedulers for MPTCP and MPQUIC share the same algorithms.

A comprehensive review of state-of-the-art schedulers in the MPTCP and MPQUIC framework has been provided in [11, 12]. In the context of this work, particular attention attracts BLEST (BLocking ESTimation) [13] and ECF (Earliest Completed First) [14], which throttle the fastest path by estimating the degree of HoL blocking. An interesting approach that overcomes the deficiency of BLEST and ECF for bursty traffic is the Peecaboo scheduler [15], which employs machine learning and an evolutionarily stable strategy to obtain an optimal split ratio. A similar approach has recently been adopted by 4D-MAP [16] and MARS [17] schedulers. In turn, a freshly developed synchronizing scheduler [18] tries to proactively find the optimal allocation of the data on particular paths.

Other works target specific scenarios, e.g., Tetris [19], which combines path and stream MPQUIC schedulers, multimedia-related [20], or priority-based ones [21]. However, cross-module approaches are outside the scope of this work.

In principle, the schedulers discussed in this paper can be supplemented by Forward Error Control (FEC) [22], or similar mechanisms [23], which allows for recovering delayed segments without retransmission. However, this substantially increases network-related demands because the scheduler algorithm must be executed at least once for every expedited packet.

5   Proposed Approach

A detailed observation of the transmission characteristics allows for recognizing the following sources of the protocol delay increase and jitter:

The SRTT Variability. The sender has a limited impact on this value. It depends on the technologies involved, the number of hops, and the activity of other users. However, the aggressiveness of the congestion control algorithm may indirectly aggravate SRTT by inducing buffer bloat phenomenon [24].

Number of Drops and Retransmissions. If the congestion control algorithm detects a packet drop, it must resend it. If it is not a spurious event, the retransmission results in a sudden delay spike. Otherwise, it affects throughput, only. However, improper activity of both the congestion controller and path scheduler may increase the drop ratio, thus causing a surplus delay.

Head-of-Line Blocking. If a path scheduler misallocates packets, the receiver queue experiences gaps, suspending the application until the gaps are filled (Fig. 2). HoL blocking is the path scheduler's exclusive responsibility and the primary source of the protocol delay increase.

As HoL blocking is the primary source of the delay in multipath communication, particular attention should be directed to constrain this phenomenon. To do so, most existing path schedulers try to assess the current path properties and make the corresponding judgments on their basis. However, the information concerning a path is outdated due to the non-negligible time between sending a packet and receiving the acknowledgment. Moreover, the relation between the path properties (SRTT, *inflight* data, drop ratio) and HoL blocking is not apparent. Thus, instead of relying on volatile information, we propose to use direct feedback from the receiver's queue state. In our proposal, all the packets are spread randomly on the paths, but the receiver controls the probability of using a given channel.

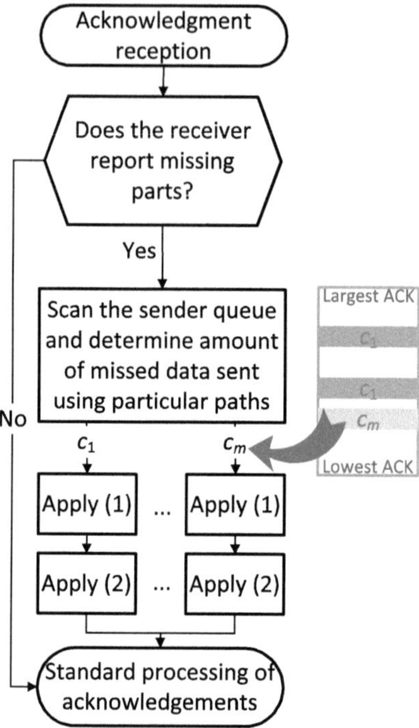

Fig. 3. Algorithm of receiver state analysis used by the probabilistic scheduler.

The probabilistic scheduler performs the following actions illustrated in Fig. 3:

1. Initially, no information concerning both the receiver queue and paths is available. Hence, the packets are sent randomly using each path i with probability $p_i = 1/m$, where m is the number of established paths.
2. After receiving the standard acknowledgment frame (right side of Fig. 3), the path scheduler analyses its content.
   (a) It computes the receiver queue length $q = \text{LargestACK} - \text{LowestACK} + 1$, where LargestACK is the sequence number of the last packet that arrived at the receiver, and LowestACK is the first packet not yet directed to the receiver application.

(b) The packets arrive at the peer in the order that depends on the temporal SRTT in each path. If the order at the receiver follows the sender, or the frame does not contain the most recent information, go to the point 3.

(c) Otherwise, the acknowledgment of the last received packets includes the information concerning the gaps (see Fig. 2). It is a similar mechanism as in the SACK TCP option [25] widely used today. Then, the gaps are mapped to the paths the packets were initially sent and summed up, obtaining quantities $c_1, ..., c_m$ (Fig. 3).

(d) For each path i, the probability of using the path is reduced as:

$$p_i \leftarrow p_i \frac{q - c_i}{q}. \tag{1}$$

(e) To preserve the requirement $\sum_{i=1}^{m} p_i = 1$, probabilities are scaled as:

$$p_i \leftarrow \frac{p_i}{\sum_{j=1}^{m} p_j}. \tag{2}$$

3. The acknowledgment frame is processed in the standard manner, i.e., it removes acknowledged packets from the sender queue and triggers the retransmissions, if necessary.

4. During the attempt to send the next packet, the path scheduler generates the random number $r_i \in [0, p_i)$ for each path.

5. The path scheduler selects path j, corresponding to $r_j = \max_i r_i$.

The path schedulers closely cooperate with congestion controllers, which control the adjustment of flow rates and the recovery of lost packets. Such cooperation falls outside the scope of this study. Any standard congestion controller [21, 22] can be paired with the proposed solution.

6 Evaluation

The designed scheduler has been implemented and verified in a real networking environment using the test setup illustrated in Fig. 4. The protocol stack at the peers has been built using de Coninck code [26]. The client device is equipped with two communication interfaces. Independent bottlenecks are found at the cellular and DSL (Digital Subscriber Line) links, respectively. The segments sent through the DSL connection reach the destination in 8 hops, and those conveyed by LTE in 16–18 hops, depending on the Internet Service Provider. The bottleneck capacity for either channel equals ~8 Mbps. Various agents (MS Windows-based laptops, tablets, Ubuntu laptops, Raspberry Pi) and servers (Windows Server, Ubuntu Server high-end computers) have been tested, giving similar results. The outcomes reported in Sect. 7 reflect the case of an MS Windows tablet communicating with a Windows Server 2019 server machine. Also, two distinct mobile network providers have been tested with no apparent measurement discrepancy. The tests have been performed on different days and at various times of the day (rush and wee hours). For the sake of presentation, the following cases have been selected:

- Best-effort (network-restricted) transmission as a reference.

- Constrained (application-restricted) transmission, wherein the first 5 s, the application demands are within the single path capacity (5 Mbps), and for $t > 5$ s, both paths must be engaged (10 Mbps).

All other modules and system settings have been left to the default.

A single test comprises four runs: 1) best-effort traffic, default scheduler, 2) best-effort traffic, competitive scheduler, 3) constrained traffic, default scheduler, and finally, 4) constrained traffic, competitive scheduler. Subsequent runs were performed immediately after completing a previous one, which increases the probability that the network remains in a similar state. 40 tests were conducted on different days and hours.

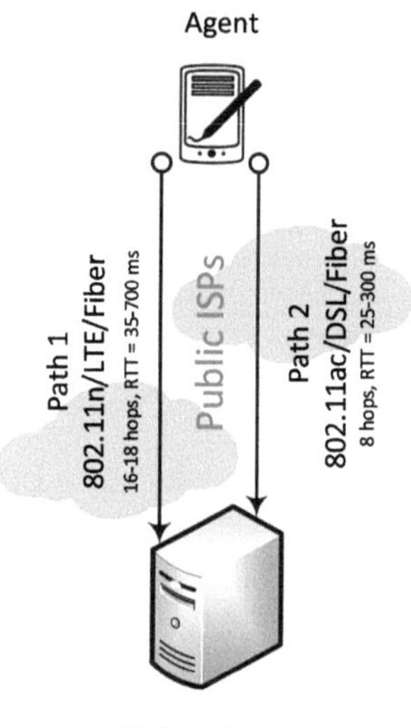

Fig. 4. Experimental setup. The first mile – wireless links operating in different bands. Internet Service Providers are unrelated to each other. The paths have a bottleneck on the DSL and LTE links. Agents include low-end Raspberry Pi, Ubuntu-based Linux, and Windows-10 powered laptops. The server includes both Linux and Windows 2019 Server high-end machines.

7   Results

Although the presented solution is not intended for best-effort transmission, where the network constrains the throughput and induces delays, it is necessary to conduct tests for such the case because most users do not want to bother selecting the transmission stack modules according to detailed application demands. Hence, any new scheduler must promise properties similar to the default solution for best-effort traffic. As evidenced in Fig. 5 – which presents the typical signal evolution in such cases – this requirement is achieved. Usually, the application of the competitive scheduler even increases the effective throughput because we have observed substantially lower drop incidents. Particular attention should be put to the lower graph, where the evolution of probabilities computed by the proposed algorithm is sketched.

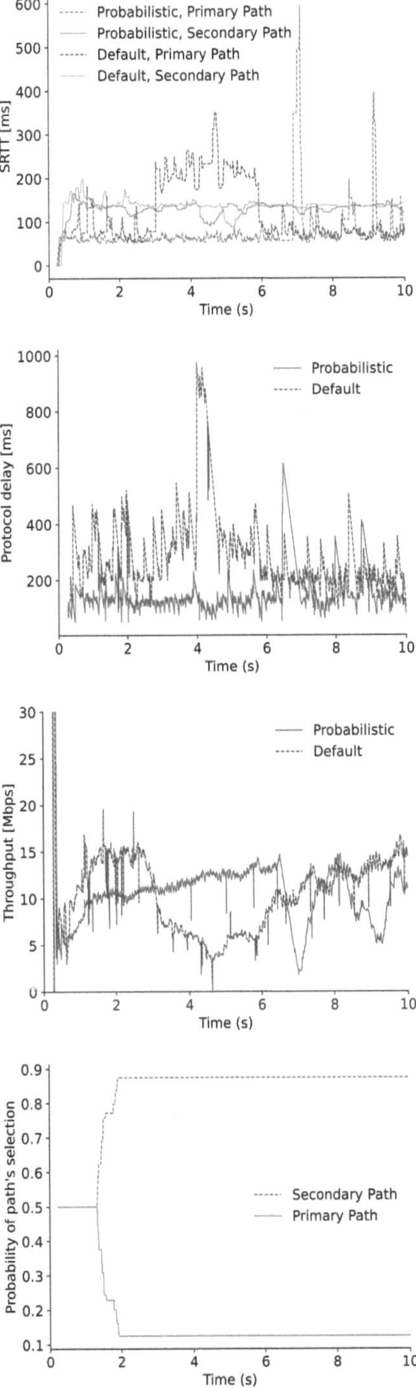

Fig. 5. Typical transmission properties observed for probabilistic and default schedulers for best effort traffic.

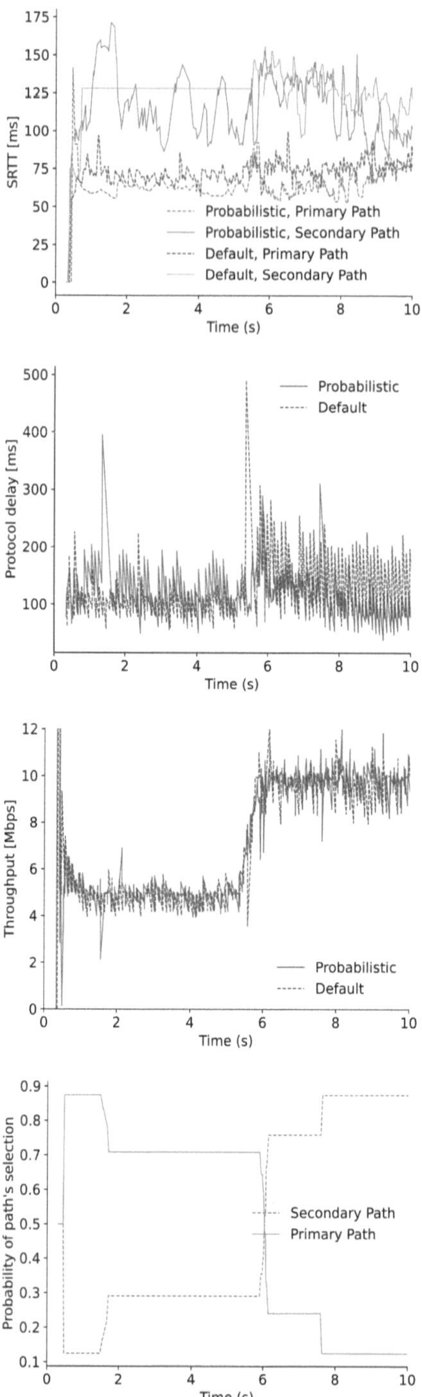

Fig. 6. Typical variability of the transmission properties observed for probabilistic and default schedulers for the application-restricted traffic.

The typical evolution of application-restricted transmission is illustrated in Fig. 6. For the first 5 s, the default scheduler engages only one path. Hence, the path delay equals protocol delay. However, if the second path must be employed, in the case of the default scheduler, the protocol delay increases substantially due to the HoL blocking. In the case of the probabilistic scheduler, the protocol delay remains unchanged, which was the desirable outcome. The perturbations mentioned above do not affect the throughput. As discussed above, particular attention should be focused on the lower graph, especially around $t = 6$ s, when the probabilistic scheduler changes its preferences as an effect of perturbations on the primary path.

Regrettably, we have noticed that during all the runs, the default congestion controller (OLIA) generates spurious retransmissions, decreasing the throughput but not impacting protocol delay. However, their impact on the transmission is low because the problem concerns <1% of packets. One should notice that the observed protocol delay is beneficially lower for the probabilistic scheduler, even for best-effort traffic.

Although the assumed goals have been accomplished, further work is necessary in two directions. First, congestion controllers should be modified to avoid spurious retransmissions that are too frequent. Second, the modification of probabilities (lower graphs in Fig. 5 and Fig. 6) are too fast. Such sudden changes may be undesirable in some cases, e.g., due to the likelihood of overshooting. Therefore, we plan to modify formulae (1).

8 Conclusion

The paper introduces a probabilistic scheduler for multipath communication systems implemented within the MPQUIC protocol framework. Unlike conventional approaches, it does not rely on path characteristics such as SRTT or the volume of *in-flight* data to infer the receiver's state. Instead, it employs direct feedback from the receiver. Scheduling decisions are made through competition among involved paths, where the likelihood of a path being selected is inversely proportional to its backlog. This approach allows the data to be delivered to the receiver application faster than with the default solution, thereby enhancing the quality of user experience. Moreover, as feedback is derived from any acknowledgment received at any interface, the scheduler's performance is only marginally affected by lost or delayed feedback. Its implementation is straightforward and imposes a low computational overhead.

Acknowledgments. This work has been performed in the framework of a project "Robust control solutions for multi-channel networked flows" no. 2021/41/B/ST7/00108 financed by the National Science Centre, Poland.

References

1. Morawski, M., Ignaciuk, P.: Reducing impact of network induced perturbations in remote control systems. Control Eng. Prac. **55**(10), 127–138 (2016)
2. Blake S., et al.: An Architecture for differentiated services, RFC 2475, (1998)

3. Bernet Y., et al.: A Framework for Integrated Services Operation over diffserv networks, RFC 2998, (2000)
4. Nguyen, V., Mohammed, D., Omar, M., Dean, P.: Net neutrality around the globe: a survey. In: 3rd International Conference on Information and Computer Technologies (ICICT), pp. 480–488 (2020)
5. Xu, C., Zhao, J., Muntean, G.: Congestion control design for multipath transport protocols: a survey. IEEE Comm. Surv. Tut. **18**(4), 2948–2969 (2016)
6. Ford A., et al.: TCP extensions for multipath operation with multiple addresses, RFC 8684, (2020)
7. Barré, S., Paasch, C., Bonaventure, O.: MultiPath TCP: from theory to practice. In: IFIP Networking, pp. 444–457, Valencia, Spain (2011)
8. De Coninck, Q., Bonaventure, O.: Multipath QUIC: design and evaluation. In: In 13th International Conference Emergency Networking EXperiments Technology (CoNEXT 2017), pp. 160–166, New York, USA (2017)
9. Ferlin, S., Dreibholz, T., Alay, Ö.: Multipath Transport over Heterogeneous Wireless Networks: Does it Really Pay off? In IEEE GLOBCOM, Austin, TX, USA (2014)
10. Morawski, M., Ignaciuk, P.: Choosing a proper control strategy for multipath transmission in industry 4.0 applications. IEEE Trans. Industr. Inform. **18**(6), 3609–3619 (2022)
11. Rabitsch A., Evaluation of Packet Schedulers for Multipath QUIC, Dissertation, (2018). https://api.semanticscholar.org/CorpusID:64664128. Accessed 1 Oct 2024
12. Zeng, H., Cui, L., Po, T.F., Zhang, Z.: Optimizing multipath QUIC transmission over heterogeneous paths. Comput. Netw. **215**(109198) (2022)
13. Ferlin, S., Alay, Ö., Mehani, O., Boreli, R.: BLEST: blocking estimation-based MPTCP scheduler for heterogeneous networks. In: 2016 IFIP Networking Conference and Workshops, pp. 431–439 (2016)
14. Lim, Y.-S., Nahum, E.M., Towsley, D., Gibbens, R.J.: ECF: An MPTCP Path Scheduler to Manage Heterogeneous Paths , ACM CoNEXT, pp. 147–159 (2017)
15. Wu, H., et al.: PEEKABOO: learning-based multipath scheduling for dynamic heterogeneous environments. IEEE J Sel Areas Commun. **38**(10), 2295–2310 (2020)
16. Song, C.-X., Han, B., Su, J.-S.: 4D-MAP: multipath adaptive packet scheduling for live streaming over QUIC. Journal of Computation Science and Technology. **39**(1), 159–176 (2024)
17. Han, X., Han, B., Li, R., Ji, X.: MARS: an adaptive multi-agent DRL-based scheduler for multipath QUIC in dynamic networks. In: IEEE/ACM 31st International Symposium on Quality of Service (IWQoS), Orlando, FL USA (2023)
18. Morawski, M., Ignaciuk, P.: A synchronizing scheduler for reduced protocol delay in multipath transmission. In: 17th International Conference on Control, Automation, Robotics and Vision Singapore, pp. 553–558 (2022)
19. Liu, Y., Su, W., Tan, L.: Tetris: near-optimal scheduling for multi-path deadline-aware transport protocol. In: International Conference on Networking and Network Applications (NaNA), pp. 34–40, Lijiang City China (2021)
20. Lee, S., Yoo, J.: Sensors. **22**(6333), Reinforcement Learning Based Multipath QUIC Scheduler for Multimedia Streaming (2022)
21. Xing, Y., et al.: A stream-aware MPQUIC scheduler for HTTP traffic in Mobile networks. IEEE Trans. Wirel. Commun. **22**(4), 2775–2788 (2023)
22. Vu, V.A., Wolff, J.: Supporting delay-sensitive applications with multipath QUIC and forward erasure correction. In: 17th ACM Symposium on QoS and Security for Wireless and Mobile Networks, Q2SWinet 2021, pp. 95–103 (2021)
23. Michel, F., Bonaventure, O.: QUIRL: flexible QUIC loss recovery for low latency applications. IEEE/ACM Trans. Netw. **5555** (2024)

24. Høiland-Jørgensen T., Bufferbloat and beyond. removing performance barriers in real-world networks. PhD Thesis, Karlstadt University (2018).
25. Mathis M., Mahdavi J., Floyd S., Romanov A., TCP Selective Acknowledgment Options, RFC 1996 (1996).
26. De Coninck Q., MPQUIC code. https://github.com/qdeconinck/mp-quic. Accessed 29 May 2024

Network-Orchestrated Security Protocol for the Internet of Drones in O-RAN

Nathan Donaghy, Oluwafemi Olukoya, Karen Rafferty, Trung Q Duong, and Vishal Sharma[✉]

School of Electronics, Electrical Engineering and Computer Science, Queen's University Belfast, Northern Ireland, UK
{ndonaghy12, o.olukoya, k.Rafferty, trung.q.duong, v.sharma}@qub.ac.uk

Abstract. The rapid evolution of open radio access network (O-RAN) technology has produced many innovations and increased adoption of drones across various industries, including delivery systems, search and rescue, and surveillance. However, as the adoption of drones becomes more widespread, there is an increased likelihood of security breaches, which can be disastrous, particularly in disaggregated scenarios. Compromised communication channels can make drone communications vulnerable to attacks by an adversary, leading to sensitive data leaks or disruption of services. This paper examines the current approaches to solve this problem and their associated drawbacks, such as requiring computationally expensive cryptographic operations unsuitable for resource-constraint drones. Following this, an efficient and secure scheme is proposed that employs chameleon hash functions to enable mutual authentication and key agreement between user and drone that allows access to real-time information. To demonstrate the protocol's resilience against known security attacks, both an informal and formal analysis utilising *Tamarin* have been presented. A *proof of concept* has been implemented to display the feasibility of the solution along with a comparison to the state-of-the-art approaches.

Keywords: Mutual Authentication · Security Protocol · Unmanned aerial vehicles · O-RAN · Internet of Drones (IoD)

1 Introduction

The recent rapid development in the open radio access network (O-RAN) has led to an ever-expanding list of military and civilian applications using drones[1]. O-RAN architecture has two RAN intelligent controllers (RICs) - non-real-time RIC (non-RT RIC) and near-real-time RIC (near-RT RIC) [1,2]. Within this architecture, non-RT RIC is part of the Service Management and Orchestration (SMO) that relies on rApps for its operations, and near-RT RIC forms the midhaul and fronthaul components of the networks and is expected to operate

---

[1] This article refers to Unmanned Aerial Vehicles when using the term 'drones'.

© ICST Institute for Computer Sciences, Social Informatics and Telecommunications Engineering 2026
Published by Springer Nature Switzerland AG 2026. All Rights Reserved
S. Li et al. (Eds.): BROADNETS 2024, LNICST 674, pp. 14–32, 2026.
https://doi.org/10.1007/978-3-032-14350-1_2

numerous xApps. The near-RT RIC offers wider application scenarios, allowing space for multi-vendor support and allowing xApps to drive individual use cases and applications. However, disaggregating services via xApps is a critical component of network security, which needs careful assessment of the existing standards and security procedures for efficient operability [3,4].

Within O-RAN scenarios, highly efficient drones can form part of the near-RT RIC [5], and be utilised for network slicing or support disaggregation via payload placement involving radio unit (RU), distributed unit (DU), central unit (CU), or next-generation node B (gNB), and in specific use case, these act as user equipment (UE) being on the receiving end of the services.

For drones, the ease of deployment and the ability to traverse without a human pilot, controlled only through wireless communications, has garnered attention in high-risk military operations, including surveillance and search and rescue. In addition to military uses, drones have been extensively explored for integrated sensing and communication [6]. The communication setup on the Internet of Drones (IoD) can involve a Ground Control Station (GCS), a user that connects to the drone, or any other entity depending on the use case [7]. The GCS calculates the flight path for the drone, and the user can obtain real-time information from the deployed drone. In O-RAN facilitation, GCS services are hosted on a non-terrestrial network (NTN) gateway.

However, drones communicating over an unsecured public channel are susceptible to adversarial attacks. These include man-in-the-middle, impersonation, replay, and privileged insider attacks [8]. Moreover, drones can also be hijacked by an adversary and therefore have sensitive information stored in memory exposed [9]. The consequences of these attacks can be disastrous. Therefore, the transferred data must be protected, and all entities in the Internet of Drones (IoD) network must be authenticated before transmission.

For authentication and to ensure confidentiality between communicating entities, an authenticated key exchange protocol can help establish a shared cryptographic session key across an unsecured communication channel. A secure channel is created between the entities using the session key, in which messages transmitted can be protected from adversaries. This has been achieved in a range of protocols for vehicular ad hoc networks (VANETs) and wireless sensor networks (WSNs). However, these are not suitable for IoD as many are too expensive concerning communication overhead due to the unique constraints of drones, such as energy, bandwidth, or limited computing power.

In recent years, lightweight, efficient key exchange protocols in the context of IoD authentication have become a popular research area. An exemplary illustration of IoD authentication is shown in Fig. 1. Most protocols authenticate a single entity at a time, using Diffie-Hellman or recent developments such as elliptic curve cryptography (ECC) [10]. In such an approach, two entities, one verifier and one prover, work to establish mutual authentication. However, in [11], a new type of authentication procedure was proposed named Group Authentication (GA). GA was designed to support group communications by efficiently authen-

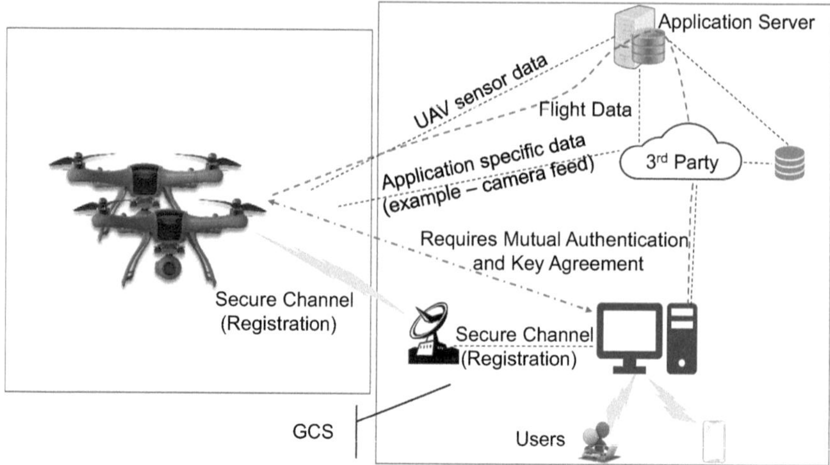

Fig. 1. An exemplary illustration of the IoD authentication scenario as a subset of services supported over RU in the near-RT RIC.

ticating all entities in the group at once, using a trusted centralized authentication server (CAS).

Looking into the use of drone cases and with the rising popularity of one-day and faster delivery, it is clear that consumers have become accustomed to and demand to receive their orders at a quicker pace than ever before. Therefore, the adoption of drone delivery systems to further speed up this process is inevitable. Secure access to real-time information from drones is crucial to facilitate many applications, particularly in a drone delivery network. However, numerous potential attack vectors must be safeguarded against adversaries before the implementation of a network of this kind. The main contributions of this paper are outlined below:

- A secure and efficient mutual authentication and key agreement (MAKA) protocol is proposed based on chameleon hash functions [12] that facilitate the mutual authentication between the user and drone.
- The security properties of the proposed protocol are verified through informal analysis, as well as being formally analysed using the security protocol verification tool, *Tamarin* [13] by taking into account a network-orchestrated drone delivery system.
- The proposed protocol is compared with state-of-the-art schemes in terms of satisfied security properties, computational efficiency and communication overheads, followed by a proof of concept.

2   Related Works

Within the context of near-RT RIC, IoD environments can be compared with IoT networks, WSNs, and VANETs because the overall architectures are alike. However, the great mobility of drones with brief lifetimes creates a disparity. Hence, key exchange protocols developed for those environments can be compared with and may be used for IoD with some modifications, and this has been the focus of interest in our related works. In [14], Lamport designed a single-factor password AKA to provide security and authentication over an unsecured channel by utilising a one-way hash function. However, this scheme depends solely on the security of the password and is therefore vulnerable to offline password-guessing attacks.

To address these flaws, two two-factor AKA schemes were proposed using a mobile device, such as a smartphone or smart card, and a password. In [15], Turkanovic et al. developed a two-factor password and smart card protocol using lightweight cryptographic primitives with low computational cost and proposed a scheme without the help of a trusted CAS. However, Faresh et al. [16] concluded that [15] was susceptible to impersonation, man-in-the-middle and stolen smart card attacks and did not deliver user anonymity. Faresh et al. [16] presented a new AKA scheme with similar functionality to [15] but overcoming its weaknesses. Later, in Amin et al. [17], this was found to have some vulnerabilities, including temporary information disclosure and offline password-guessing attacks. Therefore, two-factor AKA protocols in IoT environments were shown to be weak to numerous security exploits.

Hyang et al. [18] suggested a generic framework to upgrade two-factor to three-factor authentication. Researchers have since adopted biometric-based three-factor systems, including Amin et al. [17]. They proposed a three-factor AKA protocol employing a password and biometric-hashing function in conjunction with a smart card. However, this was found to be susceptible to stolen smart cards and offline password-guessing attacks by Jiang et al. [19].

In Dodis et al. [20], the authors proposed the idea of generating strong keys from biometrics using "fuzzy extractors". This is a cryptographic method of securely authenticating biometric data through a generate (Gen) and a reproduce (Rep) function. Gen creates a private and a public key from a user's biometric input, and Rep takes a noisy biometric input along with a public key and reproduces the original private key associated with a user's biometric information, provided that the number of differing symbolic positions between the original and noisy biometrics is less than a predetermined error threshold, known as the hamming distance.

In recent years, this method appears to be the staple for the user registration and login phase for IoD AKA protocols such as in Wazid et al. [8]. Here, the authors proposed a novel, lightweight AKA protocol that enables an authenticated user to receive data collected by a drone directly rather than through a separate server connection. This is important since most applications involving IoD are focused on receiving near real-time information. However, it was shown by Hussain et al. [21] that this scheme was not secure against traceability, impersonation and session key disclosure attacks, and no formal security analysis was provided. Hussain et al. [21] proposed a new scheme for smart city surveillance to overcome these limitations using symmetric encryption operations. Nonetheless, this scheme was found to be susceptible to drone capture and impersonation attacks by Wu *et al.* [22].

Gassend *et al.* [23] presented the notion of silicon physical random functions, also known as physically unclonable functions (PUF), which are used to create a random bit string that cannot be easily reproduced or reversed and removes the necessity of storing keys in device memory [24]. Of late, the use of PUFs has been employed as a security primitive for IoT devices, as they require minimal or no additional hardware, with a low power supply and little process time needed to generate [25]. In Mall *et al.* [26], PUF-based authentication schemes in the IoT setting were reviewed to compose an in-depth insight regarding the security concerns and vulnerabilities as well as the computational costs and security features of these protocols.

Numerous public-key cryptography (PKC) protocols have also been proposed in recent years, such as Won *et al.* [27] who designed a certificate-less ECC-based protocol for the IoD smart city setting, and Ever [9] who designed an ECC and bilinear pairing protocol for the IoD setting. These PKC protocols involve computationally expensive operations and, hence, are not practical due to the energy constraints of drones.

Krawczyk and Rabin [12] presented a novel cryptographic scheme by introducing the concept of chameleon hash functions. These are a variation of collision-resistant hash functions with an associated public and secret (trapdoor) key pair. This enables anyone with knowledge of the public key to generate the hash function, which remains collision-resistant for all those who do not possess knowledge of the trapdoor key. However, knowledge of the trapdoor key grants the ability to compute collisions for any input efficiently.

3   Preliminaries

This section will provide a detailed explanation of each of the cryptographic primitives and values utilised in the proposed protocol, which may not be widely known. Furthermore, Table 1 outlines the protocol's symbolic notations and describes the primitives and values used.

The proposed protocol employs the "fuzzy extractor" reproduce function (Rep), which can reproduce the user's private key from the original public key and noisy biometric input, provided the number of different bits between the original and noisy biometrics is within a pre-specified threshold. This function is used within the login phase to authenticate the user to the mobile device.

The HGen(.) function is used by the drone in the registration and MAKA phases of the protocol. This function takes as input a challenge value (C) provided by the GCS and the internal hardware key of the drone (IHK) and produces a challenge-response value (CR). We assume that IHK is stored in tamper-proof memory on the drone that cannot be accessed by an adversary. There is also the assumption that the GCS has a database of all drone IHK values. This property is used to identify the drone during the registration phase.

Table 1. Symbols and Functions used for the proposed protocol.

Symbols	Description
$<$user$>$, $<$Drone$>$	User, Drone
PK, SK	Public key and secret key
$ID_{<user>}$, $ID_{<Drone>}$	Identity of user and drone
$PID_{<user>}$, $PID_{<Drone>}$	Pseudonym identity of user and drone
C	Challenge generated by server
CR	Challenge response from drone
m	Message generated during registration
$h_{<i>}$, $r_{<i>}$	Chameleon hash value and randomness
PWD, BIO	User password, biometrics
UCheck, SCheck	User login authentication and GCS authentication
IHK	Drone Internal Hardware Key
n_1, n_2	Generated nonces used in DH
t_1, t_2, t_3	Timestamps
Δt	Maximum time delay for a request
x, mdr, rdr	Nonce and message
rdr	Randomness
Session	Session key between user and drone
$\|$, $\oplus$	Concatenation and bitwise XOR function
h(.)	One-way hash function
HGen(.)	Internal hardware challenge response function
CHash(.)	Chameleon hash function
Adapt(.)	Adapt chameleon randomness function
Check(.)	Verifies chameleon hash values
Gen(.)	PK and SK generation function
Rep(.)	Fuzzy extractor SK reproduce function

The proposed protocol uses certain functions that are associated with chameleon hashing. These are CHash(.), Adapt(.) and Check(.) which are defined as follows:

- CHash(.) takes a public key and a random message as input and produces a hash and a randomness value. This function is collision-resistant without knowledge of the associated trapdoor key.
- Adapt(.) is used to efficiently compute collisions for a message hashed using the associated CHash(.) function. This function takes as input the trapdoor key, the originally hashed message, a new message and the randomness value from the originally hashed message. From these inputs, a new randomness value is produced that has a collision with the originally hashed values.

- Check(.) is used to verify that two pairs of message and randomness values produce an identical hash value. As such, it takes two messages and two randomness values as input and returns True if these values produce a matching hash, or False otherwise.

4   Proposed Protocol

The proposed protocol works in five phases as follows:

4.1   Initialisation Phase

The GCS specifies the Diffie-Hellman key generation system [10] to be used in the initial phase. It selects a large prime number, p, the root modulo, g, and the prime-order subgroup size, q. The GCS then selects a one-way hash function that takes a single value as input and returns the hash value. This system is publicly distributed to all entities. This is shown in Fig. 2.

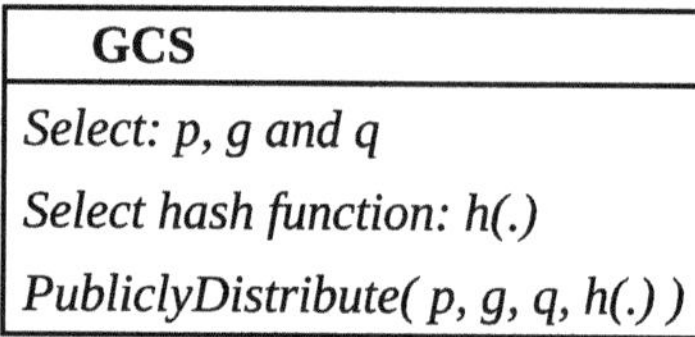

Fig. 2. Initialisation Phase.

4.2   Drone Registration Phase

This phase occurs across a secure channel for each drone, $Drone_i$, and is shown in Fig. 3.

Step 1: $Drone_i$ sends a registration request to the GCS.

Step 2: Upon receiving the registration request, the GCS generates a challenge C and a pseudonym $PID_{<Drone>}$ and responds with the registration reply $(C, PID_{<Drone>})$.

Step 3: After receiving the reply, $Drone_i$ computes a challenge response using an internal hardware key, $CR = HGen(C, IHK)$. The assumption is that an adversary cannot retrieve this IHK from memory. $Drone_i$ then generates $(PK_{<Drone>}, SK_{<Drone>}) = GEN(CR)$, selects a message $m_{<Drone>}$ and computes its chameleon hash and randomness value by $(h_{<Drone>}, r_{<Drone>}) = CHash(PK_{<Drone>}, m_{<Drone>})$. $Drone_i$ stores $(PID_{<Drone>}, h_{<Drone>}, r_{<Drone>}, PK_{<Drone>}, m_{<Drone>})$ in memory and sends $(PID_{<Drone>}, PK_{<Drone>}, h_{<Drone>}, CR)$ to the GCS.

Step 4: It is assumed that the GCS has a secure database of all drone IHKs. The GCS searches for $Drone_i$ in its database by computing CR = HGen(C, IHK), and if found, select $ID_{<Drone>}$. Finally, the GCS stores ($ID_{<Drone>}$, $PID_{<Drone>}$, C, $PK_{<Drone>}$, $h_{<Drone>}$) and sends $ID_{<Drone>}$ to $Drone_i$.

Step 5: $Drone_i$ computes SCheck = $h(ID_{<Drone>}$ || $PID_{<Drone>}$ || $SK_{<Drone>})$ which is used to authenticate the GCS during the key agreement phase. Finally, $Drone_i$ stores ($ID_{<Drone>}$, SCheck).

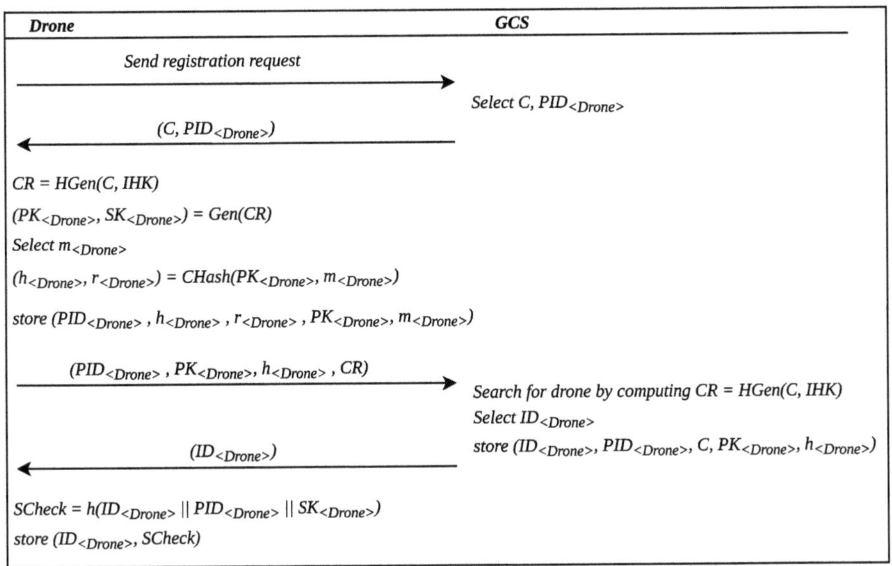

Fig. 3. Drone Registration Phase.

4.3   User Registration Phase

This phase occurs across a secure channel for each user $User_i$, and is shown in Fig. 4.

Step 1: $User_i$ selects $ID_{<user>}$, PWD and imprints BIO into the mobile device before generating ($PK_{<user>}$, $SK_{<user>}$) = Gen(BIO). $User_i$ then selects a message $m_{<user>}$ and computes its chameleon hash and randomness value by ($h_{<user>}$, $r_{<user>}$) = CHash($PK_{<user>}$, $m_{<user>}$). Next, $User_i$ computes UCheck = $h(ID_{<user>}$ || $SK_{<user>}$ || PWD), which is used to authenticate the user on the mobile device during the login phase. $User_i$ stores ($PK_{<user>}$, $h_{<user>}$, $r_{<user>}$, $m_{<user>}$, UCheck) in mobile device memory and sends the registration request ($ID_{<user>}$, $PK_{<user>}$, $h_{<user>}$) to the GCS.

Step 2: Upon receiving the registration request, the GCS generates a pseudonym $PID_{<user>}$, stores $(ID_{<user>}, PID_{<user>}, PK_{<user>}, h_{<user>})$ and responds with the registration reply $(PID_{<user>})$.

Step 3: Finally, $User_i$ computes $PID'_{<user>} = PID_{<user>} \oplus h(PWD \,||\, SK_{<user>})$ and stores $(PID'_{<user>})$ on the mobile device.

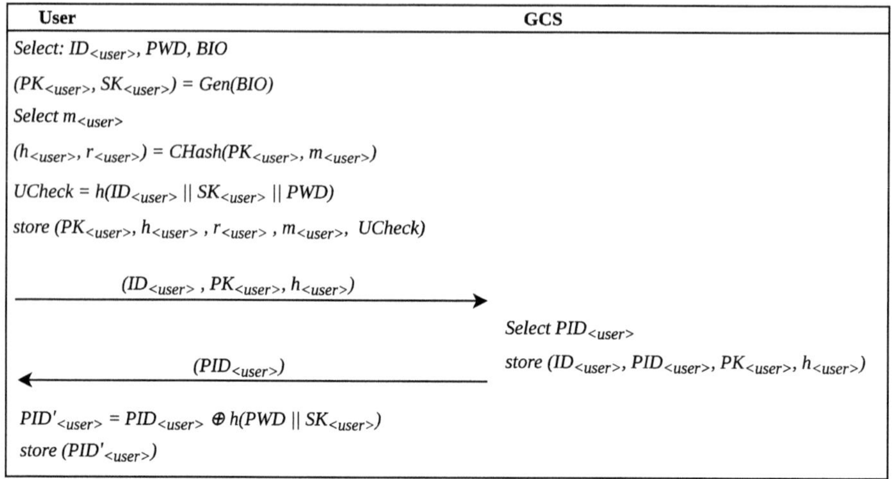

Fig. 4. User Registration Phase.

4.4   Login, Authentication and Key Agreement Phase

A registered user, $User_i$, initiates the mutual authentication and key agreement phase to acquire a shared session with a drone to obtain live information from that deployed drone. The GCS acts as a trusted CAS to facilitate this proposed authentication scheme. This is shown in Fig. 5.

Step 1: $User_i$ inputs $ID_{<user>}$ and PWD, and imprints BIO into the mobile device, which computes $SK_{<user>} = Rep(BIO, PK_{<user>})$. Next, $UCheck' = h(ID_{<user>} \,||\, SK_{<user>} \,||\, PWD)$ is computed and compared with the stored value UCheck. If the values match, the password and biometric checks are successful; otherwise, login is aborted. If successful, values n_1, mdr and x are randomly selected along with the current timestamp t_1 and $User_i$ then computes $exu = h(n_1 \,||\, SK_{<user>})$, $dhu = (g^{exu} \bmod p)$, $t_1x = h(t_1 \,||\, x)$. Next, $User_i$ generates a collision for its chameleon hash value by computing $r'_{<user>} = Adapt(SK_{<user>}, m_{<user>}, t_1x, h_{<user>}, r_{<user>})$ which is used to authenticate the user to the GCS. $User_i$ computes $PID_{<user>} = PID'_{<user>} \oplus h(PWD \,||\, SK_{<user>})$, $(hdr, rdr) = CHash(PK_{<Drone>}, mdr)$, $x' = x \oplus h(ID_{<user>} \,||\, PID_{<user>})$. Subsequently, $User_i$ computes $PK'_{<user>} = h(PK_{<user>} \,||\, t_1)$,

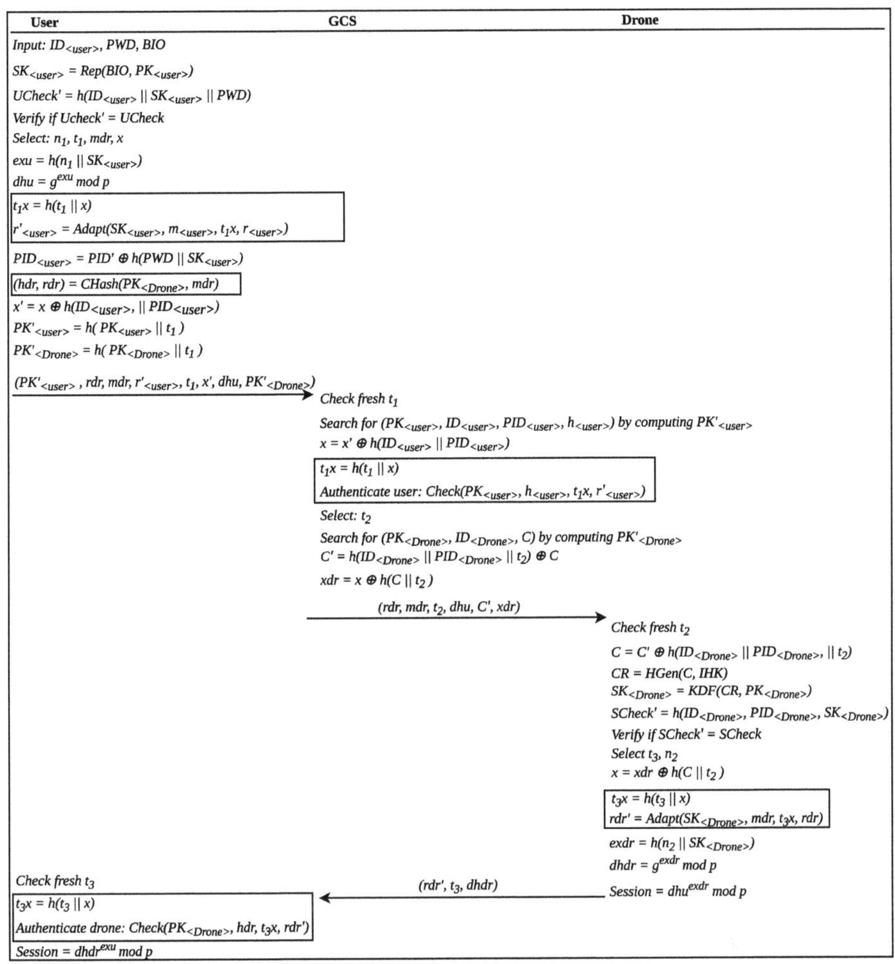

Fig. 5. Mutual Authentication and Key Agreement Phase.

$PK'_{<Drone>} = h(PK_{<Drone>} \| t_1)$ and sends $(PK'_{<user>}, rdr, mdr, r'_{<user>}, t_1, x', dhu, PK'_{<Drone>})$ to the GCS.

Step 2: Upon receiving the login request, the GCS verifies the time freshness $(t_1 - currentTime) < \Delta t$, and if successful, the GCS searches for the registered user in the database by computing $PK'_{<user>}$. If a user is found, GCS computes $x = x' \oplus h(ID_{<user>} \| PID_{<user>})$, $t_1x = h(t_1 \| x)$ and attempts to authenticate $User_i$ by $Check(PK_{<user>}, h_{<user>}, t_1x, r'_{<user>})$. If this fails, the key agreement is aborted, otherwise $User_i$ is authenticated. Now, GCS selects timestamp t_2 and searches for a deployed drone by computing $PK'_{<Drone>}$. If found, GCS computes $C' = h(ID_{<Drone>} \| PID_{<Drone>} \| t_2) \oplus C$, $xdr = x \oplus h(C \| t_2)$ and sends $(rdr, mdr, t_2, dhu, C', xdr)$ to $Drone_i$.

Step 3: $Drone_i$ verifies the time freshness of the received message, $(t_2$ - currentTime$) < \Delta t$, and if successful computes the challenge $C = C' \oplus h(ID_{<Drone>}$ $\parallel PID_{<Drone>} \parallel t_2)$ and the challenge-response $CR = HGen(C, IHK)$. Now, $Drone_i$ reproduces its secret key $SK_{<Drone>} = KDF(CR, PK_{<Drone>})$ and computes $SCheck' = h(ID_{<Drone>}, PID_{<Drone>}, SK_{<Drone>})$. Next, the server is authenticated by comparing $SCheck' = SCheck$, and if successful, $Drone_i$ selects a random nonce n_2 and a timestamp t_3. Following this, $Drone_i$ computes $x = xdr \oplus h(C \parallel t_2)$, $t_3x = h(t_3 \parallel x)$ and generates a collision for its chameleon hash value against message t_3x by computing $rdr' = Adapt(SK_{<Drone>}, mdr, t_3x, rdr)$ which will be used to authenticate $Drone_i$ to $User_i$. Subsequently, $Drone_i$ computes $exdr = h(n_2 \parallel SK_{<Drone>})$, $dhdr = (g^{exdr} \bmod p)$ and finally the shared session key, $Session = (dhu^{exdr} \bmod p)$, before sending $(rdr', t_3, dhdr)$ to $User_i$

Step 4: $User_i$ verifies the time freshness of the received message, $(t_3$ - currentTime$) < \Delta t$. If successful, $User_i$ computes $t_3x = h(t_3 \parallel x)$ and attempts to authenticate $Drone_i$ by $Check(PK_{<Drone>}, hdr, t_3x, rdr')$. Finally, upon successful authentication, $User_i$ computes the shared session key, $Session = (dhdr^{exu} \bmod p)$.

4.5   De-registration Phase

Upon successful drone delivery, $User_i$ initiates this phase by sending a de-registration request to $Drone_i$ that is encrypted using the shared session key. Upon successful decryption of this request, $Drone_i$ responds with an encrypted acknowledgement message before deleting the session. Finally, $User_i$ deletes the session from memory after successful decryption of the acknowledgement.

5   Security Evaluation

In this section, informal analysis is used to prove the security of the protocol against many adversarial attacks. This is followed by a formal analysis using Tamarin [13].

5.1   Informal Evaluation

Mutual authentication between $User_i$ and $Drone_i$ is achieved through the assistance of the trusted GCS. $User_i$ is authenticated by the GCS by verifying the user-adapted chameleon hash randomness value. Next, the GCS is authenticated by $Drone_i$ by validating the generated $SCheck'$ against the stored $SCheck$. Finally, $User_i$ authenticates $Drone_i$ by verifying the drone-adapted chameleon hash randomness value and thus achieving mutual authentication.

Replay Attacks. The protocol is resistant to replay attacks through the use of timestamps t_1, t_2, t_3 to verify the freshness of the received messages. If an adversary intercepts and re-sends a message, the timestamp will be declared invalid. Furthermore, if the timestamp is modified by the adversary so that it would be validated as a fresh message, the values required to authenticate the original honest entity can not be reached with the use of the modified timestamp.

Stolen Device and Password Guessing Attacks. Assuming a $User_i$'s mobile device has been lost or stolen, and an adversary has obtained the stored data through power analysis [28], namely ($PK_{<user>}$, $PID'_{<user>}$, UCheck, Gen(.), Rep(.), h(.)). The adversary can only be authenticated on the device through knowledge of the secret credentials to verify UCheck = $h(ID_{<user>} \parallel SK_{<user>} \parallel PWD)$. Therefore, the password cannot be deduced without the knowledge of both $ID_{<user>}$ and BIO to reproduce the secret key, which is mathematically impractical to generate.

Drone Capture Attacks. Assuming a $Drone_i$ has been physically captured and an adversary has obtained the stored data through power analysis [28], namely $PK_{<Drone>}$, $ID_{<Drone>}$, $PID_{<Drone>}$, HGen(.), KDF(.), h(.). The assumption is that the IHK of the drone is stored in tamper-proof memory and, hence, cannot be recovered by an adversary. However, even if we ignore the assumption and an adversary can obtain this value, they cannot compute CR and by extension $SK_{<Drone>}$ without knowledge of the challenge C. Furthermore, as discussed in [8], since every drone has a unique ID, PID and C generated by the GCS, if we assume that $Drone_i$ has been captured with its session key to $User_i$ compromised, other sessions between that user and uncompromised drones remain secure. Therefore, the protocol can resist drone capture attacks.

User Impersonation Attacks. For an adversary to send a valid message from $User_i$ to the GCS, they must know $SK_{<user>}$, PWD, and $ID_{<user>}$, to successfully adapt the chameleon hash randomness value, reproduce $PID_{<user>}$ and compute a valid x' that can be utilised by the GCS in the authentication phase. As outlined in Sect. 4, this is not feasible.

GCS Impersonation Attacks. For an adversary to impersonate the GCS and send a valid message to $Drone_i$, they must have knowledge $ID_{<Drone>}$, $PID_{<Drone>}$ and the drone challenge value C, which are never transmitted across the open channel. It is computationally infeasible to generate these valid values, thus the protocol is secure against this attack.

Drone Impersonation Attacks. To successfully impersonate $Drone_i$ and send a valid message to $User_i$, an adversary must reproduce x and use this value to adapt the chameleon hash randomness value. This is not possible without knowledge of drone challenge C and $SK_{<Drone>}$. Thus, an adversary cannot impersonate a valid drone.

Anonymity and Untraceability. An adversary cannot trace any user or drone as new timestamps and random nonces are generated for each session leading to unique messages. Furthermore, identities, pseudonyms and public keys are not openly transmitted. Hence, the properties of anonymity and untraceability are upheld.

5.2   Formal Evaluation Using Tamarin

Tamarin [13] has been used to provide a formal analysis of the proposed protocol to verify it is secure against key disclosure attacks, that perfect forward secrecy is upheld and that anonymity is provided. Tamarin has been well-researched and used to formally prove the security of many protocols including, 5G-AKA [29], TLS1.3 [30] and WPA2 [31]. In Tamarin, a system's state is modelled as a multiset of facts with protocol operations specified as multiset rewriting systems. The adversary is a Dolev-Yao attacker that can intercept all network traffic between entities and update, remove, inject or replay messages as an authorized party. The adversary cannot, however, read messages sent over a secure channel. Furthermore, if the adversary derives secret keys, it can send encrypted messages or decrypt messages sent using those keys [32]. The initialisation, user registration, drone registration, and the login and mutual authentication phases have each been modelled inside a Tamarin secure protocol verifier. The proved Lemmas and traces are shown in Figs. 6 and 7. The green background on the Lemma indicates that Tamarin cannot find any potential counterexamples to the Lemma; hence, the Lemma holds true.

Man-in-the-Middle Attacks and Key Secrecy. Figure 6 shows the Tamarin trace and Lemma for key secrecy. The Lemma disallows the adversary from knowing the secret key of the user and drone. The output indicates that an adversary could not intercept or inject messages in any way that would result in a discovered session key.

Perfect Forward Secrecy. Figure 7 shows the Tamarin trace and Lemma for perfect forward secrecy. The Lemma allows the adversary to reveal the secret key of the user and drone after a session has been established. The output indicates that past sessions remain secure from adversaries even after revealing the secret keys. Hence, perfect forward secrecy is upheld.

User and Drone Anonymity. This Lemma is modelled by disallowing the adversary from knowing the user and drone identities - $ID_{<user>}$, $PID_{<user>}$, $PK_{<user>}$, $ID_{<Drone>}$, $PK_{<Drone>}$ or $PID_{<Drone>}$. The output indicates that an adversary could not intercept or inject messages in any way that would result in the identity of a user or drone being discovered, hence anonymity is achieved in the protocol.

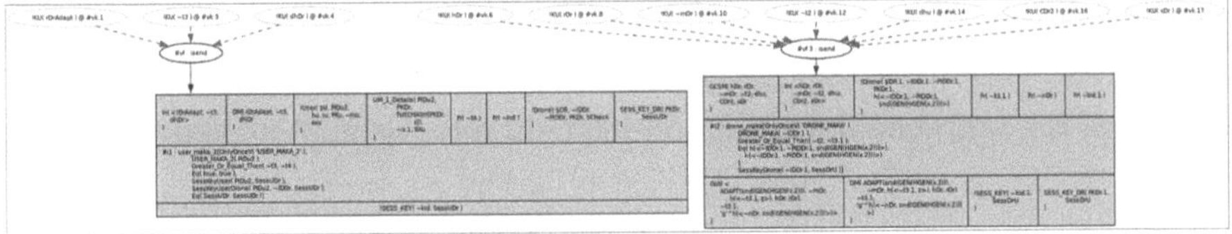

Fig. 6. Tamarin Key Secrecy Lemma verification and trace.

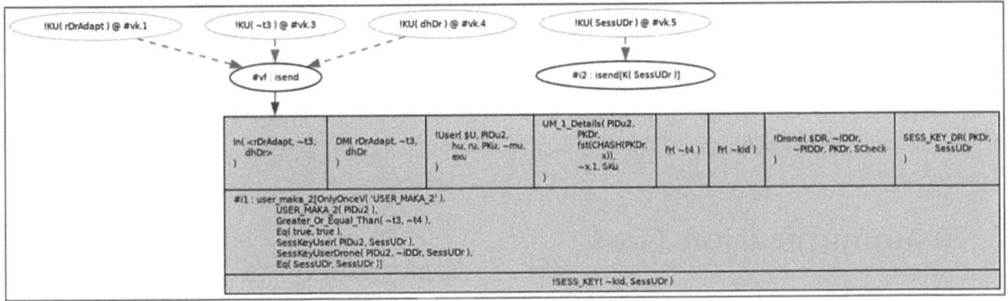

Fig. 7. Tamarin Perfect Forward Secrecy Lemma verification and trace.

Table 2. Comparison of Security Properties (Note: SP_1: Mutual authentication; SP_2: Replay attacks; SP_3: Stolen device attacks; SP_4: Password guessing attacks; SP_5: Drone capture attacks; SP_6: User impersonation attacks; SP_7: GCS impersonation attacks; SP_8: Drone impersonation attacks; SP_9: Man-in-the-middle attacks; SP_{10}: Session key secrecy; SP_{11}: Perfect forward secrecy; SP_{12}: Anonymity; SP_{13}: Untraceability; SP_{14}: Formal security analysis).

Property	Ever [9]	Wazid *et al.* [8]	Hussain *et al.* [21]	Ours
SP_1	✓	✗	✓	✓
SP_2	✓	✓	✓	✓
SP_3	✗	✗	✓	✓
SP_4	✓	✓	✓	✓
SP_5	✓	✓	✗	✓
SP_6	✓	✗	✓	✓
SP_7	✓	✗	✓	✓
SP_8	✓	✗	✗	✓
SP_9	✓	✓	✓	✓
SP_{10}	✗	✗	✗	✓
SP_{11}	✗	✗	✗	✓
SP_{12}	✗	✗	✓	✓
SP_{13}	✗	✗	✓	✓
SP_{14}	✗	✓	✓	✓

6   Security Properties Comparison

This section presents a comparison of the security properties that have been fulfilled in the proposed approach and related protocols in [8,9], and [21], which is summarised in Table 2. The protocol proposed by Ever *et al.* [9] was found to be vulnerable to session key disclosure and drone capture attacks as well as not providing anonymity or untraceability [10]. Moreover, this scheme does not provide any formal security analysis. In Hussain *et al.* [21], it was shown that Wazid *et al.* [8] was not secure against traceability, impersonation and session key disclosure attacks, and does not provide mutual authentication. The protocol of Hussain *et al.* was discovered to be susceptible to impersonation attacks and drone capture attacks by Wu *et al.* [22]. Consequently, it is shown that the presented protocol fulfils a greater number of security properties in comparison to these related schemes.

7   Communication Cost

The communication overheads of our proposed protocol are evaluated in comparison to [8,9,21] concerning the bits transmitted in the login and mutual authentication phase. Identities and pseudonyms for both user and drone are considered to be 160 bits, timestamps are 32 bits, random nonces and generated messages are 160 bits, SHA-1 [33] hash digest is 160 bits, chameleon hash and randomness are 160 bits, and modular exponentiation utilizes RSA1024 with a prime order of 160 bits. RSA1024 is shown to have similar security to ECC curves with field sizes of 160 bits [34], hence, ECC points (x, y) require 320 bits. Table 3 summarises the overall communication costs and shows that our proposed protocol incurs a greater overhead compared with [8], and a similar overhead to [21], whereas it has a lower communication cost when compared with [9]. However, including a larger number of security features validates the additional overheads in the proposed protocol.

Table 3. Communication Cost Comparison.

Protocol	Number of messages	Bits exchanged
Ever [9]	6	2592
Wazid *et al.* [8]	3	1696
Hussain *et al.* [21]	3	2336
Ours	3	2336

Table 4 displays the average computation time for each cryptographic primitive. The experiments were conducted on an ASUS GL503GE laptop running Ubuntu 20.04, equipped with an Intel i5-8300H quad-core CPU operating at

Table 4. Cryptographic Primitives Experimental Performance.

Primitive	Symbol	Performance (ms)
Bilinear pairing	T_{bp}	3.8976
FE reproduce ham = 4	T_{fe}	2.7034
Chameleon hash adapt	T_{ca}	2.4747
ECC scalar multiplication	T_{sm}	1.7297
Chameleon hash	T_{ch}	1.6554
Modular exponentiation	T_{me}	0.8432
Key derivation function	T_{kdf}	0.0706
Symmetric encryption	T_{bp}	0.0373
Symmetric decryption	T_{bp}	0.0329
Random number generation	T_r	0.0035
SHA1 hash	T_h	0.0022
XOR	T_{xor}	0.0005

2.30 GHz and 16GB RAM, with all non-essential background processes terminated. Every primitive was tested 10,000 times, with the highest and lowest 10% of timings removed before calculating the average. The primitives were implemented using Python, with MIRACL [35] utilized for ECC scalar multiplication and bilinear-pairing timings.

8   Computational Cost

Table 5. Computation Cost Comparison.

Protocol	User	GCS	Drone	Total Operations	Time (ms)
Ever [9]	$2T_{bp} + T_r + 5T_h + 6T_{xor}$	$2T_{bp} + 4T_{sm} + 9T_h + 4T_{xor}$	$2T_{bp} + 3T_h$	$6T_{bp} + 4T_{sm} + T_r + 17T_h + 10T_{xor}$	30.35
Wazid et al. [8]	$T_{fe} + 16T_h + T_r + 11T_{xor}$	$9T_h + T_r + 5T_{xor}$	$6T_h + T_r + 3T_{xor}$	$T_{fe} + 31T_h + 3T_r + 19T_{xor}$	2.792
Hussain et al. [21]	$T_{fe} + T_r + 15T_h + 10_{xor}$	$2T_r + T_{se} + T_{sd} + 11T_h + 5_{xor}$	$T_r + 7T_h + 4_{xor}$	$T_{fe} + 3T_r + T_{se} + T_{sd} + 33T_h + 19_{xor}$	2.866
Proposed	$T_{ca} + 2T_{ch} + T_{fe} + 2T_{me} + 3T_r + 6T_h + 2T_{xor}$	$T_{ch} + 4T_h + 3T_{xor}$	$T_{ca} + 2T_{me} + T_{kdf} + T_r + 6T_h + 2T_{xor}$	$2T_{ca} + 3T_{ch} + T_{fe} + 4T_{me} + T_{kdf} + 4T_r + 16T_h + 7T_{xor}$	16.11

The computational cost of our proposed protocol is evaluated in comparison to [8, 9], and [21] for the login and mutual authentication phase. The results in Table 5 show the proposed protocol demands a considerably lower cost compared with the scheme in [9], however, the protocols in [8, 21] achieve better performance. Nonetheless, the inclusion of a larger number of security features validates the additional computational requirements of the proposed protocol.

The proposed method of providing anonymity and untraceability in the MAKA phase requires, in the worst case, the GCS to compute $h(PK_{<user>} \| t1)$ and $h(PK_{<Drone>} \| t1)$ for every registered entity in its database when searching for $User_i$ and $Drone_i$. This highlights the significance of finding a more efficient method of achieving anonymity and untraceability as a large number of registered entities can lead to degraded performance, which is a limitation of the proposal protocol. It is to be noted that the experimental results obtained show the performance of modular exponentiation faster than ECC scalar multiplication, which is contrary to usually expected research. A possible reason for this is that MIRACL's Python implementation of ECC is not efficient, which is detailed on the official GitHub repository [35]. Future work can involve bringing the platform to a common implementation of each primitive for comparison.

9   Conclusion

This research discussed the security of the Internet of Drones (IoD) in O-RAN. A MAKA scheme was proposed that utilised the properties of chameleon hash functions for securing drones via network-orchestrated protocol. The security properties of this scheme were proven through an informal analysis and a formal analysis using Tamarin. Finally, a comparative analysis was performed between the proposed and related schemes using security properties, communication overheads and computational efficiency as metrics. The results demonstrate the proposed protocol has enhanced security properties at the expense of slightly reduced computational efficiency. As the current approach requires the GCS to compute additional hashes for each registered user and drone in its database during the MAKA phase, future work will investigate the design of a more effective way to achieve anonymity and untraceability. Consequently, this can lead to decreased performance with many registered entities, which is highly likely given the expectation that multi-vendor systems will evolve in the near-real-time RIC component of O-RAN.

Acknowledgment. This work was partly supported by the UK Department for Science, Innovation and Technology under the Future Open Networks Research Challenge project TUDOR (Towards Ubiquitous 3D Open Resilient Network), and partly by the Cyber security academic startup accelerator programme funded by Innovate UK and DSIT. The views expressed are those of the authors and do not necessarily represent the project or the funding agency.

References

1. Polese, M., Bonati, L., D'oro, S., Basagni, S., Melodia, T.: Understanding o-ran: architecture, interfaces, algorithms, security, and research challenges. IEEE Commun. Surv. Tutorials **25**(2), 1376–1411 (2023)
2. O-RAN Working Group 1: O-RAN architecture specifications, O-RAN Alliance, Tech. Rep., June 2023 (Last Accessed: March 2024). https://orandownloadsweb. azurewebsites.net/specifications

3. Yungaicela-Naula, N.M., Sharma, V., Scott-Hayward, S.: Misconfiguration in o-ran: analysis of the impact of ai/ml. Comput. Networks, 110455 (2024)
4. Megarry, M., Masaracchia, A., Fahim, M., Sharma, V., Duong, T.Q.: Understanding the security implications in o-ran with abusive adversaries. In: 10th EAI International Conference on Industrial Networks and Intelligent Systems. Springer (2024)
5. Pham, C., Fami, F., Nguyen, K.K., Cheriet, M.: When ran intelligent controller in o-ran meets multi-uav enable wireless network. IEEE Transactions on Cloud Computing **11**(3), 2245–2259 (2022)
6. Mu, J., Zhang, R., Cui, Y., Gao, N., Jing, X.: UAV Meets Integrated Sensing and Communication: challenges and Future Directions. IEEE Commun. Mag. **61**(5), 62–67 (2023)
7. Yin, D., Yang, X., Yu, H., Chen, S., Wang, C.: An air-to-ground relay communication planning method for UAVs swarm applications. IEEE Trans. Intell. Vehicles **8**(4), 2983–2997 (2023)
8. Wazid, M., Das, A.K., Kumar, N., Vasilakos, A.V., Rodrigues, J.J.P.C.: Design and analysis of secure lightweight remote user authentication and key agreement scheme in internet of drones deployment. IEEE Internet of Things J. **6**(2), 3572–3584 (2019)
9. Kirsal Ever, Y.: A secure authentication scheme framework for mobile-sinks used in the internet of drones applications. Comput. Commun. **155**, 143–149 (2020)
10. Deebak, B., Al-Turjman, F.: A smart lightweight privacy preservation scheme for iot-based uav communication systems. Comput. Commun. **162**, 102–117 (2020). https://www.sciencedirect.com/science/article/pii/S0140366420319034
11. Harn, L., Lin, C.: An efficient group authentication for group communications. Int. J. Network Secur. Appl. **5**, 06 (2013)
12. Krawczyk, H., Rabin, T.: Chameleon hashing and signatures. Cryptology ePrint Archive, Paper 1998/010, 1998, https://eprint.iacr.org/1998/010. https://eprint.iacr.org/1998/010
13. Meier, S., Schmidt, B., Cremers, C., Basin, D.: The tamarin prover for the symbolic analysis of security protocols. In: Sharygina, N., Veith, H. (eds.) Computer Aided Verification, pp. 696–701. Springer, Heidelberg (2013)
14. Lamport, L.: Password authentication with insecure communication. Commun. ACM **24**(11), 770–772 (1981)
15. Turkanović, M., Brumen, B., Hölbl, M.: A novel user authentication and key agreement scheme for heterogeneous ad hoc wireless sensor networks, based on the internet of things notion. Ad Hoc Netw. **20**, 96–112 (2014)
16. Farash, M.S., Turkanović, M., Kumari, S., Hölbl, M.: An efficient user authentication and key agreement scheme for heterogeneous wireless sensor network tailored for the internet of things environment. Ad Hoc Netw. **36**, 152–176 (2016)
17. Amin, R., Islam, S.H., Biswas, G., Khan, M.K., Leng, L., Kumar, N.: Design of an anonymity-preserving three-factor authenticated key exchange protocol for wireless sensor networks. Comput. Networks **101**, 42–62 (2016). industrial Technologies and Applications for the Internet of Things
18. Huang, X., Xiang, Y., Chonka, A., Zhou, J., Deng, R.H.: A generic framework for three-factor authentication: preserving security and privacy in distributed systems. IEEE Trans. Parallel Distrib. Syst. **22**(8), 1390–1397 (2011)
19. Jiang, Q., Zeadally, S., Ma, J., He, D.: Lightweight three-factor authentication and key agreement protocol for internet-integrated wireless sensor networks. IEEE Access **5**, 3376–3392 (2017)

20. Dodis, Y., Reyzin, L., Smith, A.: Fuzzy Extractors: How to Generate Strong Keys from Biometrics and Other Noisy Data. In: Cachin, C., Camenisch, J.L. (eds.) EUROCRYPT 2004. LNCS, vol. 3027, pp. 523–540. Springer, Heidelberg (2004). https://doi.org/10.1007/978-3-540-24676-3_31
21. Hussain, S., Mahmood, K., Khan, M.K., Chen, C.-M., Alzahrani, B.A., Chaudhry, S.A.: Designing secure and lightweight user access to drone for smart city surveillance. Comput. Stand. Interfaces **80**, 103566 (2022). https://www.sciencedirect.com/science/article/pii/S0920548921000611
22. Wu, T., Guo, X., Chen, Y., Kumari, S., Chen, C.: Amassing the security: an enhanced authentication protocol for drone communications over 5g networks. Drones **6**(1) (2022). https://www.mdpi.com/2504-446X/6/1/10
23. Gassend, B., Clarke, D., van Dijk, M., Devadas, S.: In: Silicon physical random functions, pp. 148–160. Association for Computing Machinery, New York (2002)
24. Tehranipoor, F., Karimian, N., Yan, W., Chandy, J.A.: Dram-based intrinsic physically unclonable functions for system-level security and authentication. IEEE Trans. Very Large Scale Integr. VLSI Syst. **25**(3), 1085–1097 (2017)
25. Shamsoshoara, A., Korenda, A., Afghah, F., Zeadally, S.: A survey on physical unclonable function (puf)-based security solutions for internet of things. Comput. Netw. **183**, 107593 (2020)
26. Mall, P., Amin, R., Das, A.K., Leung, M.T., Choo, K.-K.R.: Puf-based authentication and key agreement protocols for iot, wsns, and smart grids: a comprehensive survey. IEEE Internet Things J. **9**(11), 8205–8228 (2022)
27. Won, J., Seo, S.-H., Bertino, E.: Certificateless cryptographic protocols for efficient drone-based smart city applications. IEEE Access **5**, 3721–3749 (2017)
28. Messerges, T., Dabbish, E., Sloan, R.: Examining smart-card security under the threat of power analysis attacks. IEEE Trans. Comput. **51**(5), 541–552 (2002)
29. Basin, D., Dreier, J., Hirschi, L., Radomirovic, S., Sasse, R., Stettler, V.: A formal analysis of 5G authentication. In: Proceedings of the 2018 ACM SIGSAC Conference on Computer and Communications Security, ser. CCS 2018, pp. 1383–1396. Association for Computing Machinery, New York (2018)
30. Cremers, C., Horvat, M., Scott, S., van der Merwe, T.: Automated analysis and verification of TLS 1.3: 0-rtt, resumption and delayed authentication. In: 2016 IEEE Symposium on Security and Privacy (SP), pp. 470–485 (2016)
31. Cremers, C., Kiesl, B., Medinger, N.: A formal analysis of ieee 802.11's WPA2: countering the kracks caused by cracking the counters. 29th USENIX Security Symposium (USENIX Security 20), pp. 1–17 (2020)
32. Dolev, D., Yao, A.: On the security of public key protocols. IEEE Trans. Inf. Theory **29**(2), 198–208 (1983)
33. N. I. of Standards and Technology: Secure hash standard (SHS), U.S. Department of Commerce, Washington, D.C., Tech. Rep. Federal Information Processing Standards Publications (FIPS PUBS) 180-4, August 2015
34. Mallouli, F., Hellal, A., Sharief Saeed, N., Abdulraheem Alzahrani, F.: A survey on cryptography: comparative study between rsa vs ecc algorithms, and rsa vs elgamal algorithms. In: 2019 6th IEEE International Conference on Cyber Security and Cloud Computing (CSCloud)/ 2019 5th IEEE International Conference on Edge Computing and Scalable Cloud (EdgeCom), pp. 173–176 (2019)
35. Multiprecision integer and rational arithmetic cryptographic core library - miracl core. https://github.com/miracl/core. Accessed 10 Mar 2023

BITS-HAR: Human Activity Recognition Using Explainable Deep Learning Models

Devrajsinh Jhala[✉], Gladwin Kurian, Yogesh Kumar Agrawal, Ishan Jat, and Hemant Rathore

Department of CS & IS, BITS Pilani, Goa Campus, Goa, India
{h20240120, h20240040, h20240106, h20240102, hemantr}@goa.bits-pilani.ac.in

Abstract. Human Activity Recognition systems have applications in various domains ranging from health and fitness to medical applications. Many of the existing work focuses only on model building and benchmarking. However, in this study, we aimed to design and develop an effective human activity recognition system that is explainable and deployable in a real-time setting. Our work used the capability of joint learning algorithms like the joint multi-head memory models to classify complex human activity recognition tasks. We designed and developed the Joint Convolutional Neural Networks and Long Short Term Memory model that achieved an accuracy of 99.03% on the UCI human activity recognition dataset. We also focussed on model and data explainability using SHapley Additive exPlanations and Local Interpretable Model-agnostic Explanations algorithms. The explainability module highlights the top 15 features that are critical in the model's thinking and decision-making. Finally, we developed an android application for real-world human activity recognition based on phone sensor data that achieved an accuracy of 91.75%.

Keywords: Convolutional Neural Networks · Gated Recurrent Units · Long Short Term Memory Units · SHapley Additive exPlanations · Local Interpretable Model-agnostic Explanations

1 Introduction

A recent report by the Center for Disease Control and Prevention (CDC) suggests that 80% of adults fall short of meeting recommended physical activity levels, leading to significant public health challenges. Inactive behavior and improper physical activity are leading to a global health crisis, like a surge in chronic diseases, obesity, and lower well-being. At such a time of advancing technology and growing sedentary lifestyles, we wish to have more accurate and convenient methods for monitoring physical activity. Thus, Human Activity Recognition (HAR) systems based on sensor data have gained prominence, especially with the advent of wearable technology and the IoT [26].

S. Li et al. (Eds.): BROADNETS 2024, LNICST 674, pp. 33–51, 2026.
https://doi.org/10.1007/978-3-032-14350-1_3

Researchers have explored a range of models like convolutional autoencoders (ConvAEs), attention-based models, LSTMs, and CNNs for developing human activity recognition systems. Thakur et al. [21] proposed a deep learning approach named ConvoAE-LSTM that combined convolutional auto-encoder along with LSTM units and achieved 98.14%. Benhaili et al. [5] proposed a novel lightweight deep stacked LSTM network achieving an accuracy of 97.15%. Wang et al. proposed a novel structure named hierarchical deep LSTM (H-LSTM) and were able to achieve an accuracy of 91.65%. Thus, it became evident from existing studies that combining Convolutional Neural Networks (CNNs) and Long Short-Term Memory (LSTM) networks is particularly effective for handling time-series data in human activity recognition tasks. However, none of the existing works have explored data and model explainability. It is essential to explain the model's derivations and inferences when deciding on the prediction label. Also, very few studies have deployed the human activity recognition model to test it in real-world scenarios.

In our work, we proposed two novel architectures for human activity recognition, namely multi-head Convolutional Neural Networks (CNN) with Long Short Term Memory (LSTM) and Convolutional Neural Networks (CNN) with Gated Recurrent Unit (GRU). The proposed human activity recognition system performs better than most of the state-of-the-art models. Later, we also focused on data and models using SHapley Additive exPlanations (SHAP) [13] and Local Interpretable Model-agnostic Explanations (LIME) [17] algorithms. We have also developed an android mobile application that captures data from phone sensors and performs human activity recognition. The HAR application turns sensor data into a frame and predicts the activity along with explanations using feature importance, prediction probability, etc. Finally, our work has made the following contributions to the domain:

- We designed two novel architectures, namely: multi-head CNN-LSTM and multi-head CNN-GRU, for human activity recognition that achieved an overall accuracy of 99.06% and 98.47%, respectively. The proposed systems perform better than most of the state-of-the-art models in the existing literature.
- Our proposed architecture incorporates data and model explainability using SHAP and LIME algorithms. The designed system also lists the top 15 features that are essential in model's thinking and decision-making.
- We have also developed an Android mobile application that captures real-time phone sensor data and performs human activity recognition with an accuracy of 91.75%. The android application converts sensor data into frames of 73 features and predicts human activities along with essential features, prediction probability, etc.

The paper will now introduce the proposed framework architecture in Sect. 2. We will then explain the theoretical concepts utilized in the study in Sect. 3. The experimental setup which includes the dataset and various components is described in Sect. 4. The experimental results are illustrated in Sect. 5, followed by the literature survey and comparison with existing work in Sect. 6. Finally, concluding remarks and future scope are listed in Sect. 7.

2   Proposed Framework for BITS-HAR

The framework architecture for the proposed human activity recognition system is shown in Fig. 1. First, the publicly available signal data was downloaded and combined in a data frame to form the dataset. Next, the pre-processing and standardization step was performed on the dataset using the sci-kit learn [15] library. Subsequently, two deep learning models, multi-head CNN + LSTM and multi-head CNN + GRU were designed and developed for human activity recognition. The two developed models were then evaluated using common evaluation metrics such as classification report, confusion matrix, accuracy vs. epochs, and loss vs. epochs plots. Later, the model explainability was performed using SHAP and LIME algorithms.

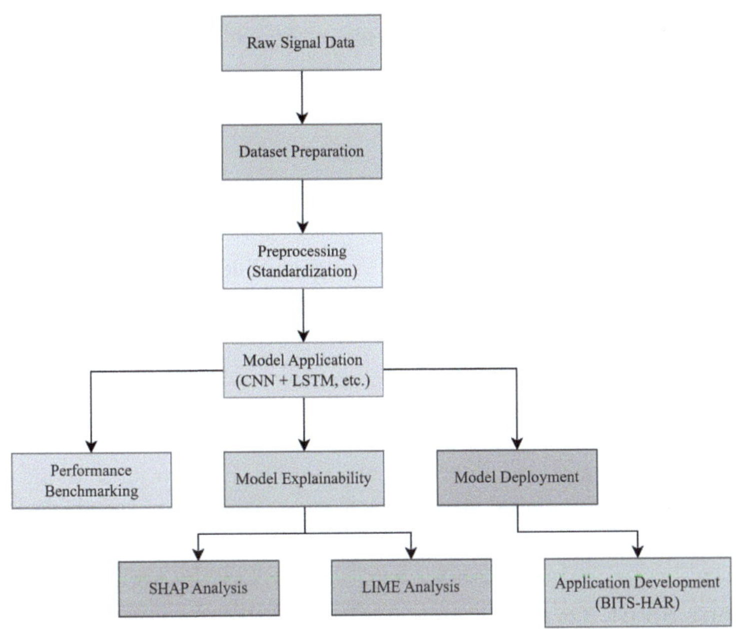

Fig. 1. Framework architecture for human activity recognition system

Both SHAP and LIME improve model understanding and explain how the model thinks, what important features the model considers for prediction, etc. It provides a deep understanding of the nature of prediction and the feature set of the dataset. Finally, an android mobile application was developed that collects real-time sensor data and processes it for real-time human activity prediction. The application is developed using React Native as the front end, and the back end is built using Python and Flask [9]. The deep learning-based HAR model was deployed on the backend. The entire backend is hosted on a platform as a web service called render.

3 Proposed Method for BITS-HAR

In this section, we will discuss the main theoretical concepts and the model architecture utilized in this study. We will expand on different components and modules in detail which are the basic blocks of our model how we used them in our model to get desired advantages and how these modules come together to form a model architecture.

3.1 Convolutional Neural Network (CNN)

Convolutional Neural Networks (CNNs) are the most applied in image processing and other spatial data applications due to their ability to extract local dependencies and hierarchical structures of data [12]. For more granular spatial feature extraction, methods like those proposed in [3] employ multi-headed CNN architectures to capture complex local patterns. The CNNs use the convolutional layers, where filters are moved over the input data to generate feature maps, which determine the spatial features, such as edges, corners, and textures. This is mathematically stated as:

$$(f * g)(x) = \sum_i f(i) \cdot g(x - i) \tag{1}$$

where f is the input and g the filter. Using pooling layers reduces the spatial dimension while including max-pooling, for example, the highest value in the region is reserved. Pooling layers enable model generalization by focusing on big features:

$$h_{ij}^{\text{pool}} = \max(x_{i:i+p,\,j:j+p}) \tag{2}$$

Here p refers to the pool size. Spatial downsampling has proven to reduce computation while having increased spatial invariance. This has particularly benefited in transfer learning and multi-domain applications.

3.2 Long Short Term Memory Units (LSTMs)

Long Short-Term Memory (LSTM) networks are a class of recurrent neural networks (RNN) particularly designed to capture long-term dependencies over sequences. Therefore, they are suitable for applications such as time-series analysis and natural language processing [10] and hence since recent times, complex LSTM architecture like explored in [23] finds more and more attention in HAR works. LSTMs have memory cells that retain information across sequence steps, which helps alleviate the problem of vanishing gradients often associated with traditional RNNs. The LSTM cell structure comprises an input, output, and forget gate whose operations over the information flow are as follows.

Forget Gate: This gate decides what part of the cell state to forget.

$$f_t = \sigma(W_f \cdot [h_{t-1}, x_t] + b_f) \tag{3}$$

Input Gate: Decide what new information to inject.

$$i_t = \sigma(W_i \cdot [h_{t-1}, x_t] + b_i) \tag{4}$$

Output Gate: Determines the cell's output.

$$o_t = \sigma(W_o \cdot [h_{t-1}, x_t] + b_o) \tag{5}$$

Recent research pays more attention-augmented LSTM architectures for better performance in video recognition tasks and processing sensor data.

3.3   Gated Recurrent Units (GRUs)

Gated Recurrent Units, GRUs, are an implementation of LSTM networks minus the internal structure complexity of LSTMs. GRUs were introduced by Cho et al. in 2014 [7] and have fewer gates and no internal memory cells, thus training faster and better use of memory. Because of their efficiency, they are applicable in real-time applications and handling long sequences in speech recognition and sensor data analysis tasks.

The two primary gates within a GRU cell are the update gate and the reset gate

Update Gate: This gate indicates what percentage of the previous state to carry along into the current state:

$$z_t = \sigma(W_z \cdot [h_{t-1}, x_t] + b_z) \tag{6}$$

Reset Gate: This determines at what level the past state impacts the current input:

$$r_t = \sigma(W_r \cdot [h_{t-1}, x_t] + b_r) \tag{7}$$

Candidate Activation: Introduce another hidden state to the candidate

$$\tilde{h}_t = \tanh(W_h \cdot [r_t * h_{t-1}, x_t] + b_h) \tag{8}$$

Hidden State Update: It combines the previous state and the candidate state:

$$h_t = z_t * h_{t-1} + (1 - z_t) * \tilde{h}_t \tag{9}$$

3.4   Additional Components

Fully Connected Layers: Fully connected layers are also called dense layers. In this case, each neuron connects with each neuron in the previous as well as the next layer. They are mainly used at the end of the network for compiling a higher-level abstraction of the features into a prediction. The output of a fully connected layer is given by:

$$h = \sigma(W \cdot x + b) \tag{10}$$

where W is the weight matrix, x is the input vector, b is the bias vector, and σ is the activation function (e.g., softmax for classification). Although fully connected layers are good at feature summarization, pruning methods have been proposed in recent works to remove redundancy and make dense layers more efficient [8, 18, 19].

Batch Normalization: The BatchNorm normalizes the layer inputs to have zero mean and unit variance, which stabilizes and accelerates training [11]. Different Normalization strategies such as Instance Normalization [24] are also helpful in different and diverse classification problems. It reduces the internal covariate shift, which enables faster convergence as well as adjusts learnable parameters to scale and shift values for optimal representation. Variants of this, such as group normalization, improve performance for various batch sizes and tasks.

3.5   Proposed Model Architecture

Joint Learning Between Multi-head CNN and Multi-head LSTM: In this architecture, we have a six-head CNN paralleled with a six-head LSTM that is used to concurrently learn spatial information captured by the multi-head CNN and temporal information captured by the multi-head LSTMs built using Tensorflow [1]. We have different Conv1D layers with varying kernel sizes in the CNN part that capture different types of local patterns. Finally, we used batch normalization to improve stability in training. It has a flattening layer that takes the 2D outputs, converts them to a 1D format, and then concatenates all of the outputs from the six CNN heads.

Six LSTMs provide output for each of the sequences. L2 regularization will add a caveat against overfitting. Output from LSTM heads get further concatenated. These two outputs of the multi-head CNN and multi-head LSTM are passed to a dense layer of 256 units and ReLU activation functions to process the merged features. More regularization is applied by the dropout function, and finally, softmax activation is applied in the output layer for classification purposes. The model is compiled using the SGD optimizer specifically with a learning rate of 0.01 and a momentum of 0.9. Here are detailed descriptions with values for each of the hyperparameters used in model building.

The model was trained with a batch size of 64 using the SGD optimizer, configured with a learning rate of 0.01 and momentum of 0.9. The training spanned 120 epochs with Categorical Crossentropy as the loss function and a validation split of 0.1. Regularization was applied to the LSTM layers using L2 with a λ of 0.001, along with a dropout rate of 0.5. A ReduceLROnPlateau learning rate scheduler adjusted the learning rate by a factor of 0.2 when improvement plateaued, with a minimum learning rate of 1e-5. Six CNN heads incorporated Conv1D layers with kernel sizes of 3, 5, and 7, each containing 64 filters and "same" padding. Six GRU heads, each with 64 units, were also included. Activation functions included ReLU [4] for Conv1D and Dense layers, with Softmax at the output layer.

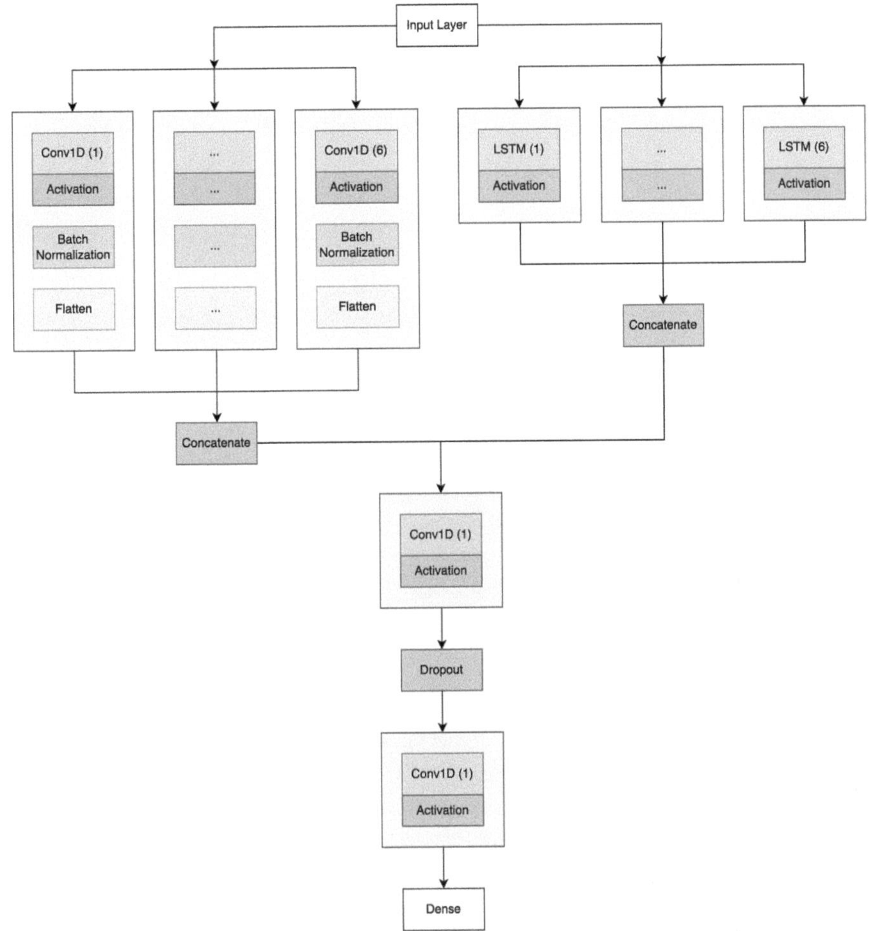

Fig. 2. Model architecture for multi-head CNN+LSTM

Joint Learning Between Multi-head CNN and Multi-head GRU: This architecture is a follow-up of the above model; where the LSTM layers are replaced by GRU layers to test the effectiveness of the joint learning mechanism. The architecture is very similar to the above-mentioned, it is just more simple. In this architecture as well, we have divided our input branch into 12 layers with 6 layers being CNN layers and 6 layers being GRU layers. The 6 CNN layers have the same kernel sizes also mentioned in the table below as above but lack BatchNormalization as seen from the figure. Using CNN we aim to capture spatial patterns and important data patterns in the dataset. As usual Flatten layer is utilized to convert data from a higher dimension to a lower dimension.

The GRU layer is considered a little weak to the LSTM layer as it has only two gates: Update Gate and Forget Gate. Still, the performance of this model

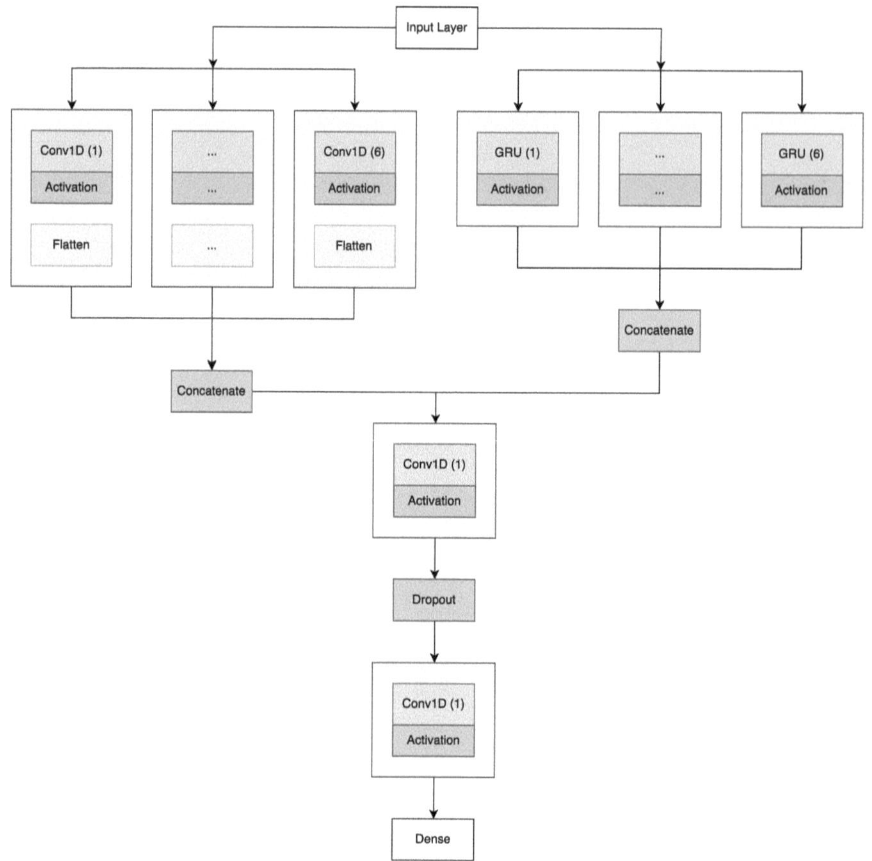

Fig. 3. Model architecture for multi-head CNN+GRU

beats most of the other models in the literature indicating promising capabilities of joint learning mechanisms in classifying complex classification problems. A detailed description of the hyperparameters utilized and their values are given below:

The model was trained using a batch size of 64 and optimized with the Adam optimizer at a learning rate of 0.001. Categorical Crossentropy was used as the loss function over 70 epochs, with a validation split of 0.1 and a dropout rate of 0.5 to prevent overfitting. Activation functions included ReLU for Conv1D and Dense layers, while Softmax was applied at the output layer. The model utilized six CNN heads, each with Conv1D layers having kernel sizes of 3, 5, and 7, and 64 filters per layer, along with padding set to "same." Additionally, six GRU heads were incorporated, each with 64 units, to enhance temporal sequence modeling.

4 Experimental Setup for BITS-HAR

In this section, we will discuss the important components of the project, like the dataset we have used, and a detailed explanation and in-depth analysis of the dataset, the dataset used for the mobile application since it needs to be faster and with low computational cost, the mobile application development details and how we are going to analyze the performance of our models after training.

4.1 Train Dataset Description

The dataset is built using sensor data collected from the Samsung Galaxy-S(II) smartphone tied to the waist of 30 subjects belonging to the age group of 19–48 years. Each of the subjects performed various activities like Sitting, Walking, Laying, etc. The sensor recordings were sampled at 50 Hz frequency for 2.56 s. The sensor readings with 50% overlap or 128 readings per window were then passed to Butterworth filters with 0.3 Hz cutoff frequency. There are a total of 6 activities whose count and percentage distribution is given in the table below. The dataset was made in shape using Pandas [14, 22] (Table 1).

Table 1. Activity distribution in training dataset

Activity	Count	Percentage (%)
Walking	1722	16.72
Walking Upstairs	1541	14.97
Walking Downstairs	1406	13.65
Sitting	1944	18.88
Standing	1773	17.22
Laying	1913	18.56

4.2 Computational Resources and Environment

We have used the publicly available UCI-HAR dataset [16] for designing and developing the deep learning models. All the experiments were executed in the Kaggle Notebook environment. All the deep learning models were trained on GPU-100 GPU from Kaggle.

4.3 Mobile Application Dataset

For the mobile application, the dataset utilized is a subset of the original UCI HAR dataset. When the sensor data comes from the front end, it is processed in real-time in the backend where we extract the features from the data. The features are extracted from 3 sensors: accelerometer, gyroscope, and magnetometer in 3 axes: X, Y, and Z. Also, 8 feature sets are extracted like mean, skewness, etc. Hence total features extracted is 72 (8*3*3) + 1 (Target class). These features are then sent to the CNN + LSTM model for prediction.

4.4 Mobile Application Development

For the development of the mobile application BITS-HAR, we utilized React-Native with Expo version 6.3.12. Backend development was done using Python version 3.12.5 and Flask version 3.0.3. The development was done in VS-Code code editor and Kaggle Jupyter Notebook. A more detailed description of the application is given in the Application Development section.

4.5 Performance Metrics

Confusion Matrix: A confusion matrix is somewhat like a plot. We see where our model makes incorrect predictions. Ideally, the matrix should have maximum values across its diagonal cells (true positives) and minimum values for any other cells.

$$\text{Accuracy} = \frac{\text{Correct Predictions}}{\text{Total Samples}} \tag{11}$$

Classification Report: A classification report provides metrics like Precision, Recall, and F1-score for each class, along with overall accuracy. These metrics help assess the model's performance:

$$\text{Precision} = \frac{\text{True Positives}}{\text{True Positives} + \text{False Positives}} \tag{12}$$

$$\text{Recall} = \frac{\text{True Positives}}{\text{True Positives} + \text{False Negatives}} \tag{13}$$

$$\text{F1-Score} = 2 \cdot \frac{\text{Precision} \times \text{Recall}}{\text{Precision} + \text{Recall}} \tag{14}$$

Accuracy vs Epoch: An Accuracy vs. Epoch plot shows the training and validation accuracy over time. Ideally, both curves should increase and approach high accuracy without overfitting.

$$\text{Accuracy for each epoch } t = \frac{\text{Correct Predictions}_t}{\text{Total Predictions}_t} \tag{15}$$

Loss Vs Epoch: A Loss vs. Epoch plot shows the training and validation loss over time. Ideally, both curves should decrease and approach a low loss value.

$$\text{Loss for each epoch } t = L_t = \frac{1}{n} \sum_{i=1}^{n} -\text{Loss}(\text{Prediction}_i, \text{Actual}_i) \tag{16}$$

5   Results Obtained for BITS-HAR

This section details the performance of the proposed models following rigorous evaluation. We compared our models with a recognized state-of-the-art (SOTA) model for Human Activity Recognition (HAR) and used various evaluation metrics Accuracy and F1-Score to assess the models' strengths and limitations. Additionally, we analyzed model size and parameter count to evaluate computational efficiency and suitability for mobile applications.

5.1   Model Performance Evaluation

In this section, we explored the performance parameters in detail which are also given in the table below. We then proceed to describe each of the parameters in detail including Accuracy and F1 score, Accuracy and Loss vs Epochs, and Confusion matrix as well.

Accuracy and F1-Score Evaluation: Both Accuracy and F1-Score were selected as key metrics for evaluating prediction performance. While Accuracy measures the proportion of correct predictions across all classes, F1-Score accounts for both Precision and Recall, making it a more robust measure, especially for imbalanced datasets. Multi-head CNN + LSTM achieves 99.06% Accuracy and 99.05% F1-Score, indicating that this model consistently predicts each activity with high precision. Multi-head CNN + GRU, though slightly lower in Accuracy at 98.47%, shows a similar trend with an F1-Score of 98.40%, maintaining competitive performance at a fraction of the parameter count (Table reftab:modelspsaccuracy).

Table 2. Brief summary on model performances

Approaches	Accuracy (%)	F1-Score (%)	Total Parameters	Size (MB)	Accuracy Change (SOTA) (%)
CNN + LSTM	99.06	99.05	4,908,046	18.72	0.92
CNN + GRU	98.47	98.40	2,114,438	8.07	0.33

Model Complexity and Mobile Suitability: The models vary significantly in size and parameter count, directly impacting computational efficiency: The CNN + LSTM model has over 4.9 million parameters and requires 18.72 MB of storage. Although this larger model offers slightly superior accuracy, it may be resource-intensive for mobile deployment. CNN + GRU, with only 2.1 million parameters and 8.07 MB in size, offers a more compact and computationally efficient solution, making it better suited for mobile applications with only a marginal loss in accuracy.

State-Of-The-Art Comparison:

Comparative Analysis of Confusion Matrices: Using confusion matrices for both models, we observed nearly perfect prediction rates for most classes. However, sitting and standing classes presented challenges for both models due to overlapping sensor signal characteristics, possibly due to the stationary nature of these activities. Despite these challenges, the CNN + LSTM model slightly outperforms the CNN + GRU, attributable to its larger parameter space and complexity

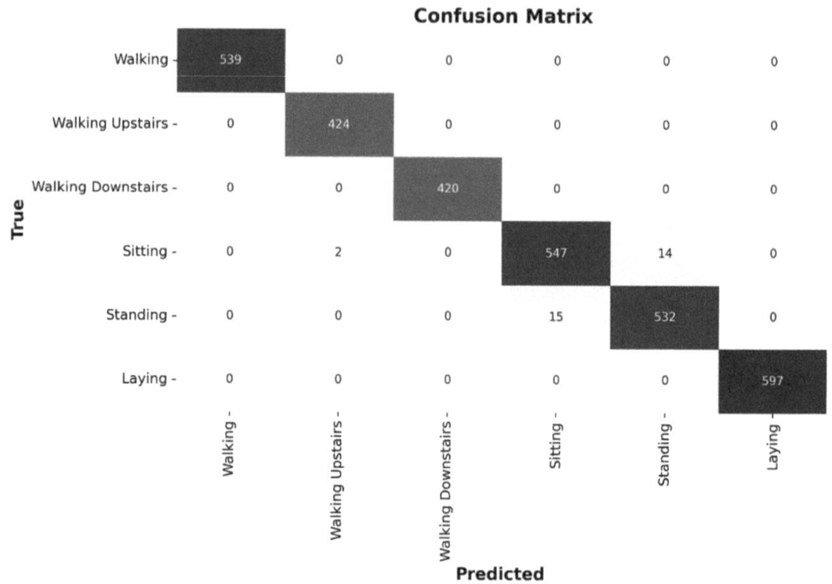

Fig. 4. Confusion matrix for multi-head CNN+LSTM

Accuracy and Loss over Epochs: The validation of the Multi-head CNN + LSTM model is shown in the above figure. These figures show accuracy and loss over the span of 120 epochs for the CNN+LSTM model where we have scored an accuracy of 99.06% which is the current state-of-the-art accuracy score with a loss of 0.01. There are few spikes in validation accuracy, that can occur due to several reasons like learning rate fluctuations, data shuffling and regularization techniques like dropout can cause these fluctuations but on the running average the accuracy goes up with the increase in epochs and Thus, these spikes are temporary, random and epoch specific due to above-mentioned reasons.

The accuracy and loss score for the Multi-head CNN + GRU model is shown in the above figure which shows that the accuracy of this model is 98.47% with

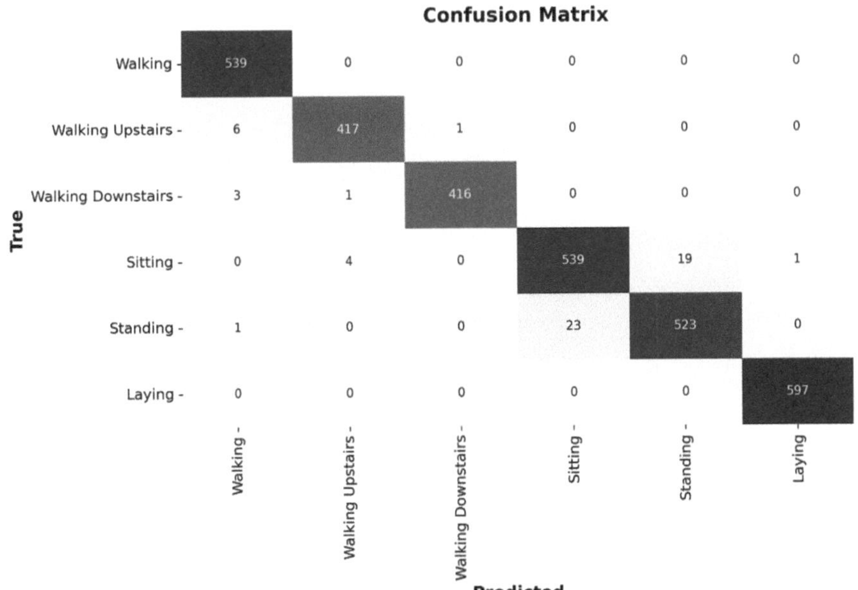

Fig. 5. Confusion matrix for multi-head CNN+GRU

a loss score of 0.02. As we can see the performance of the model over time is not as smooth as CNN+LSTM that is because this model is of lesser size and faster which is ideal for a mobile application at the cost of slight cost in prediction accuracy.

Our results suggest that while the CNN + LSTM model provides the highest predictive accuracy, the CNN + GRU offers a balanced trade-off between performance and efficiency, essential for mobile application use. These findings support the practical utility of both models: the CNN + LSTM for high-accuracy applications and the CNN + GRU for lightweight, efficient deployment with minimal accuracy compromise.

5.2 Explainability Analysis: SHAP Applied to Multi-Head CNN+LSTM

In this SHAP summary plot, the contributions of individual features toward the classification of various human activities are displayed. Each bar represents a feature, with its length indicating the average impact on model predictions, expressed in terms of SHAP values. The features with the highest SHAP values, such as tBodyGyroJerk-entropy()-X and fBodyGyro-entropy()-X, contribute the most to the model's predictions, suggesting that they are key factors in distinguishing between activities. The color segmentation within each bar illustrates the feature's contribution across different activities, namely "Sitting," "Standing," "Walking Upstairs," "Walking," "Laying," and "Walking Downstairs." For

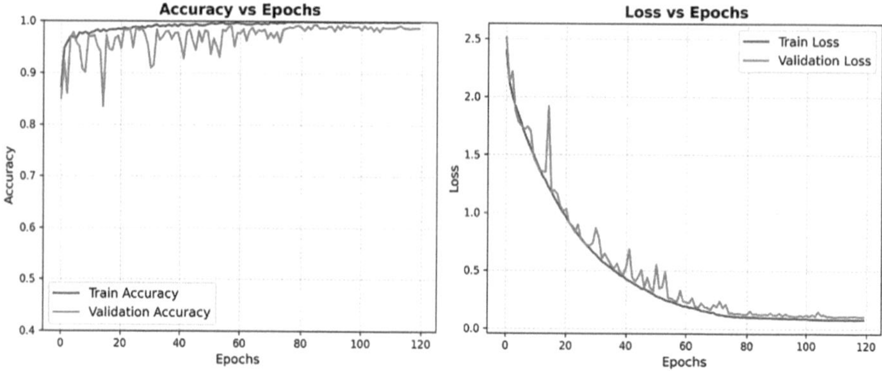

Fig. 6. Accuracy and loss vs epoch for multi-head CNN+LSTM

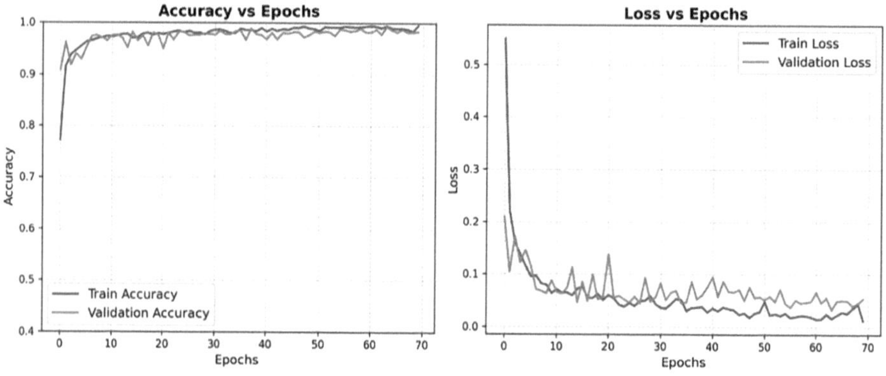

Fig. 7. Accuracy and loss vs epoch for multi-head CNN+GRU

example, tBodyGyroJerk-entropy()-X has the greatest impact across multiple activities, particularly distinguishing between "Sitting" and "Standing." This indicates that entropy values derived from body gyroscope jerk data play a crucial role in capturing unique characteristics of stationary versus dynamic postures. Similarly, fBodyGyro-entropy()-X exhibits high importance, highlighting that frequency-domain entropy features from the gyroscope sensor provide significant insights for activity differentiation, likely due to their sensitivity to changes in motion patterns.

5.3   Mobile Application Development

The mobile app is built with React-native which will give us cross-platform flexibility in the future. For capturing the sensor data, we are using the Expo-Sensor package. We are using data from three different sensors namely Accelerometer, Gyroscope. When the user clicks start recording, the app starts collecting data

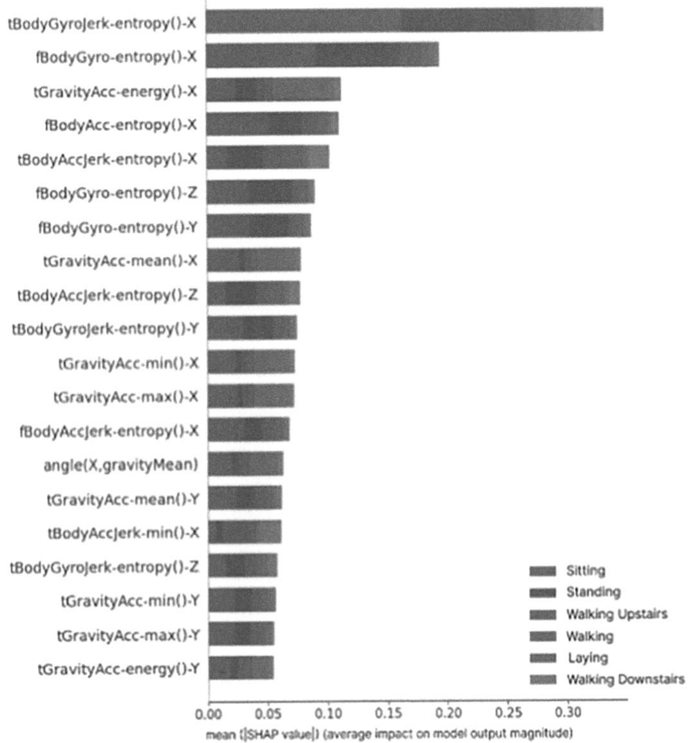

Fig. 8. SHAP summary plot analysis of CNN+LSTM model

from the sensor at a rate 50 Hz for 2.56 s and the data is stored as a list of objects. This data is then sent to the backend for prediction.

At the backend, which is built with Flask and Python will extract eight features from the three sensors for the three different axes. In this manner, we are able to get $8*3*3 + 1($ target feature$) = 73$ features from the mobile app. But our proposed model above had 562 features, so for our mobile app we had to make the model with reduced features to incorporate it for the mobile development. Thus with reduced features our accuracy was also reduced slightly to 92.57%. All our backends are hosted on a platform known as render as a web service. After the prediction, we send the prediction back to the front end to display the result. We are also using the LIME package for real-time model explainability which gives us the probability of activities and also the feature contributions against each prediction.

6   Related Work

The field of Human Activity Recognition is a very explored sector in the field of literature. Initially, various classification machine learning algorithms were

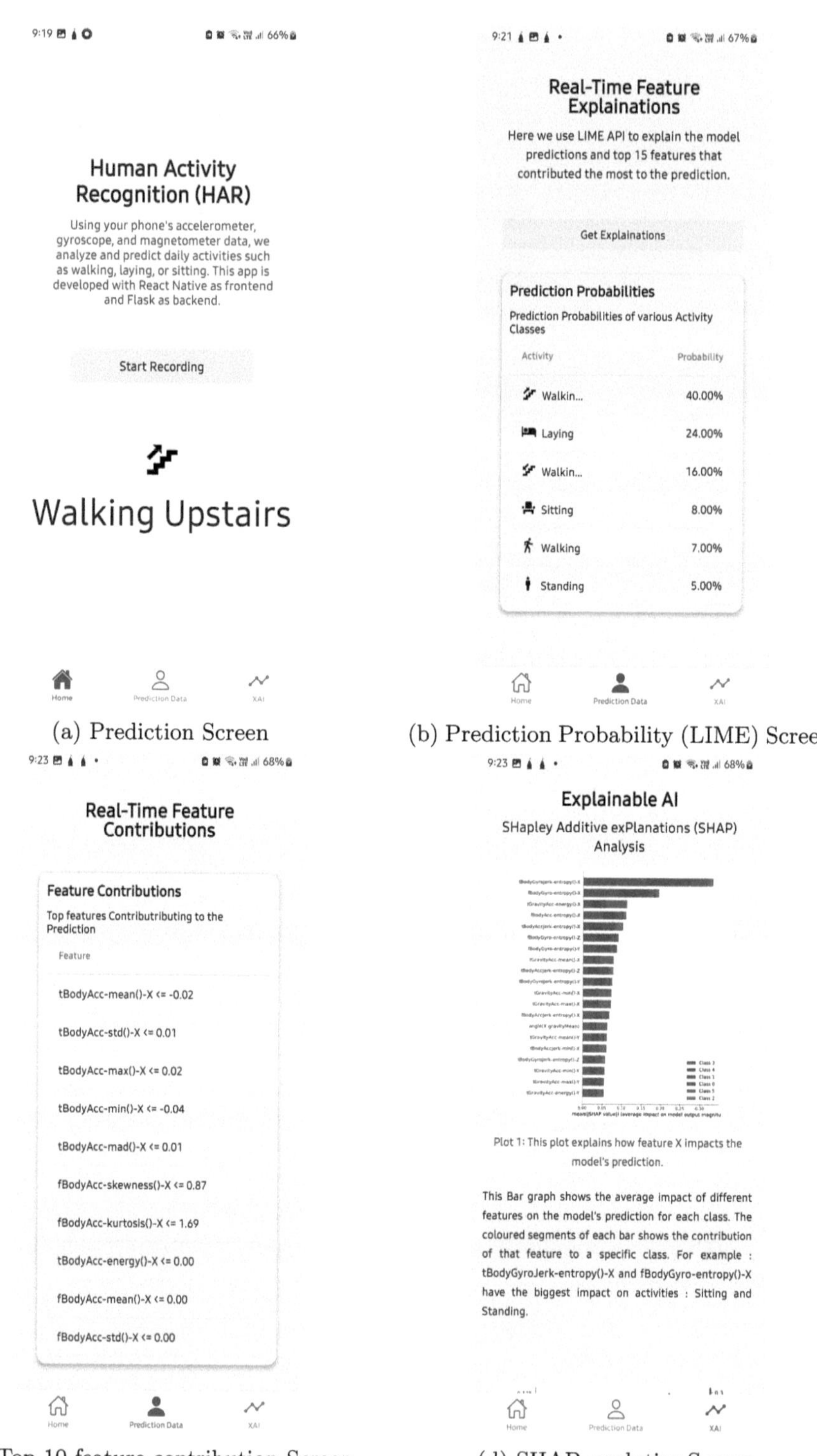

(a) Prediction Screen

(b) Prediction Probability (LIME) Screen

(c) Top 10 feature contribution Screen

(d) SHAP analytics Screen

Fig. 9. BITS-HAR android application interface displaying real-time predictions and prediction probabilities screen of different classes

Table 3. Comparison with existing literature survey

Author	Approach Utilized	Dataset Utilized	Accuracy (%)	F1-Score (%)	Explainability	Application Developed
Wang et al. (2019) [25]	HDL model, coupling CNN - LSTM	UCI-HAR	91.65	Not mentioned	✗	✗
Basset et al. (2021) [2]	Deep stacked LSTM	UCI-HAR WISDM	97.15 99	97 99	✗	✗
Bi et al. (2021) [6]	ConvoAE-LSTM	UCI-HAR OPPORTUNITY PAMPL WISDM	98.14 95.69 94.33 95.86	97.67 95.54 94.46 98.14	✗	✗
Benhaili et al. (2022) [5]	AIM-CNN	UCI-HAR WISDM	95.38 98.18	95.37 97.20	✗	✗
Thakur et al. (2023) [20]	Conv LSTM-PmwA	UCI-HAR WISDM	96.71 95.86	Not mentioned	✗	✗
Our proposed models	Multihead CNN+LSTM Multihead CNN+GRU	**UCI-HAR**	**99.06** **98.47**	**99.05** **98.40**	✓	✓

proposed to classify activities. However with the advent of deep learning algo-rithms, the performance and architecture both improved very much. Models such as Multi-layer perceptron, Convolutional Neural Networks, etc., and their combinations made huge strides in improving the classification extent, and this is also visible in the literature survey we performed below.

Most of the works listed below utilize deep learning approaches; however, the achieved accuracy and F1-Score hovers around 91% – 99%. However, our multi-head CNN and multi-head LSTM achieved an average accuracy of 99.06% and 99.05% F1-Score after five iterations.

Also, none of the works touched upon the explainability of the model, which is explored in the sections below. We performed both data and model explainability using SHAP and LIME, which gives us plots to better understand what features were given more preference by the model for prediction; moreover, it also gives us prediction probabilities of various class labels, which helps us understand how the model came to a particular conclusion on prediction. Also, we developed a mobile application that takes real-time phone sensor data and predicts activities which is also explored in the sections below.

Yin, X. et al. [26] proposed a novel convolutional neural network with Bi-LSTM units along with a parallel attention mechanism (Conv LSTM-PmwA), which achieved an impressive accuracy of 96.71% on the UCI HAR dataset. How-ever, we were able to achieve 99.06% accuracy using a combination of multihead CNN and multihead LSTM. Thakur, D. et al. [21] proposed an innovative deep learning approach named ConvoAE-LSTM, which is a combination of a con-volutional auto-encoder along with long short-term memory units. This model achieved an impressive accuracy of 98.14% and F1 score of 97.67%. However, with our multi-head CNN – multi-head LSTM model, we were not only able to get slightly better accuracy and F1 score, but we also performed SHAP and LIME analysis to explain the data and the model's decision-making. Xia, K. et al. built a DL algorithm that has three parallel CNNs for providing local features and for subsequent merging to establish feature fusion models of varying kernel size and scored an accuracy of 97.49%. We were able to deploy our model into an android application which gave live SHAP and LIME analysis for features impacting the prediction and probability of classes. In the next section, we will discuss the methodology followed during the entire span of the study, and we will provide a high-level overview of the processes followed and their achieved outcomes (Table 3).

7   Conclusion and Future Work

In conclusion, we aimed to present a comprehensive analysis and potential of Joint learning algorithms like Joint multihead CNN and LSTM or GRU in analyzing complex classification problems. We not only performed better than the State-Of-The-Art model in terms of accuracy and F1-scores but also explored model and data explainability to provide better insights into how the model works. We also developed an application that predicts activities based on real-time phone sensor data. The sensor data is processed into a data frame and then sent to the model for prediction in the backend. Our main objective here was to check how many of the features of the original UCI-HAR dataset we extracted in real time. Still, some of the limitations of our paper include:

- In our mobile application, we were able to extract only 73 features out of 144 features (some of the features were not there in the UCI-HAR dataset and some were giving NaN values sometimes which would break the model).
- In the future, we would like to not only extract more features consistently but also add new features which would make the prediction much more refined and better.
- Joint learning is a mechanism, not a model, so there can be a lot of combinations made. In this study, only CNN, LSTM, and GRU are utilized, but transformers can also be explored in the future.

We hope in the future we are able to solve some of the problems listed above or improve upon the existing methodology utilized in the paper.

References

1. Abadi, M., et al.: Tensorflow: Large-scale machine learning on heterogeneous systems (2015)
2. Abdel-Basset, M., Hawash, H., Chakrabortty, R.K., Ryan, M., Elhoseny, M., Song, H.: St-deephar: deep learning model for human activity recognition in ioht applications. IEEE Internet Things J. **8**(6), 4969–4979 (2020)
3. Abdulwahab, S., Rashwan, H.A., Sharaf, N., Khalid, S., Puig, D.: Deep monocular depth estimation based on content and contextual features. Sensors **23**(6), 2919 (2023)
4. Agarap, A.F.: Deep learning using rectified linear units (relu). arXiv preprint arXiv:1803.08375 (2018)
5. Benhaili, Z., Abouqora, Y., Balouki, Y., Moumoun, L.: Basic activity recognition from wearable sensors using a lightweight deep neural network. J. ICT Standardization **10**(2), 241–260 (2022)

6. Bi, H., Perello-Nieto, M., Santos-Rodriguez, R., Flach, P.: Human activity recognition based on dynamic active learning. IEEE J. Biomed. Health Inform. **25**(4), 922–934 (2020)
7. Cho, K.: Learning phrase representations using rnn encoder-decoder for statistical machine translation. arXiv preprint arXiv:1406.1078 (2014)
8. Goodfellow, I., Bengio, Y., Courville, A.: Deep Learning. The MIT Press (2016)
9. Grinberg, M.: Flask web development: developing web applications with python. Inc, O'Reilly Media (2018)
10. Hochreiter, S.: Long short-term memory. Neural Computation MIT-Press (1997)
11. Ioffe, S.: Batch normalization: Accelerating deep network training by reducing internal covariate shift. arXiv preprint arXiv:1502.03167 (2015)
12. LeCun, Y., Bottou, L., Bengio, Y., Haffner, P.: Gradient-based learning applied to document recognition. Proc. IEEE **86**(11), 2278–2324 (1998)
13. Lundberg, S.: A unified approach to interpreting model predictions. arXiv preprint arXiv:1705.07874 (2017)
14. Wes McKinney: Data Structures for Statistical Computing in Python. In: 9th Python in Science Conference, pp. 56 – 61 (2010)
15. Pedregosa, F., Varoquaux, G., Gramfort, A., Michel, V., Thirion, B., Grisel, O., Blondel, M., Prettenhofer, P., Weiss, R., Dubourg, V., Vanderplas, J., Passos, A., Cournapeau, D., Brucher, M., Perrot, M., Duchesnay, E.: Scikit-learn: Machine learning in Python. J. Mach. Learn. Res. **12**, 2825–2830 (2011)
16. Reyes-Ortiz, J.L., Anguita, D., Ghio, A., Parra, X.: Human activity recognition using smartphones data set. UCI Machine Learning Repository (2012)
17. Ribeiro, M.T., Singh, S., Guestrin, C.: "Why should i trust you?" explaining the predictions of any classifier. In: 22nd ACM SIGKDD International Conference on Knowledge Discovery and Data Mining, pp. 1135–1144 (2016)
18. Sewak, M., Sahay, S.K., Rathore, H.: In: Value-approximation based deep reinforcement learning techniques: an overview, pp. 379–384. IEEE (2020)
19. Sewak, M., Sahay, S.K., Rathore, H.: Policy-approximation based deep reinforcement learning techniques: an overview. Information and Communication Technology for Competitive Strategies, pp. 493–507 (2022)
20. Thakur, D., Biswas, S., Ho, E.S.L., Chattopadhyay, S.: Convae-lstm: convolutional autoencoder long short-term memory network for smartphone-based human activity recognition. IEEE Access **10**, 4137–4156 (2022)
21. Thakur, D., Guzzo, A., Fortino, G.: Attention-based multihead deep learning framework for online activity monitoring with smartwatch sensors. IEEE Internet Things J. **10**(20), 17746–17754 (2023)
22. The Pandas Development Team: pandas-dev/pandas: Pandas, February 2020. https://doi.org/10.5281/zenodo.3509134
23. Tian, Y., Song, S., Zhou, D., Pang, S., Wei, C.: Canonical triangular interval type-2 fuzzy set linguistic distribution assessment todim approach: A case study of fmea for electric vehicles dc charging piles. Expert Syst. Appl. **223**, 119826 (2023)
24. Ulyanov, D., Vedaldi, A., Lempitsky, V.S.: Instance normalization: The missing ingredient for fast stylization. arXiv preprint arXiv:1607.08022 (2016)
25. Wang, L., Liu, R.: Human activity recognition based on wearable sensor using hierarchical deep lstm networks. Circuits Syst. Signal Process. **39**(2), 837–856 (2020)
26. Yin, X., Liu, Z., Liu, D., Ren, X.: A novel cnn-based bi-lstm parallel model with attention mechanism for human activity recognition with noisy data. Sci. Rep. **12**(1), 7878 (2022)

PhishBuster: Phishing Detection Based on URL Embeddings and Deep Learning Models with Explainability

T. M. V. S. G Pavan[(✉)], Tanikella Sai Charan, Ayush Agarwal, Ajith Vivekanandan, and Hemant Rathore

Department of CS and IS, BITS Pilani, Goa Campus, Goa, India
{h20240131,h20240138,h20240125,h20230072,hemantr}@goa.bits-pilani.ac.in

Abstract. Today, internet users are becoming increasingly vulnerable to phishing attacks. Phishing is a five-star crime involving stealing sensitive information from internet users, leading to heavy economic losses. Many recent reports suggest that the number of phishing attacks doubles yearly. Therefore, effective and efficient methods are needed to detect these phishing attacks. This paper proposes a novel approach to detect phishing websites with high-performance solutions. We developed a framework that extracts embeddings of Uniform Resource Locators (URL) generated using several embedding creation techniques. Later, the existing features and URL embeddings were concatenated and used to train several deep learning models (FFNN, RNN, and LSTM). Our proposed RoBERTa embeddings based LSTM model for phishing website detection achieved an accuracy of 99.98% and an F1-score of 99.991%. We also focused on model explainability and performed the faithfulness check to validate model reliability. We used the integrated gradient algorithm to explain the performance of the designed models to various stakeholders. The faithfulness of the model was evaluated by removing the top 5 attributes with the highest attribution scores iteratively and observing the performance change in accuracy.

Keywords: Phishing website detection · Deep learning · Explainability · Faithfulness · URL embeddings

1 Introduction

Since its inception, the Internet has evolved into an integral and critical infrastructure, providing its users with many sublime benefits. However, the number of phishing attacks on the internet has also increased exponentially in the last few years. Phishing is a type of fraudulent activity in which spoofed websites are created by mimicking legitimate websites to steal users' sensitive information such as passwords, bank account credentials, credit card details, etc. According to the FBI, phishing was the largest crime in 2017, resulting in a loss of 54 million dollars [4]. The primary targets of any phishing attack are identity

S. Li et al. (Eds.): BROADNETS 2024, LNICST 674, pp. 52–71, 2026.
https://doi.org/10.1007/978-3-032-14350-1_4

theft and the economy of users. These are performed through malicious links in emails/messages, QR codes on mobile applications, and links in online advertisements and tweets. According to the Symantec Security Threat Report, 1 in 170 URLs in 2018 was used to perform a phishing attack [6]. Nowadays, phishing is used to steal sensitive information and spread malicious software, such as ransomware.

In India, nearly 700 million people out of 1.3 billion use the Internet due to increased availability and affordable data rates. People in rural areas who are mostly unaware of the technicalities of internet services are the primary targets of phishing attackers. A recent report by APWG (Anti-Phishing Working Group) stated that the number of phishing attacks from 2021 to 2022 has nearly doubled, and the per month attack rate from 2004–2016 has seen a growth of 5753% [1]. According to Kaspersky's lab report for 2019, nearly 30% of the users faced at least one phishing attack. Many educational institutions had their vulnerable details stolen and later traded on the dark web [5]. So, seeing the magnitude of the loss of wealth and information occurring due to phishing attacks, the importance of anti-phishing solutions to tackle them effectively has also increased over time.

Several traditional methods include an experience based approach where malicious URLs are detected using manual rules. It is a user feedback-based approach where observed malicious URLs when surfing the internet are noted down and tackled when they reappear. This method was primarily based on individual experience and thus was not so effective as the number of URLs is increasing exponentially. According to a Dofo report, nearly 5.2 million URLs were registered with new domain names during April 2020 [3]. So, The traditional methods are not effective in tackling phishing websites. Similarly, several blacklisting software was built to combat phishing websites. Still, attackers easily bypassed them by changing part of the domain names, the path of directories, and other URL information.

This work proposes a novel framework for phishing website detection using URL embeddings and deep learning models. Initially, URL embeddings were generated using embedding generation techniques like Bidirectional Encoder Representations from Transformers (BERT) based models such as BERT_CLS, Sentence-BERT (SBERT), Robustly-optimized BERT (RoBERTa), A Lite BERT (ALBERT) and Universal State Encoder (USE). These embeddings were then concatenated with additional features other than URL derived from the dataset. These features were then used to train three phishing website detection models based on deep learning (feedforward neural networks (FFNN), recurrent neural networks (RNN), and long short-term memory neural networks (LSTM)). The performance of each model was then evaluated using metrics such as accuracy and F1 score. We used the integrated gradients explainability technique that helps the users resonate with the highly accurate results provided by the deep learning models. We also conducted the faithfulness check to ensure that the explanations provided by the integrated gradients algorithm were consistent with the actual model's results.

Our key contributions in this work are as follows:

- We extracted novel URL Embeddings for phishing website detection using several methods like BERT-CLS, SBERT, USE, RoBERTa, and AlBERT. These features were concatenated with additional features derived from the dataset.
- We developed a long short-term memory model for phishing website detection using RoBERTa generated URLs that achieved an accuracy score of 99.989%.
- We also implemented model explainability using integrated gradients algorithm. We found that feature *Line of Code* contributed positively towards the decision with an attribution score of $+1.4204$ while feature *Largest Line Length* contributed negatively with an attribution score of -1.5939.
- We also performed a faithfulness check on the model by removing the top 5 attributes with the highest attribution scores iteratively. The faithfulness check resulted in accuracy degradation from 99.98% to 21.27%, which validates the reliability of the proposed model.

2   Phishbuster Framework

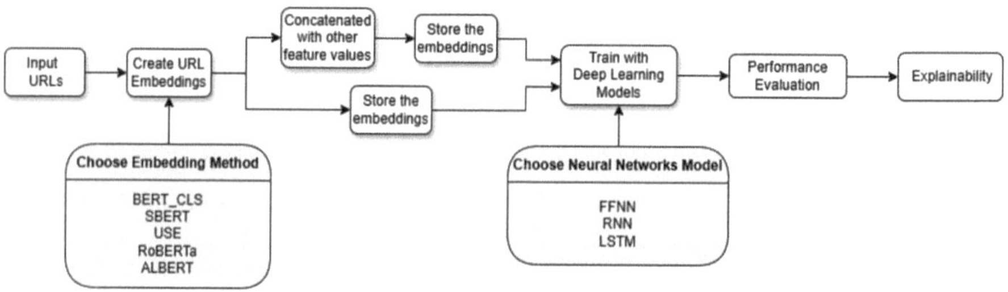

Fig. 1. PhishBuster Framework for Phishing URL Detection

Figure 1 illustrates the proposed framework that aims to provide a reliable and explainable method for phishing website detection. The process begins with data collection by utilizing a publicly available UCI phishing URL dataset. This is followed by the crucial step of converting the URLs of the dataset into URL embeddings. This initial phase is vital in representing URLs as low-dimensional vectors that capture the semantic and contextual information. During this phase, we choose to create embeddings from several embedding models like SBERT, BERT-CLS, RoBERTa, ALBERT, and USE. It allows a comparative study of how different embedding techniques contribute to the effectiveness of various deep learning models. The resulting URL embeddings are then stored for further phases.

The URL embeddings are concatenated with other features extracted from the dataset that can provide additional context for phishing website detection and potentially improve the model's performance. These new embeddings and feature sets are then introduced to different neural network models like feedforward neural networks (FFNN), recurrent neural networks (RNN), and long short-term memory neural networks (LSTM) in the model training phase. This phase intends to examine the suitability of various neural network architectures to handle URL embeddings obtained from different embedding models and extract patterns that distinguish phishing and legitimate URLs.

After the training phase, the proposed framework has a performance evaluation step in which metrics like accuracy and f1-score are used to assess the performance and effectiveness of the model. Following this evaluation, the last step involves the explainability and faithfulness check. In this step, the integrated gradients algorithm was used to provide insights into the contribution of individual features in making the final decision. This enhances transparency and is crucial for building trust in phishing website detection systems when deploying them in real-world scenarios. The experiment ended with a faithfulness check of the phishing detection model in which explanations provided by the integrated gradients algorithm were validated.

3   PhishBuster Modules

This section will elaborate on PhishBuster modules, such as embedding models used to create URL embeddings, classification models used for phishing detection, and the key parameters and techniques used to train neural networks.

3.1   URL Embedding Generation Techniques

Embedding is a way of representing data in a lower-dimensional vector space to make it easier for deep learning algorithms to process. It captures the meaning or context of the data. We have used the following pre-trained deep learning models to create the embeddings.

BERT (Bidirectional Encoder Representations from Transformers): Devlin et al. developed BERT to understand the context of the word based on neighboring words [12]. BERT uses the transformer model, which consists of multiple layers of feed-forward neural networks and allows the model to generate embeddings of the entire sequence at once. We will now examine different embedding generation methods that individually provide a fixed-length embedding vector (Table 1):

- **BERT_CLS**: A special classification (CLS) token will be added at the start of each input text. The final hidden state corresponding to these tokens is used as the representation of inputs to perform our binary classification [12].
- **SBERT** (Sentence-BERT): It is a slight modification of BERT_CLS which is used to create dense vectors to represent texts. The major difference is that SBERT doesn't use CLS tokens but will use a triplet network structure to optimize the cosine similarity between the text embeddings generated [21].

Table 1. Comparison of different embedding methods

Model	Length of Embeddings	Specialization	Embedding Level	Efficiency (Memory)	Training Speed
SBERT	384	Sentence similarity	Sentence	Moderate	Moderate
BERT_CLS	768	General-purpose sentence embedding	Sentence (CLS)	Moderate	Moderate
ALBERT	768	Efficiency-focused, smaller model	Token or CLS	High	Faster
RoBERTa	768	Enhanced BERT for robustness	Token or CLS	Moderate	Slower
USE	512	General-purpose sentence encoding	Sentence	High	Moderate

- **ALBERT**: A lightweight variant of BERT that reduces the number of parameters and ensures the performance has a negligible loss. It initiates parameter sharing between layers to reduce the size of the model and also factorizes embeddings with respect to parameters to reduce memory usage, making it easier to develop and deploy fast [15].
- **RoBERTa**: RoBERTA is a robustly optimized BERT model [10]. It is an extension of the BERT model and is useful in optimal pre-training and in processing large data sets. It also removes the next text prediction task of BERT. It uses a transformer as its base and is good at understanding semantics. It improves the performance of NLP/ML tasks by generating optimal embeddings.

USE (Universal Sentence Encoder): A sentence embedding model from Google that provides fixed-length embeddings for sentences, optimized for various semantic similarity and sentence-level tasks. It uses any of the transformer or deep averaging networks to capture the semantics of a text input [11].

3.2 Deep Learning Models Used for Phishing Detection

We have designed and developed three deep learning models (FFNN, RNN, and LSTM) to detect whether a given URL is **Malicious** or **Legitimate**. The classification models detail are as follows:

- **FFNN** (Feed-Forward Neural Network): It is a neural network where information flows only in one direction and has no cycles between nodes [14]. It is used in tasks without sequential or temporal dependency like image classification and regression.
- **RNN** (Recurrent Neural Network): It is a neural network that is designed for sequential data. It is trained to process and convert sequential data into specific output by forming cycles or internal loops, enabling it to maintain the memory of previous inputs. It is suitable for temporal dependencies and sequential data and can be applied in speech recognition and sequence prediction tasks.

– **LSTM** (Long Short-Term Memory): LSTM is an advanced type of RNN that stores the memory of previous layers [25]. It incorporates memory cells that can hold information for extended periods and are thereby capable of learning long-term dependencies in sequential data. This model is applied in text generation, speech prediction, and speech synthesis.

3.3   Other Parameters in Deep Learning Models

Some of the key parameters and techniques used in the training process of deep neural networks in the proposed framework are:

– **Batch Size**: The number of training samples processed in a single pass before the model's internal parameters are updated. Depending on the model size and capability of hardware it ranges from 16 to 512 samples.
– **Learning Rate**: The step size at which the model's parameters are adjusted to minimize the loss function. It needs fine-tuning often as it significantly affects the performance of the model.
– **Early Stopping**: A technique particularly used in neural networks to stop training once the model performance on the validation set stops improving. Overfitting is prevented by stopping the training even when the model has not completed all the epochs.
– **Dropout**: Dropout is an effective technique to restrict overfitting in a model [24]. It is a process in which neurons are turned off automatically during training to prevent overfitting.
– **Optimizer**: ADAM (Adaptive Moment Estimation) is an optimization algorithm that adjusts the learning rate based on the first and second moments of the gradients. It is used for a wide range of tasks as it balances speed and stability. ADAM uses AdaGrad and RMSProp to make it more robust and scalable and generally works with a learning rate of 0.01.

4   Experimental Setup

This section describes the experimental setup, including dataset description, model details, experimental details, and performance metrics used in the work.

4.1   Phishing URL Dataset

We have used a publicly available *Phishing Websites* dataset from the UCI Machine Learning Repository [2]. The Dataset has 235794 URL entries which contains 134850 Benign (Legitimate) website URLs and 100945 Malicious website URLs. This dataset is a collection of 54 attributes distributed as 4 Categorical, 4 Continuous, and 46 Integer features. This dataset by default has no missing values in it. As fake URL detection is a binary classification task, the class label contains two entries, *Label 0* corresponds to a phishing/malicious URL, and *Label 1* to a legitimate URL.

4.2   PhishBuster Details

The different stages involved in setting up the model start with input generation from different embedding techniques. These embeddings are then concatenated with feature values and then used to train the corresponding FFNN, RNN, and LSTM models.

Input URL Extraction: Initially, we only select the URL from the dataset. It is to be noted that all the other features except URL and label (like URL length, domain length, number of digits, etc.) are lexical features (which are derived from the base URL). This highlights the importance of working on URLs and converting them to improve the model performance.

It can be done by using various embedding generation techniques that convert URLs into vectorized continuous numerical inputs that can be recognizable by the models during training. These embeddings are generated using different techniques like BERT_CLS, SBERT, USE, RoBERTa, and ALBERT. We store all these generated embeddings in pickle(.pkl) files. These embeddings are then concatenated with the remaining feature values of the rest of the attributes other than URLs. For instance, BERT_CLS technique will result in a fixed length embedding vector of size 768 units for each URL. After concatenating them with the available 46 rational features, the size of each embedding vector becomes 814 units. Numpy functions (precisely np.hstack) were used to perform this concatenation operation. So, by the end of this task, we were able to generate two input sets. The first is the URL embeddings, and the second one is the concatenated version of URL embeddings and features.

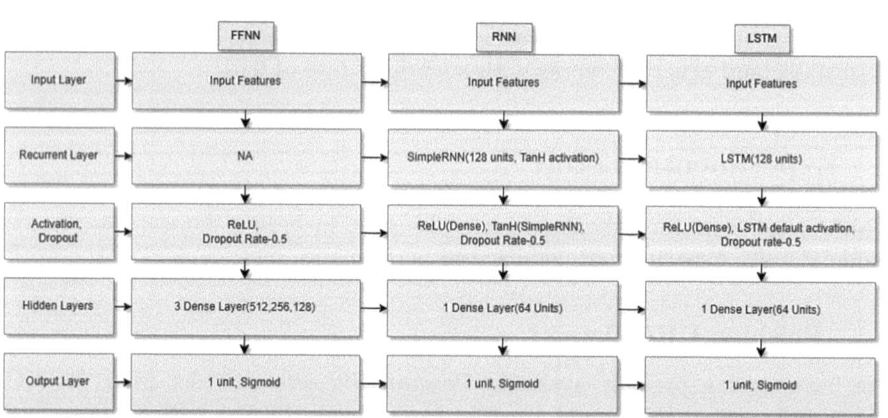

Fig. 2. Architecture of FFNN, RNN and LSTM models

Architecture of Deep Learning Models: The three deep learning models used in the experiments are Feed Forward Neural Networks (FFNN), Recurrent Neural Networks (RNN), and Long Short-Term Memory Neural Networks (LSTM). The architecture of these models is illustrated in Fig. 2. So, with the two input sets we generated, we train them on all of the neural network models. Coming to the hyperparameters, we have used Adam optimizer with a learning rate 0.01 and loss function as binary cross entropy. Neural network models were set to be trained for 50 epochs with an early stopping criteria applied at a patience value of 5. The validation split was at 0.1 with batch size 32.

4.3   Experimental Details

We have used various tools and libraries to develop phishing URL detection models. Python (version: 3.0) was our primary programming language. We used platforms such as Google Collab, Kaggle, and VSCode to develop our project. Many Python libraries were heavily used starting from numpy which was used for data manipulation and also during concatenation which is one of the novel parts of this project. Pandas was used to create a data frame for the dataset and also to complete preprocessing tasks. Matplotlib and Seaborn were extensively used in different parts of the projects for visualization purposes. Deep learning models were developed using TensorFlow [7], Keras, and PyTorch [19]. Scikit-Learn (Sk-learn) was used to create train and test data and also to evaluate the performance of the models developed [20].

4.4   Performance Evaluation

We evaluate the performance of phishing URL detection models in a Legitimate or Phishing URL using the confusion matrix containing four entries: True Positives, False Positives, True Negatives, and False Negatives. We have also used additional metrics such as accuracy, precision, recall, and F1-score to evaluate the deep learning models.

- **True Positives** (TP): TP is the number of phishing instances that are correctly predicted as phishing ones.
- **False Positives** (FP): FP is the number of phishing instances that are incorrectly predicted as legitimate ones.
- **True Negatives** (TN): TN is the number of legitimate URLs that are correctly predicted as legitimate ones.
- **False Negatives** (FN): FN is the number of legitimate instances that are incorrectly predicted as phishing ones.

All these variables are mutually exclusive and the sum of them will result in the number of URLs in the test split. Accuracy and F1-score can be defined using these parameters:

– **Accuracy**: It is defined as the proportion of correctly predicted phishing and legitimate URLs out of the number of all URLs.

$$\text{Accuracy} = \frac{TP + TN}{TP + TN + FP + FN} \tag{1}$$

– **F1-Score**: It is defined as the harmonic mean of precision and recall.

$$\text{F1-Score} = \frac{2 * Precision * Recall}{Precision + Recall} \tag{2}$$

- **Precision**: It is the ratio of the number of phishing URLs that are correctly predicted out of the total number of predicted phishing URLs.

$$\text{Precision} = \frac{TP}{TP + FP} \tag{3}$$

- **Recall** (Sensitivity): It is the ratio of the number of phishing URLs that are correctly predicted out of the total number of phishing URLs.

$$\text{Recall} = \frac{TP}{TP + FN} \tag{4}$$

5   Experimental Results

The section starts with the results of exploratory data analysis. Then, the three phishing URL detection models were trained and evaluated using the performance metrics. The results are then visualized using different plots. This section ends with the explainability and faithfulness check of the developed phishing URL detection models.

5.1   Exploratory Data Analysis

Exploratory Data Analysis (EDA) is a fundamental concept that helps observe and analyze data to draw meaningful conclusions. EDA is important as it helps look at the data before making any assumptions (or) conclusions. We can detect outliers, errors, and anomalies in our data beforehand by performing EDA. The primary purpose of EDA is to detect any interesting relations among our attributes, which can significantly help select models and increase accuracy. The first step in EDA is to check whether the dataset contains NULL values or any duplicate values. It was performed using pandas library functions, and our dataset was free of any NULL or duplicate values. The final stage was the comparison of attributes with each other. It was performed through plots like scatterplots or heat maps. Observing these plots, we derived inferences and draw conclusions. Sometimes, attributes can be functions of each other, which can be visually observed by plots. Some attributes were derived as a combination of multiple already present attributes. At this stage, we were able to determine the importance of each attribute and what kind of feature would be most valuable to the model.

Barplot (Count vs Label): We generated a Barplot (Count vs Label) to get better insight about the nature and distribution of URLs.

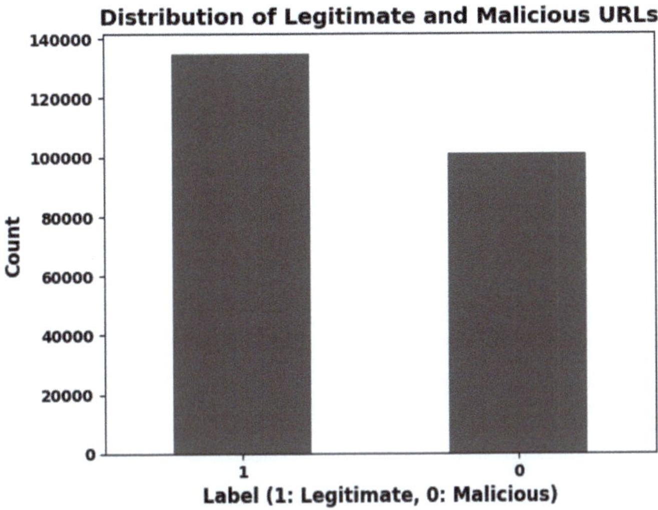

Fig. 3. Distribution of Malicious and Legitimate URLs in Dataset

The bar plot in Fig. 3 shows the distribution of Legitimate and Malicious URLs. We observed that the count of legitimate URLs is 134850 while the count of malicious URLs is 100945. Considering our problem statement, we can observe that the proportion of Legitimate and Malicious URLs is good.

Correlation Heatmap: We generated a correlation heatmap (Fig. 4) between different features and identified some strong relationships between the numerical features. This correlation heat map shows the relationship between attributes, the intensity of color represents the correlation coefficient ranging from -1 to 1.

- ▪: Represents a strong positive correlation between attributes (close to +1).
- ▪: Represents a weak or no correlation between attributes (close to 0).
- ▪: Represents a strong negative correlation between attributes (close to -1).

We observed that the diagonal blocks are dark red, indicating a strong positive correlation coefficient when the same attributes are plotted against themselves. Additionally, some other attributes like NoOfLettersinURL and URLLength also have a strong positive correlation when plotted against each other.

We also observed that some attributes, like 'SpacialCharacterRatioInURL' and 'CharContinuationRate' have a strong negative correlation when plotted against each other while attributes such as 'NoOfObfuscatedChar' and 'NoOfPopUp' showed almost zero correlation. The plot was dominated by the points indicating either a little positive correlation or zero correlation.

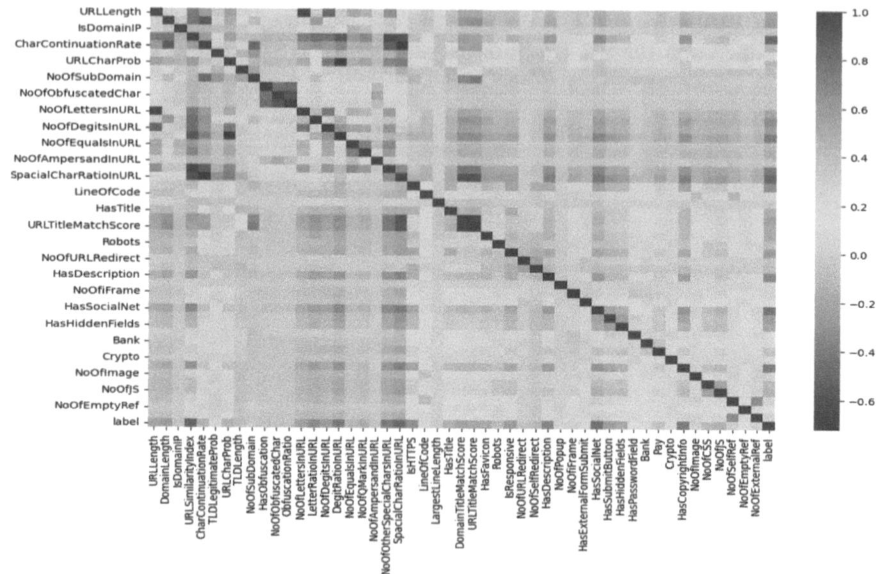

Fig. 4. Attribute Relationships across Phishing and Legitimate URLs

Pairplot (NoOfSubDomains vs Domain Length vs URL Length): We
generated a Pairplot (Fig. 5) to visualize relationships between multiple features
and how they relate to the target label by keeping hue = 'label'.

Some of the depencies which we observed are:

- **URL Length x Domain Length**: Legitimate URLs are observed to have
  smaller domain lengths and URL Lengths, and malicious URLs were identified
  as having larger domain lengths and URL Lengths.
- **URL Length x No of Subdomains**: For legitimate URLs, the URL length
  is generally small with less number of subdomains. For malicious URLs, URL
  length and number of subdomains are spread over the domain.
- **Domain Length x No of Subdomains**: As seen in the plot, legitimate
  URLs have less number of subdomains and smaller domain lengths whereas
  malicious URLs are spread all over the place with variations in both domain
  lengths and number of number of subdomains.

Diagonal plots interpretation of the Pair Plot:

- **URL Length**: Legitimate URLs have shorter URL lengths, whereas malicious ones have pretty large URLs even until a length of 6000.
- **Domain Length**: The domain length of legitimate URLs tends to be low(0–
  50), while malicious URLs have it distributed with majority being in the
  range of legitimate ones and others with a upper bound greater than 50.
- **Number of Subdomains**: Malicious URLs have number of subdomains
  until 10, while most of the legitimate URLs have less than 3 subdomains.

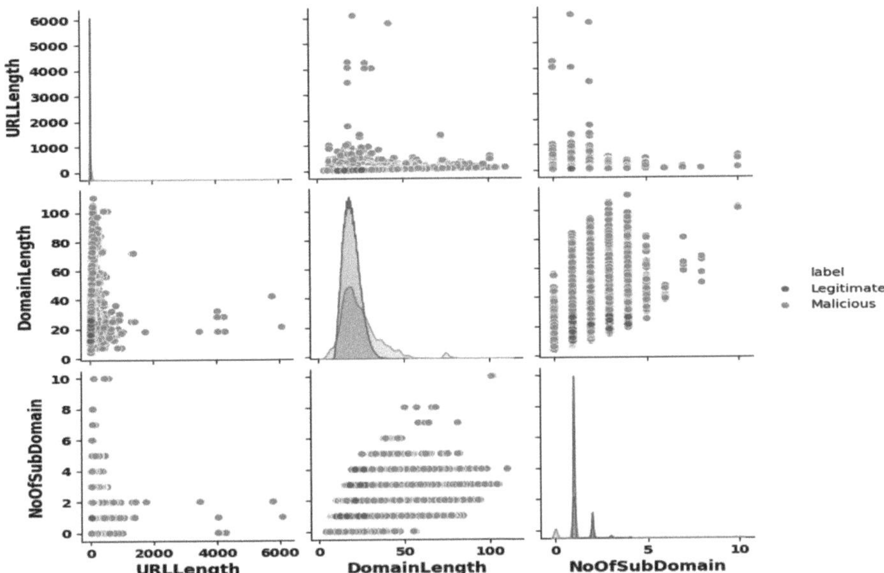

Fig. 5. Pairwise Distribution of URLs based on URL Length, Domain Length and Number of Subdomains

5.2   Performance Evaluation

All the three deep learning models were then trained and tested based on the setup discussed earlier. This section will discuss the results and observations generated using only URL embeddings and using both URL embeddings and feature values for the three models FFNN, RNN and LSTM using different embedding generation techniques.

Using only URL Embeddings: In this setup, embeddings generated through BERT_CLS, SBERT, USE, RoBERTa and AlBERT were trained using all of the FFNN, LSTM, and RNN models. RNN with RoBERTa produced the highest accuracy of 99.752% followed by LSTM with RoBERTa with an accuracy of 99.741%. SBERT embeddings performed the least with all of the deep learning models. Comparatively, BERT_CLS, RoBERTa and AlBERT embeddings had optimal and almost the same performance coefficient. The performance of the model was evaluated using accuracy and f1-score. Figure 6 contains accuracies and f1-scores of FFNN, LSTM, RNN models by using only URL embeddings.

Using both URL Embeddings and Feature Values: The first interesting observation was the growth in the accuracy of the models using USE-generated embeddings concatenated with feature values. This was the essence of concatenation in our experiment and it has proven its worth by increasing the performance of our models.

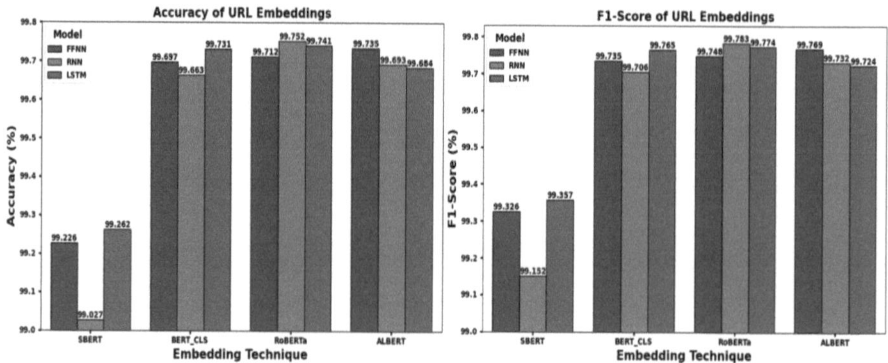

Fig. 6. Accuracy and F1-Score of FFNN, RNN and LSTM models using only URL embeddings

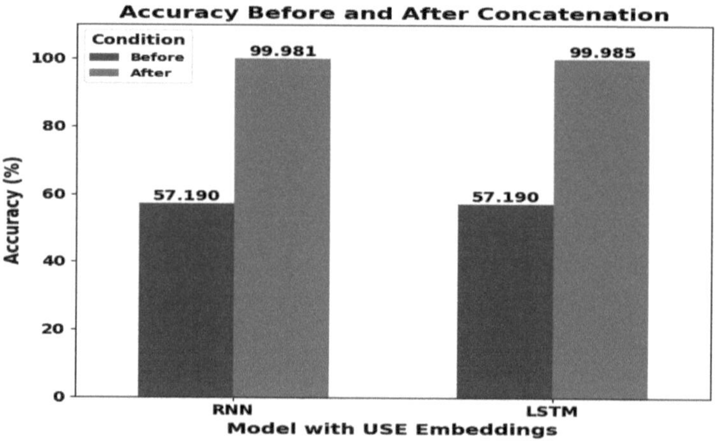

Fig. 7. Impact of URL embedding and Feature Concatenation on Accuracy

As we can see in Fig. 7, the performance of models using both URL embeddings and feature values through concatenation is better than the models using only URL embeddings. USE-generated embeddings had a severe spike in accuracy from 57.19% to 99.981% when concatenated with features, which shows that models perform better when they used the concatenated version of inputs. Now, let us evaluate the performance of the remaining models generated and trained on the concatenated version using the rest of the embedding methods. The performance of models was evaluated using the performance metrics mentioned in section **4.4**. Now, we visualise the results obtained from our experiment before deriving conclusions based on the results obtained.

As we can see in Fig. 8, the LSTM and RNN models using RoBERTa-generated embeddings concatenated with features performed the best with an accuracy score of 99.989 and an f1 score of 99.991. AlBERT embeddings were

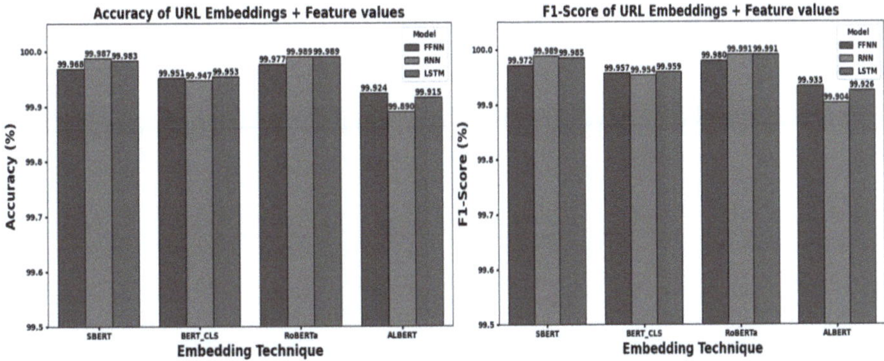

Fig. 8. Accuracy and F1-Score of FFNN, RNN and LSTM models using both URL embeddings and feature values

lagging by a bit compared to other embedding techniques, whereas RoBERTa along with USE methods performed the best and consistent for all three models. So, according to our experiment, the priority order of embedding models with respect to the generated results is RoBERTa > USE > SBERT > BERT_CLS > ALBERT. Overall, there was an all-out increase in performance when compared to the previous results. So, we were able to find the best performing model which is the RoBERTa concatenated embeddings-based LSTM model which is the proposed model of this experiment in order to tackle phishing attacks. Now, we went another step ahead and performed explainability on the proposed model to build transparency and trust with respect to the decisions made.

5.3   Explainability

To perform the explainability of our proposed model we have used the Captum explainability [8] tool and implemented its integrated Gradients algorithm and found the importance of each attribute while making the final decision. Now let us look at the flow of explaining the proposed model.

Captum: Captum is also known as 'comprehension' in Latin. It is an exclusive open-source tool that is used for model interpretability tasks. As the models become more and more complex when dealing with larger datasets, the lack of completeness (or) transparency regarding model decisions will also increase. For this reason, captum can be used to increase the visibility of a model's decision and help the users to clearly understand the answer to the question (why is the model making this decision?). Captum will perform model explainability tasks only on the models developed in Pytorch. Captum is a major strength while performing debugging tasks and makes them easier too, by standing as an important curator during benchmarking. Captum provides many state-of-the-art methods, such as the integrated gradients algorithm, to complete the task of interpretation.

Integrated Gradients: The integrated gradients algorithm is a very efficient method of interpreting the decision-making process of the model. It is a gradient-based algorithm that assigns importance scores to each attribute by approximating the integral of gradients of the model output with respect to the given inputs. Integrated gradients can be used for model debugging, feature extractions, and playing with performance metrics. The integrated gradients algorithm is available in the captum.attr library, which gives the attribution scores for each attribute with respect to the impact it has on the model's final decision. From this, we can observe the highest attribution score generating attributes which are our most important attributes and we can also observe the less important attributes. We then applied this algorithm to the proposed model of the experimental setup, and the results were obtained and plotted in Fig. 9.

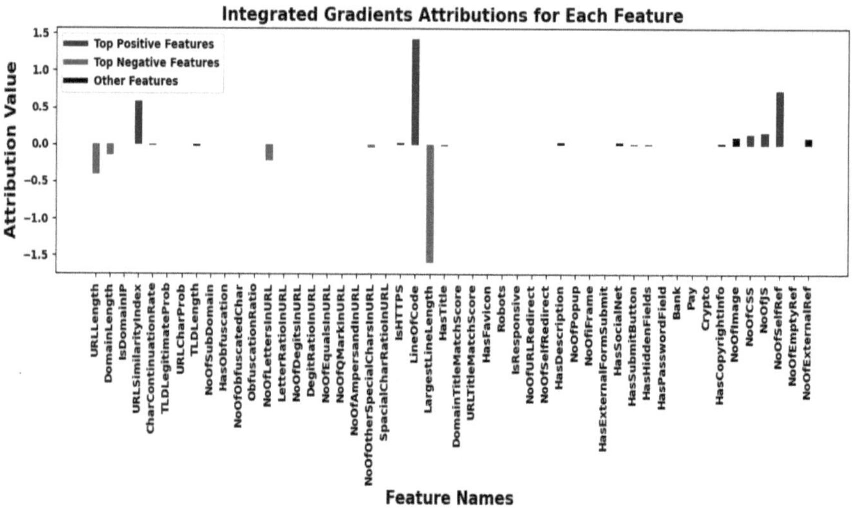

Fig. 9. Attribution scores of all features

As we can see from Fig. 9, there are some features with positive attribution values that affect the model positively in making an informed decision, and there are also some negative features with negative attribution values that are acting inversely to reduce the model's performance which means that they drive the model negatively towards its prediction.

Top positive features[Attribute, Attribution Value] = { [LineOfCode, 1.4204], [NoOfSelfRef, 0.7384], [URLSimilarityIndex, 0.5824], [NoOfJS, 0.1610], [NoOfCSS, 0.1364] }.

Top negative features[Attribute,Attribution Value] = { [LargestLineLength, −1.5939], [URLLength, -0.4082], [NoOfLettersInURL, −0.2111], [Domain-Length, −0.1465], [TLDLength, −0.0336] }.

Faithfulness Check: This is also one of our novel captures in this experiment, where we will check the faithfulness of the explanations provided by captum and justify that they are credible. The faithfulness of this model can be checked by removing the top 5 attributes with maximum attribution values one by one and then checking how the model is performing after the end of each iterative removal of top 5 attributes.

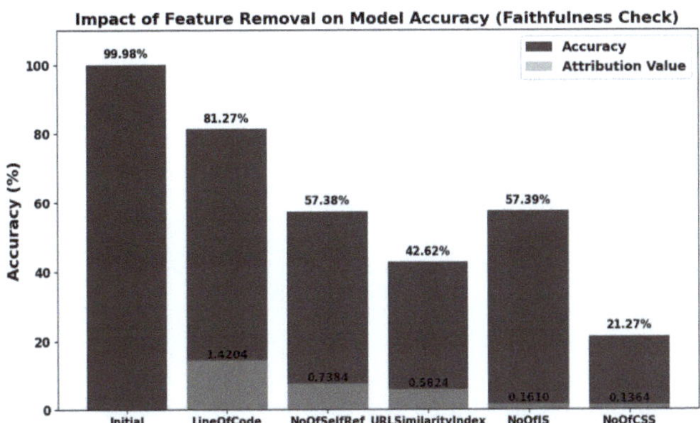

Fig. 10. Impact on Accuracy after Removing Top 5 Features Iteratively

In Fig. 10, the x-axis denotes the feature that will be removed in each iteration, and the y-axis is the accuracy of each iteration. From the plot, we can see that the accuracy is gradually going down after removing the important attributes as per the integrated gradients algorithm which implies that the explanations provided by the captum tool are reliable and correct. The initial accuracy was 99.989% which decreased to 81.27% on removing the attribute (LineOfCode) with the highest attribution value (1.4204). Similarly, the accuracy went down to 21. 27% after removing all the top five attributes with the highest attribution values. This tells us that the results provided by the integrated gradients algorithm are reliable and correct.

6 Related Work

In this section we present an overview about the existing phishing detection systems and compare them with our proposed model as in Table 2. **Yang et al.** proposed a CNN+LSTM model based on TF-IDF based embeddings and proposed a model with 98.99% accuracy [27]. Similarly, **Tang et al.** derived new features based on hyperlinks information and proposed a Random Forest model with 99.57% accuracy [25]. Both succeeded in generating highly accurate results, but with our proposed model of LSTM+RoBERTa we obtained an accuracy score of 99.98% and also went a step further and explained our results using the integrated gradients algorithm.

Table 2. Comparison of various existing Phishing Detection Systems.

Authors	Model	Accuracy	Embedding Methods	Concatenation	Explainability
Yuan et al. [28]	Word2vec	99.69%	Word2vec	×	×
Opara et al. [18]	WebPhish	98.10%	URL char + HTML word	✓	×
Aldakheel et al. [9]	1D CNN	98.77%	×	×	×
Maneriker et al. [17]	URLTran_BERT	99.67%	BERT	×	×
Gupta et al. [13]	Random Forest	99.57%	×	×	×
Shirazi et al. [22]	MobileBERT	96.30%	BERT, ELECTRA, RoBERTa	✓	×
Yan et al. [26]	UE Classifier	92%	Huffman Encoding	×	×
Somesha et al. [23]	Random Forest	99.50%	FastText, Word2vec, TF-IDF	×	×
Yinhan et al. [16]	XLNet + SG-Net	87%	RoBERTa	×	×
Ankit et al. [10]	Logistic Regression	98.42%	×	×	×
Yang et al. [27]	CNN + LSTM	98.99%	TF-IDF	×	×
Tang et al. [25]	Random Forest	99.57%	×	×	×
Our Model	RoBERTa + LSTM	99.98%	BERT_CLS, USE, SBERT, RoBERTa, AlBERT	✓	✓ (Captum)

Yuan et al. proposed a framework that uses an embedding representation of characters in URLs generated by the word2vec model to detect phishing webpages [28]. They considered five parts of the URL which are protocol, subdomain, domain, suffix, and path. Similarly, **Opara et al.** proposed WebPhish, a deep neural network trained using HTML content and embedded raw URLs [18]. However, relying solely on embeddings from these five parts of the URL may overlook deeper semantic relationships within URLs. Our approach concatenates URL embeddings with other additional feature values of our data set.

Shirazi et al. developed a model named MobileBERT which is an ANN-based model based on URL features and HTML features with an accuracy of 96.30% [22]. Furthermore, **Maneriker et al.** developed a transformer-based URLTran model and largely succeeded in doing it by producing an FPR of 0. 01% and an accuracy of 99. 67% [17]. However, they only used limited embedding generation techniques like BERT and RoBERTa which leaves us with a limitation of using a more variety of embedding methods like our model. Additionally, we concatenated URL embeddings with feature values and were able to produce a better accuracy of 98.981%.

Aldakheel et al. utilized a CNN-based approach that takes fragments of URLs as input and achieved an accuracy of 98.77% [9]. **Gupta et al.** proposed a Random forest model with 99.57% accuracy [13]. They used a very small dataset with only 9 features which may not guarantee accurate results on large datasets. Our proposed model overcomes this limitation as we trained with 54 features and also produced a better accuracy of 99.98%. Additionally, their approach did not use any embeddings but we used embeddings generated from various embedding methods like BERT_CLS, USE, SBERT, RoBERTa, AlBERT.

Yan et al. have introduced a new unsupervised learning algorithm named the UE classifier and were able to prove that their model was better than many existing algorithms such as RF, DT, SVM, and CNN [26]. **Somesha et al.** proposed a Random Forest model with TF-IDF vectorization and achieved an accuracy of 99.50% [23]. They did a vast experiment on many supervised and unsupervised learning algorithms but didn't use any deep learning models which may have produced better results than the proposed RF model which we have shown by developing a LSTM based model and achieving an accuracy of 99.98%. Additionally, we explained our results using integrated gradients algorithm, which none of the previous works implemented.

7   Conclusion and Future Work

Phishing attacks are increasing rapidly due to many online services such as internet banking, e-commerce sites, and social media apps. Therefore, a highly accurate phishing detection system is the need of the hour. We designed and developed LSTM model trained on RoBERTa-generated embeddings. For the model input, we first generated URL embeddings using several embedding techniques and then concatenated them with existing feature values. The combined features were then trained using FFNN, RNN and LSTM models. Among these, FFNN with USE-generated embeddings performed the best with an accuracy of 99.981%. RNN and LSTM models performed the best while using RoBERTa-generated embeddings with an F1-Score of 99.991%. Following this, we applied the integrated gradients algorithm to explain the decisions made by our proposed model. This algorithm generated attribution scores for all the features based on the importance they have in model's decision making process. Finally, we performed a faithfulness check on the algorithm by removing the top 5 attributes with the highest attribution values. This resulted in a performance degradation of 78.719%, indicating that the explanations provided were accurate and that our model is highly reliable and trustworthy. In the future, given that this model performs well in detecting phishing websites, we want to construct a similar experiment to detect malicious emails and spam messages. Nowadays, mobile devices are becoming more vulnerable to phishing attacks, and implementing this approach in mobile environments is a challenge that we want to take up in the future.

References

1. APWG: 2018 Report on Phishing Attack Trends. https://apwg.org/resources/apwg-reports/
2. Center for Machine Learning and Intelligent Systems: PhiUSIIL Phishing URL Dataset. https://archive.ics.uci.edu/ml/datasets/phishing+websites
3. Dofo: Report on Domains Registered in April 2020. https://dofo.com/blog/domain-industry-report-april-2020/
4. Federal Bureau of Investigation: 2020 Internet Crime Report. https://www.ic3.gov/AnnualReport/Reports/2020_IC3Report.pdf

5. Kaspersky: 2017 Security Bulletin, Overall Statistics. https://securelist.com/ksb-overall-statistics-2017/83453/
6. Symantec Corporation: 2018 Internet Security Threat Report. https://docs.broadcom.com/doc/istr-24-2019-en
7. TensorFlow: Large-scale machine learning on heterogeneous systems (2015). https://www.tensorflow.org/softwareavailablefromtensorflow.org
8. Captum: A unified and generic model interpretability library for pytorch (2020)
9. Aldakheel, E.A., Zakariah, M., Gashgari, G.A., Almarshad, F.A., Alzahrani, A.I.: A deep learning-based innovative technique for phishing detection in modern security with uniform resource locators. Sensors **23**(9), 4403 (2023)
10. Atari, M., Al-Mousa, A.: A machine-learning based approach for detecting phishing urls. In: 2022 International Conference on Intelligent Data Science Technologies and Applications (IDSTA), pp. 82–88. IEEE (2022)
11. Cer, D., et al.: Universal sentence encoder (2018)
12. Devlin, J.: Bert: Pre-training of deep bidirectional transformers for language understanding. arXiv preprint arXiv:1810.04805 (2018)
13. Gupta, B.B., Yadav, K., Razzak, I., Psannis, K., Castiglione, A., Chang, X.: A novel approach for phishing urls detection using lexical based machine learning in a real-time environment. Comput. Commun. **175**, 47–57 (2021)
14. Kamath, U., Liu, J., Whitaker, J., Kamath, U., Liu, J., Whitaker, J.: Basics of deep learning. Deep Learning for NLP and Speech Recognition, pp. 141–201 (2019)
15. Lan, Z., Chen, M., Goodman, S., Gimpel, K., Sharma, P., Soricut, R.: Albert: a lite bert for self-supervised learning of language representations. arXiv preprint arXiv:1909.11942 (2019)
16. Liu, Y.: Roberta: a robustly optimized bert pretraining approach. arXiv preprint arXiv:1907.11692 (2019)
17. Maneriker, P., Stokes, J.W., Lazo, E.G., Carutasu, D., Tajaddodianfar, F., Gururajan, A.: Urltran: improving phishing url detection using transformers. In: IEEE Military Communications Conference (MILCOM), pp. 197–204. IEEE (2021)
18. Opara, C., Chen, Y., Wei, B.: Look before you leap: Detecting phishing web pages by exploiting raw url and html characteristics. Expert Syst. Appl. **236**, 121183 (2024)
19. Paszke, A., et al.: Pytorch: an imperative style, high-performance deep learning library (2019)
20. Pedregosa, F., Varoquaux, G., Gramfort, A., Michel, V., Thirion, B., Grisel, O., Blondel, M., Prettenhofer, P., Weiss, R., Dubourg, V., Vanderplas, J., Passos, A., Cournapeau, D., Brucher, M., Perrot, M., Duchesnay, E.: Scikit-learn: Mmachine learning in Python. J. Mach. Learn. Res. **12**, 2825–2830 (2011)
21. Reimers, N.: Sentence-bert: Sentence embeddings using siamese bert-networks. arXiv preprint arXiv:1908.10084 (2019)
22. Shirazi, H., Hayne, K.: Towards performance of nlp transformers on url-based phishing detection for mobile devices. Int. J. Ubiquitous Syst. Pervasive Networks (2022)
23. Somesha, M., Pais, A.R.: Classification of phishing email using word embedding and machine learning techniques. J. Cyber Secur. Mobility, 279–320 (2022)
24. Srivastava, N., Hinton, G., Krizhevsky, A., Sutskever, I., Salakhutdinov, R.: Dropout: a simple way to prevent neural networks from overfitting. J. Mach. Learn. Res. **15**(1), 1929–1958 (2014)
25. Tang, L., Mahmoud, Q.H.: A survey of machine learning-based solutions for phishing website detection. Mach. Learn. Knowl. Extraction **3**(3), 672–694 (2021)

26. Yan, X., Xu, Y., Cui, B., Zhang, S., Guo, T., Li, C.: Learning url embedding for malicious website detection. IEEE Trans. Industr. Inf. **16**(10), 6673–6681 (2020)
27. Yang, P., Zhao, G., Zeng, P.: Phishing website detection based on multidimensional features driven by deep learning. IEEE Access **7**, 15196–15209 (2019)
28. Yuan, H., Yang, Z., Chen, X., Li, Y., Liu, W.: Url2vec: Url modeling with character embeddings for fast and accurate phishing website detection. In: IEEE ISPA/IUCC/BDCloud/SocialCom/SustainCom, pp. 265–272. IEEE (2018)

Atomic Operation Classification for Effective Legal Supervision Model Construction

Tao Qin[✉], Yunzhe Liu, Ya Gao, Yizhen Li, and Pinghui Wang

Department of Computer Science and Engineering, Xi'an Jiaotong University,
Xi'an 710049, China
qin.tao@mail.xjtu.edu.cn

Abstract. With the rapid development of big data technology, more and more complex legal supervision models are established to achieve different supervision goals. How to reduce the constructive difficulty and improve the usability is an essential challenge to be solved. In this paper, we propose a framework to classify the operations into different groups and named them as atomic operations. First, we divide the atomic operations into four different categories, including the basic operations, basic machine learning operations, specific functions and some specific operations for special areas. Secondly, for different categories, we simple give the implementation of different operations, and select specific operation as an example to issullate the detailed implementation process. Based on the atomic operations proposed in this paper, we can not only reduce the construction difficulty of the legal supervision model, but also can improve the interpretability of different constructed models, as they are formed by different atomic operations.

Keywords: Legal supervision models · Atomic operation classification · Atomic implementation

1 Introduction

Recently, significant progress has been made in the construction of legal supervision models based on multi-type data analysis. The development model primarily includes the construction of big data legal supervision models and the establishment of big data legal supervision platforms [1]. Based on various data collected, digital legal supervision models are constructed to extract knowledge from the data and improve the efficiency of the supervision models. However, despite many advances have been made in big data legal supervision, there are still several challenges to be solved. Firstly, the construction standards for big data legal supervision platforms are not well defined, thus reusability of the developed supervision model is very low; it means that the model constructed by one specific procuratorate cannot be used by other procuratorates. Secondly, as the data are collected from multiple sources, their location is different, this situation will

S. Li et al. (Eds.): BROADNETS 2024, LNICST 674, pp. 72–83, 2026.
https://doi.org/10.1007/978-3-032-14350-1_5

cause difficulty for data sharing and integration among various multi-functional departments. Third, the widely used of some end-to-end methods in those models have led to an obvious decline in their execution interpretability. In this paper, we focus on developing atomic operations to solve those challenges. The atomic operation, which is a basic functional operation in the legal supervision model, can be used to segment the supervision model. One specific atomic operation is corresponding to one data analysis function in the legal supervision model. In this way, we can combine different atomic operations to establish specific supervision model. We can not only reduce the difficulty of supervision model construction, but also improve the explanation of one specific supervision model.

Based on the basic analysis of the supervision model, we categorize the atomic operations into four different categories: basic operations, basic machine learning operations, some specific functions, and specific operations for special areas. Each category plays a distinct role in achieving specific supervision objectives. Subsequently, for different categories of atomic operations, we provide simple implementations of various operations, introduce our design goals and principles, and select specific operations as examples to illustrate the detailed implementation process. In summary, the atomic operation design method proposed in this paper aims to build a flexible, generalizable, and interpretable supervision system, providing strong support for the construction of legal supervision models in the era of big data.

The rest of this paper is organized as follows: Sect. 2 introduces the relevant work on legal supervision models and atomic operations. Section 3 presents our research framework and explains our design ideas. In Sect. 4, we present the principles and implementation methods of selected atomic basic operations. Finally, we summarize the work presented in this paper and discuss future prospects in Sect. 5.

2   Related Work

2.1   Legal Supervision Models

In recent years, legal supervision based on multi source big data has achieved significant results in social governance and the legal field. A successful case from the People's Procuratorate of Xianju County [2] highlights the application of big data in the criminal domain. Through supervision, issues related to criminal offenders improperly receiving pension insurance have been revealed, promoting a closed governance loop and providing strong support for judicial practice. The oil big data legal supervision platform constructed using a unified spatiotemporal framework in Zhejiang Province [3] analyzes electronic waybills, route trajectories, and other data related to hazardous materials vehicles, calculating and mining the locations of loading and unloading oil products, total cargo volume, and the total sales and tax amounts for each gas station. Those data are aggregated and analyzed with tax supervision data from tax authorities to accurately identify clues related to oil tax evasion. Additionally, Gibb R.G. et al. [4] utilized a unified spatio-temporal framework for anomaly detection in judicial spatio-temporal big data, discovering spatially adjacent and temporally continuous anomalies with significant attribute differences in relation to the supervised subjects. Ji Genlin et al. [5] extract valuable frequent patterns, periodic patterns, co-occurrence patterns, and association patterns within the data to uncover case clues. By clustering spatio-temporal objects with similar behaviors based on spatial and temporal similarities, they can identify case leads. These predecessors' studies have provided us with much experience and inspiration. However, there are also issues with supervision model construction, such as the lack of unified standards, limited reusability, and low promotion rates. Additionally, data sharing and integration between multiple administrative departments is another challenge to be solved.

2.2 Atomic Operations

Zhai Xiuwen proposed an innovative method named as the "Marked Directory Method" [6], aimed to address the challenges of data consistency and atomic operations in shared storage. Liu Bing et al. [7] introduced a service-oriented transaction processing model suitable for ubiquitous environments, which has broad application prospects in highly mobile, extremely heterogeneous, autonomous, and open contexts environments. Zhang Ming proposed a model evolution operation [8], classifying evolution operations into basic and composite evolution operations based on their granularity. Brunet et al. [9] proposed a set of atomic operations related to global model management, including merge, match, diff, split, and slice operations. These atomic operations provide a foundation and reference for research on model merging. Additionally, Sun Haitao et al. [10] and Beckmann et al. [11] designed a model for atomic operations, with detailed descriptions of the model structures provided in their patents, which have greatly inspired us and hold significant reference value. However, current atomic operations suffer from insufficient combinability. In practical applications, the combinations of various atomic operations may be limited, affecting overall flexibility and adaptability. Additionally, there is a lack of clear standards, resulting in inconsistent partitioning criteria and insufficient interpretability.

3 Framework for Atomic Operation Design

Atomic operations are crucial for constructing flexible and interpretable legal supervision models by dividing down complex supervision processes into a series of independently executable basic operation units. In this section, we first explain the design principles and specific content of atomic operations. And then, we present our design framework for atomic operations and introduce the implementation ideas for each type of atomic operation step by step, including the basic operations, basic machine learning operations, some specific functions and specific operations for special areas. Through this fine-grained operational design, we try to maximize the interpretability and adaptability of the legal supervision model.

Based on the analysis above, the main issues are the difficulties in data sharing and integration among multiple administrative departments, as well as the challenges in the rational partitioning of atomic operations. The atomic operation model of the legal supervision model has the following functionalities:

1) It can improve the interpretability of the legal supervision model. Since the legal supervision model is constructed from a combination of atomic operation models, and the functions of atomic operations are clear, the workflow characteristics of data within the legal supervision model can be obtained through the combination of atomic operations, thereby improving the model's interpretability.

2) It can improve the inter-department coordination. The clarity and interpretability of atomic operations can encourage data owners to contribution data among different departments, enhancing collaboration among them. Given these characteristics, the atomic operation modeling of the legal supervision model needs to consider the rationality of atomic operation partitioning while also addressing the analyzability and predictability of atomic operation specifications.

Therefore, the goal of atomic operation partition modeling design is to achieve a fine-grained decomposition of the legal supervision model. This involves divide the supervision model into combinations of atomic functions based on supervisory capabilities, where different atomic functions corresponding to a single atomic operation. Conversely, combinations can be made based on different atomic operations to create legal supervision models with specific functionalities as needed. Therefore, our design framework is illustrated in Fig. 1.

As shown in the figure above, our design framework is roughly divided into the following four steps. The first step is to determine the required supervision model based on specific supervision objectives, such as insurance fraud, healthcare insurance cases, and finished oil issues. This requires a comprehensive analysis of the unique characteristics and requirements of each case to ensure the supervision model is tailored to effectively address the identified issues. By understanding the nuances of each objective, we can create a more focused and efficient model that meets the specific needs of the legal supervision process. Next, to implement this supervision model, we need to design and detail the corresponding various atomic operations. This involves not only defining the operations themselves but also understanding how they interact within the larger framework of the supervision model. Each atomic operation serves as a building block, contributing to the overall functionality and effectiveness of the model.

In the second step, since various atomic operations are needed in the supervision model, we need to categorize these atomic operations and design different types with distinct functionalities. This categorization is crucial for organizing the operations in a way that enhances their usability and effectiveness. As shown in the figure, we have categorized the atomic operations into the following four types: basic operations, basic learning operations, functional operations, and specific operations for specialized areas. By systematically categorizing and

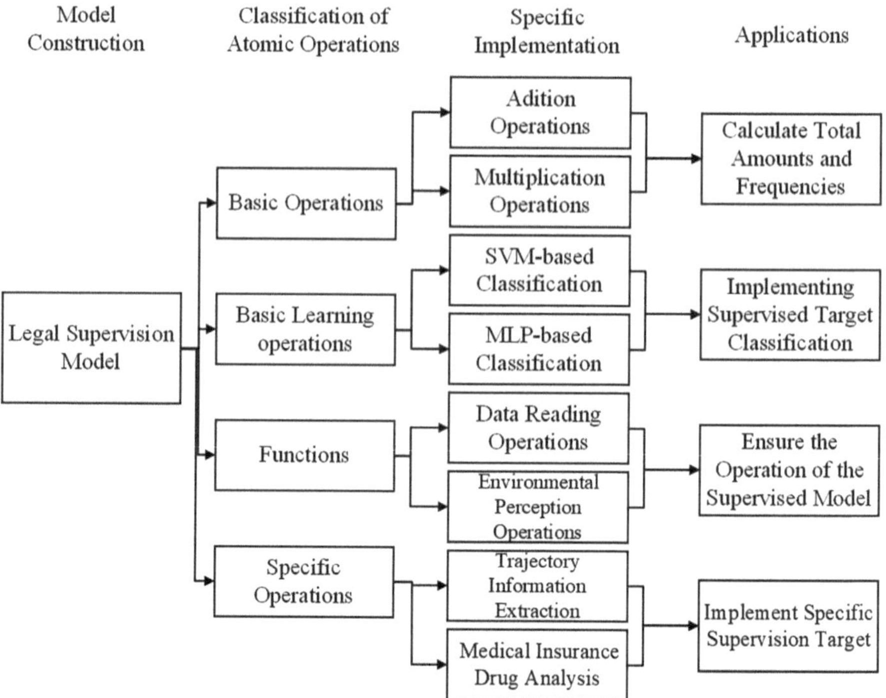

Fig. 1. Design Framework.

designing these atomic operations, we create a robust framework that facilitates the effective implementation of the legal supervision model, ultimately leading to improved outcomes in monitoring and regulatory processes.

The third and fourth steps involve the specific implementation and application scenarios of various atomic operations. The first category of operations can be divided into addition, subtraction, multiplication, and division operations to support the legal supervision system in efficiently processing numerical data. These atomic operations aim to provide basic mathematical functions for precise calculations related to financial data, statistical information, and other numerical data pertinent to legal matters. Specifically, addition operations can be used to calculate total amounts and frequencies, helping to identify the overall scale of abnormal transactions or activities; subtraction operations can be used to assess losses and discrepancies, allowing for quick determination of changes in financial status; multiplication operations are employed to calculate total costs, total outputs, etc., facilitating economic benefit analyses; while division operations assist in calculating averages and ratios to evaluate the relative importance of different factors. The second category of basic learning operations can be classified into SVM- and MLP-based classification operations, primarily aimed at enhancing the legal supervision system's capabilities in data classification and pattern recognition. These operations not only classify newly input data in real time but also generate detailed classification result evaluation reports, providing metrics such as accuracy to help users comprehensively understand the model's performance and reliability. The third category of functions is used to enhance the data processing capabilities of the legal supervision system, including operations for information reading, classification, comparison, and alerting, ensuring effective operation in different environments and improving the system's flexibility and accuracy. Finally, the specific operations for special areas are mainly targeted at specific supervision objectives, such as healthcare insurance issues and finished oil issues. In terms of implementation, we have designed different operations for different targets. For example, there are operations for reading trajectory information related to finished oil issues and for analyzing healthcare medications and reading healthcare amounts related to healthcare insurance issues.

4   Design and Implementation of Atomic Operations

4.1   Basic Operations

The basic atomic operations includes addition, subtraction, multiplication, and division. The operations can be broadly divided into four parts: addition operation, subtraction operation, multiplication operation, and division operation. These operations are designed to support the efficient processing of numerical data in legal supervision systems. In the specific implementation, we first need to input the relevant data to be processed according to the specific supervision objectives, then perform calculations based on the type of operation, and obtain the resulting data. Finally, we process the data into an appropriate structure and save it based on the actual situation. Figure 2 is the flowchart for basic arithmetic operations.

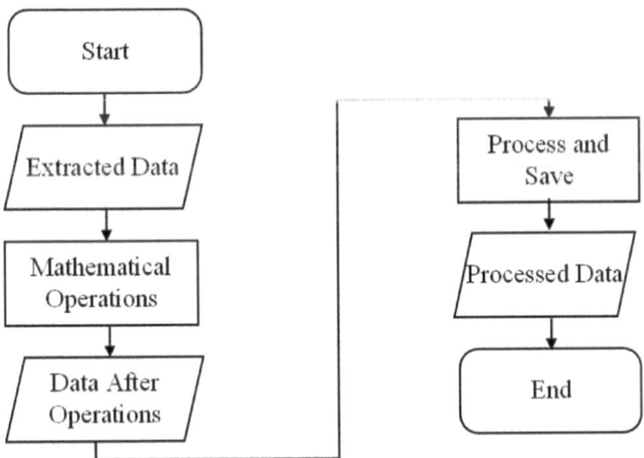

Fig. 2. Flowchart for Basic Arithmetic Operations.

These basic operations not only provide the necessary computational support for subsequent complex data analysis but also lay a solid foundation for the decision-making process in legal supervision. For example, when assessing anomalous amounts, these atomic operations can be used to calculate total amounts and frequencies, helping to identify the overall scale of abnormal transactions or activities. When processing financial data, we can multiply all transaction amounts by their respective weights and sum them to obtain the total amount, assisting us in the judgment of anomalous data.

4.2   Basic Machine Learning Operations

These atomic operations are primarily used to enhance the capabilities of legal supervision systems in data classification and pattern recognition. By utilizing machine learning methods, they can not only classify newly input data in real time but also generate detailed evaluation reports of classification results, helping users understand model performance, including metrics such as accuracy and recall. For example, in the SVM classification operation, we mainly use the Python sklearn library to implement Support Vector Machine (SVM) and encapsulate it as an atomic operation for classification functionality.

In the specific implementation process, we first load the relevant data samples based on different supervision objectives. Then, we divide the data into training and testing sets, adjusting parameters such as the random seed, the proportion of the testing set, and the number of samples in the testing set, while standardizing both the training and testing sets.

Next, we create a decision boundary plotting function based on specific classification objectives, which includes setting the marker generator and color map, plotting the decision surface, and creating scatter plots for all samples as well as the testing set samples. Finally, we train the linear SVM and obtain the classification results, outputting and saving them in both image and text formats. Figure 3 illustrates the flowchart of the SVM classification operation.

4.3   Some Specific Functions

Specific Functions play a crucial role in legal supervision systems, primarily aimed at enhancing data processing and analysis capabilities. By reading from databases, these operations effectively connect different data sources and extract information relevant to specific business contexts. Before execution, environmental perception and permission assessment ensure that the system adapts to various environments while safeguarding data security. During execution, atomic operations extract key data, providing foundational information for anomaly detection and early warning. After execution, content comparison and threshold setting help confirm abnormal information, supporting the decision-making process. These operations not only improve the system's flexibility and accuracy but also provide real-time and effective data support for legal supervision, ensuring the efficiency and correctness of supervisory work. The implementation process will be briefly illustrated through two examples below.

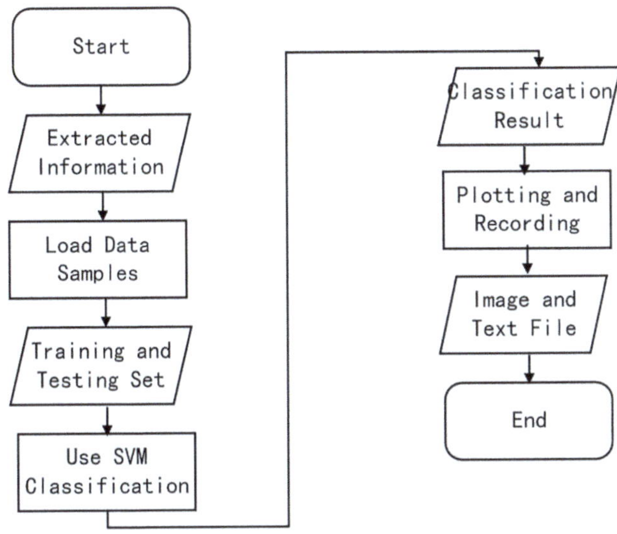

Fig. 3. Flowchart of the SVM Classification Operation.

Data Reading Operations. The main function of the data reading operation is to connect to different databases based on the selected database type, retrieve various pieces of information stored in the database, and store this data for subsequent targeted extraction and further processing. Figure 4 illustrates the flowchart of the data reading operation.

In this operation, since different problems and companies may choose different databases as information sources, we first need to determine what type of database we need to connect to. Currently, we can connect to seven types of databases: Kingbase, PostgreSQL, MySQL, GaussDB, Oracle, SQLite, and MSSQL. In the specific implementation, we adopt a redundant method. Users can input and select different database types during actual operation. For each type of database, we have written connection functions tailored to that database for execution.

Users will then need to input the required information for the selected database. For example, when using a MySQL database, users must input the MySQL hostname, port number, username, password, and database name. After successfully connecting to the database, the information stored in the database will be temporarily stored in a Python cursor, awaiting further data extraction.

Environmental Perception Operations. Among the pre-execution operations, there is a series of perceptual operations, and here we will specifically introduce **environmental perception operations**. The main function of environmental perception operations is to gather various types of environmental information, facilitating the execution of different operations in different environments and enhancing adaptability to ensure smooth operation across various

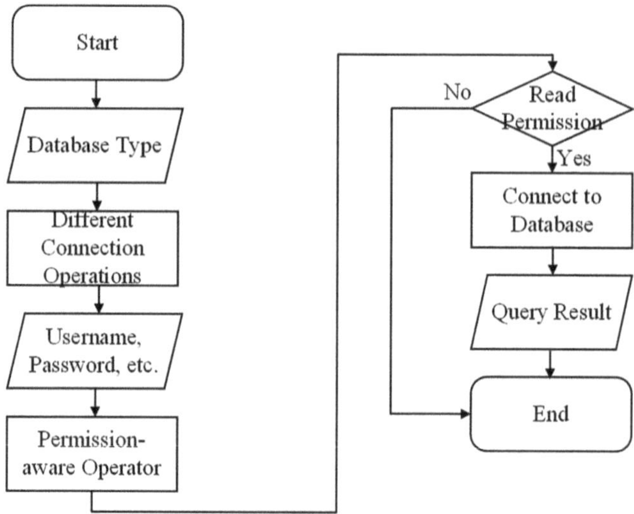

Fig. 4. Flowchart of the Data Reading Operation.

contexts. Figure 5 illustrates the flowchart of the environmental perception operations.

This operation is generally the first step after model execution. The environmental information regarding the current devices and software obtained from this operation can be provided to subsequent programs, ensuring that they can run appropriately. In this operation, by utilizing the 'platform' library in Python, we can perceive the current environment and extract basic environmental information such as the operating system name, operating system version, current Python interpreter version, machine hardware name, processor name, and current system network name. This information facilitates the use of redundant methods to ensure that the program can function normally in different environments, thereby enhancing the robustness of the model. Additionally, this information will be stored in a 'txt' file for future reference and verification.

4.4   Specific Operations for Some Specific Area

Specific operations mainly involve executing operations relevant to the field based on the supervision case and objectives. For example, in the case of finished oil issues, we have operations for reading the trajectory information of tankers. If the target case is a healthcare insurance case, it may be necessary to extract information such as insured individuals, purchasers, pharmacy names, purchase amounts, and types of medications from the database. Considering the diversity of information types across different businesses, we have various operations, but these operations share similarities. Below, we will introduce the implementation of the healthcare insurance amount reading operation, and Fig. 6 illustrates its flowchart.

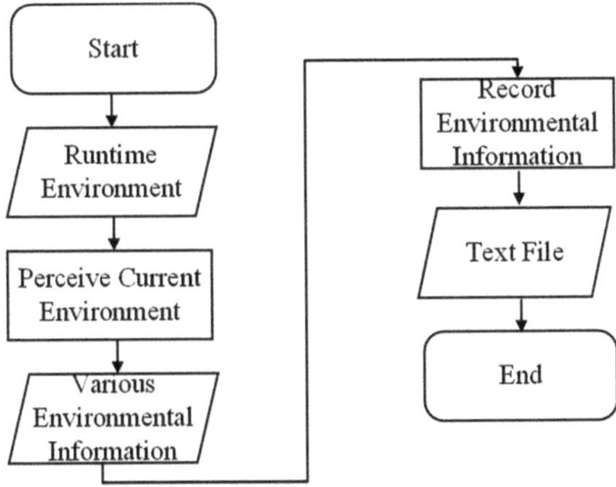

Fig. 5. Flowchart of the Environmental Perception Operation.

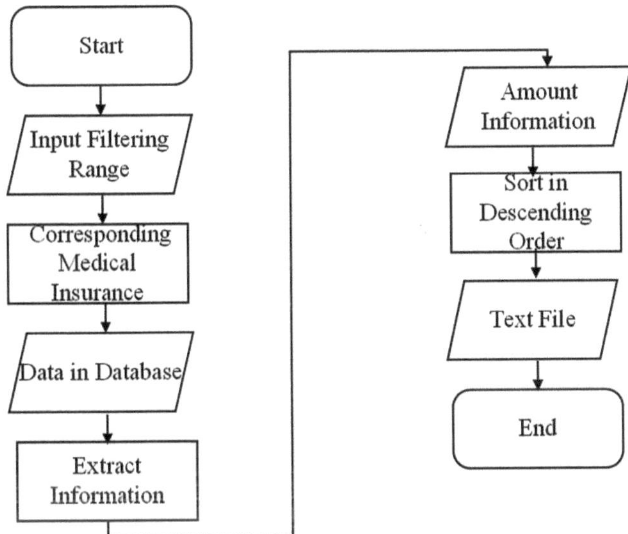

Fig. 6. Flowchart of Healthcare Insurance Amount Reading Operation.

In this operation, we first need to determine the type of information extraction operation to execute based on the supervision case and objectives. Information unrelated to the case does not need to be extracted; in this operation, we only need to extract information related to healthcare insurance. Next, we extract the corresponding information from the data reading operation based on the data stored in the database. In certain information extraction processes, such as amount extraction, the extracted information can be sorted in descending order. This method has several advantages.

First, when the target information is monetary amounts, sorting in descending order makes it easier to identify anomalies and simplifies threshold judgments. Second, when the target is a group of information containing many details, sorting by time enhances the readability of the results and facilitates subsequent operations. Third, when needing to obtain frequency information about individuals, sorting names in descending order allows similar individuals' information to be grouped together, making it easier for subsequent content comparison operations to calculate frequency statistics.

After completing the above processes, the operation will store the extracted information in a txt file for potential subsequent content comparison operations, which will yield secondary information such as similar information, excess information, and frequency data.

5   Conclusion and Future Work

We propose a design and implementation method for atomic operations design, aimed at meeting the demands of legal supervision in the context of big data. By performing fine-grained segmentation and modeling of the legal supervision process, various types of atomic operations are designed, enhancing the model's usability and interpretability, and improving the intelligence level of legal supervision.

Specifically, the main contributions of this research include the following points. First, we present a design method for a legal supervision model based on atomic operations. Through fine-grained segmentation and abstract modeling of the supervision process, we design multiple types of atomic operations, including the basic operations, basic machine learning operations, some specific function and specific operations for special areas. This lays the foundation for the intelligence of legal supervision. Moreover, the diversity of atomic operations enhances the model's flexibility and practicality, allowing the combined model to address a broader range of issues. These research outcomes not only provide valuable explorations for the intelligent practice of legal supervision in a big data environment but also offer new perspectives and methods for theoretical research in related fields.

Additionally, this study has significant theoretical implications and practical value for promoting the intelligent development of legal supervision in the era of big data. The design method for the legal supervision model based on atomic operations offers new insights for theoretical research on intelligent legal supervision. By fine-grained segmentation and modeling of atomic operations, it lays the groundwork for constructing more refined and dynamic legal supervision models in the future. The intelligent legal supervision model proposed here provides valuable explorations and practical examples for addressing legal supervision issues in the context of big data, with broad practical application prospects.

However, our research still has considerable room for improvement. In the future, the modeling methods for atomic operations can be further optimized.

Although our work lays a foundation, further refinement and enhancement are needed in the specific design and assembly of atomic operations. Future work may involve designing more general and reusable atomic operation templates to meet the practical needs of different supervision domains, thereby enhancing the model's applicability. Additionally, exploring semantic-based legal supervision reasoning mechanisms can more flexibly express legal norms, supervisory actions, and their inherent relationships, further elevating the intelligence level of legal supervision.

Acknowledgement. The research presented in this paper is supported in part by the National Key R&D Program of China (2023YFC3306100), the National Natural Science Foundation of China (62172324), Key R&D in Shaanxi Province (2023-YBGY-269, 2022QCY-LL-33HZ), Xixian New Area Science and Technology Plan Project (RGZN-2023-002, 2022-ZDJS-001).

References

1. Liu, Q.J., Liu, S., Wu, Y.R., et al.: Empowering legal supervision with big data technology. Acta Academiae Sinicae **37**(12), 1695–1704 (2022)
2. Liu, P.X.: On big data legal supervision. J. National Prosecutors College **23**(1), 76–92 (2023)
3. Gibb, R.G., Purss, M.B.J., Sabeur, Z., et al.: Global reference grids for big earth data. Earth Big Data **006**(003), 251–255 (2022)
4. Ji, G.L., Zhao, B.: A review of spatiotemporal data mining for big data. J. Nanjing Normal Univ. (Natural Science Edition) **000**(001), 1–7 (2014)
5. Zhai, X.W.: Marking target method—a new approach for achieving data consistency and atomic operations. Comput. Eng. Des. **18**(4), 9 (1997). https://doi.org/CNKI:SUN:SJSJ.0.1997-04-000
6. Liu, B.: Service-oriented Transaction Processing Technology in Pervasive Environments. Shanghai Jiao Tong University, Shanghai (2011). https://doi.org/CNKI:CDMD:2.2010.201782
7. Zhang, M.: Research on Encapsulation of Process Objects and Their Behavioral Semantics. Beijing Jiaotong University, Beijing (2014)
8. Brunet, G., Chechik, M., Easterbrook, S., et al.: A manifesto for model merging. In: GaMMa '06: Proceedings of the 2006 International Workshop on Global Integrated Model Management, pp. 5–12 (2006). https://doi.org/10.1145/1138304.1138307
9. Sun, H.T., Zhu, Z.Q., Wang, W.Q., et al.: System for Executing Atomic Operations, Atomic Operation Methods and Devices. China, CN202111433301.X[P] (2021-11-29)
10. Beckman, C.J., Suri, S.S., Hughes, C.J., et al.: Adaptive Remote Atomic Operations. China, CN202111598128[P] (2021-12-24)
11. Wu, J., Xu, Y., Zhang, Y., et al.: TIE: a framework for embedding-based incremental temporal knowledge graph completion. In: SIGIR '21: Proceedings of the 44th International ACM SIGIR Conference on Research and Development in Information Retrieval, pp. 428–437 (2021). https://doi.org/10.48550/arXiv.2104.08419

A Fake News Detection Model Based on Expert Knowledge Integration

Hui Xu, Haowen Fang, and Tao Qin[✉]

Department of Computer Science and Engineering, Xi'an Jiaotong University, Xi'an 710049, China
qin.tao@mail.xjtu.edu.cn

Abstract. The integration of expert knowledge in news classification has traditionally been a difficult problem. This paper focus on designing an expert knowledge enhanced fake news detection method. First, we classify expert knowledge into two categories: common sense knowledge and authoritative event information. For common sense knowledge, this paper designed a knowledge-reinforced transformer model that utilizes a knowledge encoding tree to embed entity knowledge into news texts and a masking mechanism to address the redundant knowledge problem brought on by over embedding. For authoritative event information, this paper uses latent semantic analysis methods to select factual information that may be used to classify fake information, and then uses the attention mechanism to fuse the selected factual information features with news text features. We verify our method on public datasets "Weibo21" and "Covid_news". The results show a 1.3% to 18% improvement in classification accuracy, verifying the effectiveness of the methods proposed in this paper.

Keywords: Fake News Detection · Expert Knowledge · KMGCN

1 Introduction

With the continuous development of social media technology, social media platforms have become many people's primary news source. Fake news publishers often base their publications on existing facts, but then distort and fabricate them to suit their narratives. Such fake news often contains the same entities as real news, but violate common sense knowledge or authoritative event information released by official media. The desire to incorporate these common-sense knowledge and authoritative event knowledge in assisting fake news detection has become a new direction in the field.

Pan et al. [1] applied knowledge graphs to the field of fake news detection. The authors derived the similarity measurement between news content and external knowledge based on the deviations between the semantic triples extracted from the news content and external knowledge. Thresholds were selected through many experiments, and classification was performed based on the thresholds and similarity. Hu et al. [2] used linear discriminant analysis (LDA) to obtain keywords of news content, and then used

S. Li et al. (Eds.): BROADNETS 2024, LNICST 674, pp. 84–99, 2026.
https://doi.org/10.1007/978-3-032-14350-1_6

entity connection to extract entity information from news text. They took into account the implicit relationship between various information on social media such as the original article, publishing users, reposting users, and comments to detect fake news. Yuan et al. [3] introduced deep neural network technology to the field of heterogeneous network fake news detection. Using the attention mechanism together with the interactive information between encoded text semantics and local structure, they then modeled it with external knowledge into a combined network structure, and finally used a classifier for classification.

In 2020, Wang et al. [4] modeled news text, expert knowledge, and visual information on a unified graph structure to obtain an enhanced multimodal representation, and constructed an external knowledge-driven, multimodal graph convolutional neural network (KMGCN). Zhang et al. [5] used the attention mechanism to integrate visual information and external knowledge into textual representation to help better understand the content of news text. Based on this idea, Dun et al. [6] further considered the actual circumstances of news content, focusing on the common-sense information of news entities, and jointly modeled news text, entity and entity context information. Finally, the multi-head attention mechanism is used for feature fusion, constructing a knowledge-augmented network (KAN) that can obtain richer semantic information.

Existing fake news detection methods that integrate expert knowledge mainly approach the problem from the perspective of either expert knowledge embedding or expert knowledge comparison. In order to solve the justification problem of fake news detection, this paper chooses the expert knowledge embedding approach. However, such methods often lead to problems with information redundancy and information loss: when the splicing position is distant from the vector space of the relevant entity information, it causes information loss; when too much information is integrated, it causes information redundancy.

Traditional fake news detection only uses the information contained in the news itself for classification and evaluation. In order to fully utilize existing external expert knowledge to improve the correctness and soundness, scholars have begun to pay attention to the introduction of expert knowledge into the field of fake news detection. Most expert knowledge embedding methods mainly perform knowledge retrieval in the knowledge graph, and then compare with the news text to identify factuality. This method only considers the difference between fake news and objective facts, but ignores the supplementary effect of expert knowledge on news content. Therefore, scholars are increasingly considering integrating expert knowledge into news texts to enhance news content. However, most methods perform feature-splicing on the selected expert knowledge and news content, and ignore the local correlation between knowledge and news content. This fails to make full use of the information enhancement effect of expert knowledge on news entities.

To answer the question of how to fully and effectively integrate expert knowledge, this paper proposes a fake news detection model that includes a knowledge-enhanced transformer module and a factual information fusion module based on authoritative knowledge. This method first uses entity information to lookup relevant knowledge in a structured knowledge base, and then uses a tree structure and annotation principle to inject structured knowledge into news texts, meanwhile using the attention mechanisms and the masking mechanisms to avoid knowledge redundancy. In the factual information fusion module, this method first uses latent semantic analysis method to lookup relevant event information in the authoritative event knowledge base, then uses the cross-attention mechanism to integrate event features with news texts, and finally classifies via a classification network. To prove the feasibility of this model, this paper runs tests on the public datasets "Weibo21" and "Covid_news", verifying the performance of the model through controlled experiments and ablation studies.

2   Knowledge Reinforcement Fake News Detection Model

Existing fake news detection algorithms commonly ignore the common-sense information that fake news often violate. The few algorithms that integrate expert knowledge simply splice expert knowledge with the news texts, without fully considering the deep semantic relationship between the expert entity knowledge and the news entity. Simultaneously, most existing methods ignore the timeliness aspect of news when considering the selection of expert knowledge (the factual information that fake news contradicts is typically recent). In such situations, the entity knowledge in the knowledge base is insufficient to judge the news' factuality, and therefore its factuality should instead be evaluated against the authoritative knowledge. In response to these problems, this chapter proposes an expert knowledge fusion algorithm that includes a knowledge-enhanced transformer [7] module and an authoritative knowledge-based factual information fusion module. Figure 1 illustrates the framework of the proposed method.

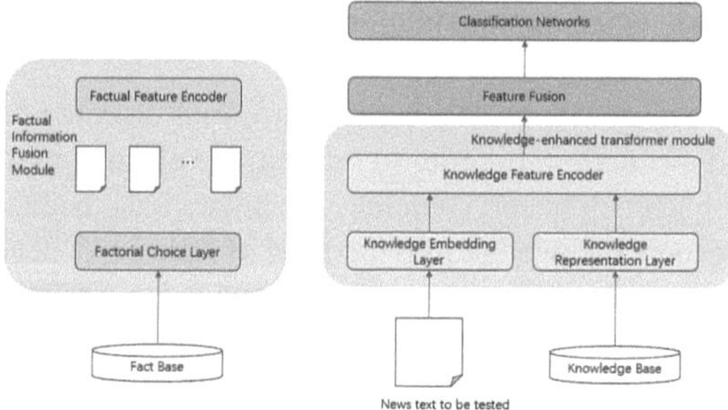

Fig. 1. The framework of this proposed fake news detection method

We define the task of fake news classification integrating expert knowledge as: given a news composed of $S = \{w_0, w_1, w_2, \cdots, w_n\}$, an external knowledge base KB, and a truth value label e, where $w_i \in V$ represents the set of words that appear in all news, $e = 0$ means the news is true, $e = 1$ means the news is fake, this chapter aims to find a mapping $f(S, KB, \theta) \rightarrow (e')$ to predict the truthfulness of a given news $((e' = 0$ or $e' = 1))$, where θ is a learnable model parameter.

Based on the model framework diagram in Fig. 1, the details of the fake news detection method integrating expert knowledge are introduced as follows. The model input is the news text set to be evaluated $\pi = \{S_0, S_1, S_2, \cdots, S_n\}$, and the truth value label set $E = \{e_0, e_1, e_2, \cdots, e_n\}$; the output is the classification model. The model in this chapter is composed of two parts. The first part is the knowledge-enhanced transformer module, used to integrate the common-sense information in the knowledge base; the second part is the authoritative knowledge-based factual information fusion module, used to integrate authoritative knowledge in real events.

2.1 Knowledge-Enhanced Transformer

This section uses the knowledge-enhanced transformer module to perform feature fusion on common sense knowledge. It mainly includes a knowledge representation layer, a text representation layer, a masking layer, and a multi-head self-attention layer with masking mechanism. The overall structure of the knowledge-enhanced transformer network is shown in Fig. 2, and its network function is defined as:

$$\begin{cases} S_{bert}{}' = S_{bert} + PE(S_{bert}) \\ S^{MULT} = Att_{mult}^{mask}\left(S_{bert}{}'\right) \\ \hat{e} = FFN\left(LN\left(S^{MULT}\right)\right) \end{cases} \tag{1}$$

where $\{\{SYM\}\}$ is a position-wise Feed-Forward neural Network (FFN), its standardized definition being:

$$FFN(x) = MAX(0, x \times W_1 + b_1) \times W_2 + b_2 \tag{2}$$

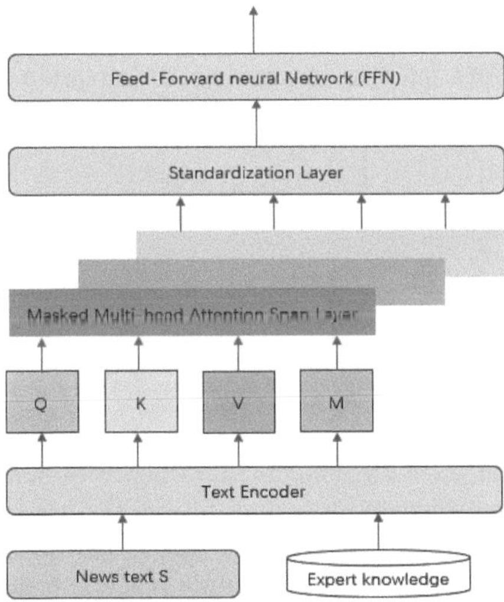

Fig. 2. The overall structure of the knowledge-enhanced transformer network

For a given news text $S = \{w_0, w_1, w_2, \cdots, w_n, P\}$, we use the text vocabulary w_i to lookup relevant structured knowledge from the "CN-DBpedia" knowledge base. The entity knowledge in this knowledge base can be represented by the tuple $\varepsilon = (\omega, \theta_0, \theta_1, \cdots, \theta_i)$, where ω represents the entity, and θ_i represents the description information of the entity ω. . For example, the entity "Baiyin City" can be described in the knowledge base as (a city under Gansu, Tongcheng, temperate continental climate, red tourism city, …). The structured knowledge retrieved from the entities in the news text S to be evaluated can be represented as:

$$\varphi = \left\{ \left(w_0, \theta_0^0, \theta_{11}^0, \cdots, \theta_i^0 \right), \left(w_1, \theta_0^1, \theta_{11}^1, \cdots, \theta_i^1 \right), \cdots, \left(w_n, \theta_0^n, \theta_{11}^n, \cdots, \theta_i^n \right) \right\} \quad (3)$$

We inject the structured knowledge into the original news text S to correlate with the corresponding entity ω_n. Here, a tree structure is used to demonstrate the text structure S after knowledge injection, as shown in Fig. 3:

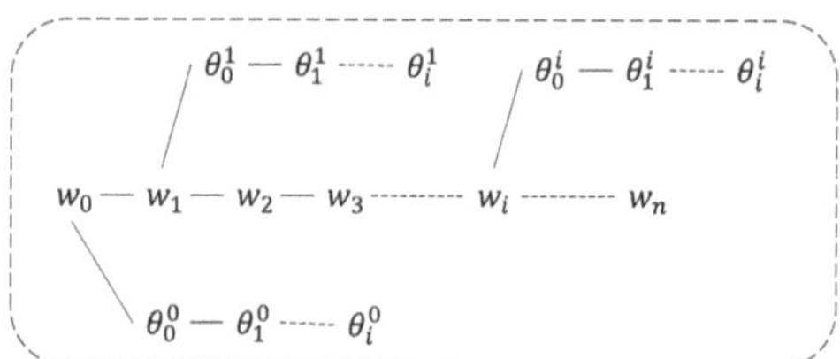

Fig. 3. The text structure S after knowledge injection

The text structure post-injection can be represented as:

$$S' = \left\{ \left(w_0, \theta_0^0, \theta_1^0, \cdots, \theta_i^0 \right), \left(w_1, \theta_0^1, \theta_1^1, \cdots, \theta_i^1 \right), \cdots, \left(w_n, \theta_0^n, \theta_1^n, \cdots, \theta_i^n \right) \right\} \quad (4)$$

The self-attention layer is the core of the transformer network. In order to construct a self-attention layer with a masking mechanism, the attention function is defined as:

$$\begin{cases} Q = S_{bert}' \times W^Q \\ K = S_{bert}' \times W^K \\ V = S_{bert}' \times W^V \end{cases} \quad (5)$$

where $W^Q \in R^{d_{model} \times d_q}, W^K \in R^{d_{model} \times d_k}, W^V \in R^{d_{model} \times d_v}, Q \in R^{L \times d_q}, K \in R^{L \times d_k}, V \in R^{L \times d_v}$, The attention function is defined as:

$$Self\ Attention(Q, K, V) = softmax\left(QK^T \Big/ \sqrt{d_q} \right) \times V \quad (6)$$

In order to fully understand the semantic information of news text, this chapter uses a multi-head attention mechanism for feature fusion. We use H self-attention heads to concurrently learn on the text information of news, and divide Q, K, and V into H different subspaces. The multi-head self-attention function is defined as:

$$MultiHead(Q, K, V) = Concat(head_1, head_2, \cdots, head_H) \times W^O \quad (7)$$

where $W^O \in R^{d_{model} \times d_q}$, $head_i$ represents the output of the ith attention head. Its learning process can be represented by:

$$head_i = Self\ Attention(Q_i, K_i, V_i) = softmax\left(Q_i K_i^T \Big/ \sqrt{\frac{d_q}{H}} \right) \times V_i \quad (8)$$

where $Q_i \in S_{bert}{}' \times W_i^Q$, $K_i \in S_{bert}{}' \times W_i^K$, $V_i \in S_{bert}{}' \times W_i^V$, $W_i^Q \in R^{d_{model} \times d_q/H}$, $W_i^K \in R^{d_{model} \times d_k/H}$, $W_i^V \in R^{d_{model} \times d_v/H}$.

Since a large amount of expert knowledge is introduced, the original news text only accounts for a small proportion after the supplementation, resulting in knowledge redundancy, causing the model to pay too much attention to the introduced knowledge text. During detection, the model should pay more attention to the semantic information in the original news text, so the masking mechanism is introduced into the self-attention function, and the self-attention function is modified as follows:

$$head_i^M = Self\ Attention(Q_i, K_i, V_i, M) = softmax\left(Q_i K_i^T + M \middle/ \sqrt{\tfrac{d_q}{H}} \right) \times V_i \quad (9)$$

Now the masking multi-head self-attention function is as follows:

$$MultiHead^{MASK}(Q, K, V, M) = Concat\left(head_i^M, head_2^M, \cdots, head_H^M\right) \times W^O \quad (10)$$

2.2 Authoritative Knowledge-Based Factual Information Integration

The original news text is supplemented using the obtained authoritative knowledge C. The supplemented text vector is obtained by concatenating the authoritative knowledge C with the original news text vector S:

$$S^{ext} = [S : C] \quad (11)$$

In the supplemented text vector, we should pay more attention to the original news text. In order to avoid information redundancy caused by the supplemented text, we use cross-attention mechanism here to integrate factual information. As shown in Fig. 4:

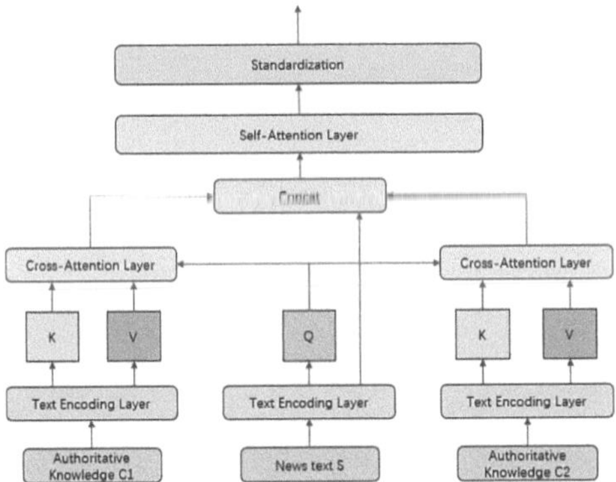

Fig. 4. Authoritative Knowledge-based Factual Information Integration Diagram

For some news text S and an authoritative knowledge C_i, the attention value function is defined as:

$$\begin{cases} Q = S \times W^Q \\ K = C_i \times W^K \\ V = C_i \times W^V \end{cases} \quad (12)$$

where $W^Q \in R^{d_s \times d_k}$, $W^K \in R^{d_c \times d_k}$, $W^V \in R^{d_c \times d_v}$. The attention is defined as:

$$Cross\,Attention(S, C_i) = softmax\left(QK^T\Big/\sqrt{d_C}\right) \times V \tag{13}$$

For k pieces of authoritative knowledge C_i, we can generate k attention representations of evidence facts. Concatenating k textual features:

$$d^{cot} = Conat(CrossAttention(S, C_i)) \tag{14}$$

where $i \in [1, k]$.

Finally, feature fusion is performed using the self-attention mechanism, and then normalized to obtain the features after integrating authoritative knowledge d^{rich}:

$$d^{rich} = LN\left(selfAttetion(d^{cot})\right) \tag{15}$$

where $LN(\cdot)$ means normalizing the results of the multi-head attention model.

Finally, we concatenate the results of the knowledge-enhanced transformer network $S^{[D]}$ and d^{rich}, and obtain the fused news text feature $[S^{[D]}, d^{rich}]$. This is fed into a Multi-Layer Perceptron (MLP) for fake news classification to obtain the predicted classification results $\hat{e}$ as follows:

$$\hat{e} = \sigma(W_1 \times (W_2 \times [S^{[D]}, d^{rich}] + b_1) + b_2 \tag{16}$$

Among them, W_1, W_2, b_1, and b_2 are the weights and biases of MLP, and the cross-entropy loss function is used to learn on the model parameters and optimize the model:

$$L_\theta(e, \hat{e}) = -\left(e\log\hat{e} + (1 - e)\log(1 - \hat{e})\right) \tag{17}$$

where e is the actual classification of this news text. The model aims to minimize the loss function L_θ and uses back propagation algorithm to train the model parameters to achieve the task of fake news classification integrating expert knowledge. The pseudo-code of the fake news detection algorithm integrating expert knowledge is shown in Algorithm 1:

Algorithm 1: Training process of fake news detection algorithm integrating expert knowledge

---

Input:

    News text S, label e, external knowledge base KB, training rounds steps

Output:

    Feature extractor E, feature classifier D

Process:

1. Randomly initialize feature extractor E and feature classifier D
2. Repeat
3. for steps do
4. Find the knowledge entity set $\{w_0, w_1, w_2, \cdots, w_n\}$ that needs to be enhanced in the news text S
5. Find the expanded common sense knowledge in CN-DBpedia; supplement news text to φ
6. Get the news text representation $S_{bert}{}'$ through the text representation layer
7. Generate the mask matrix M
8. Calculate the masked multi-head attention result $S^{[D]}$ of the text representation
9. Use the latent semantic analysis method to calculate the topic-text matrix A
10. Calculate the similarity ω between the authoritative knowledge and the news text S to be evaluated
11. If $\omega > 0.8$:
12. Concatenate the authoritative knowledge C_i with the original news text vector S to obtain S^{ext}
13. Perform feature fusion d^{rich} using the cross-attention mechanism
14. Concatenate $S^{[D]}$ and d^{rich} to form news text features with integrated expert knowledge $\left[S^{[D]}, d^{rich}\right]$
15. Make prediction $\hat{e} = \sigma(W_1 \times (W_2 \times \left[S^{[D]}, d^{rich}\right] + b_1) + b_2$ using the multi-layer perceptron
16. Use cross entropy loss function to learn model parameters $L_\theta(e, \hat{e}) = -(e \log \hat{e} + (1 - e) \log(1 - \hat{e}))$
17. Update feature classifier parameters through gradient descent
18. end for
19. Until the model converges

---

3   Model Performance Evaluation

3.1   Datasets and Knowledge Base

This section uses two public datasets, "Weibo21" and "Covid_news", and the "CN-Dbpedia" [8] external knowledge base to evaluate the model performance.

Datasets "Weibo21" dataset: This dataset is the relevant Weibo data from the Weibo Community Management Center from December 2014 to March 2021. It collects data verified as "true" by the Ruijian Rumor Identification Platform and ensures that its chronological distribution is consistent with the fake data. For each piece of data, the dataset collects information in multiple dimensions, including text content, attached pictures, timestamps, comments, and rumor-refuting information (for fake information only), which resulted in 4488 fake news and 4640 real news. The author cross-referenced multiple fact-checking websites and related research reports, and classified the news into the following 9 areas: science and technology, military, education, accidents, politics, health, finance, entertainment, and society.

"Covid_news" dataset: This dataset is a news dataset related to the Covid 19 pandemic. The dataset collects news data related to the pandemic published on platforms such as Weibo and Weixin public accounts. Each piece of data includes fields such as

Weibo text, comments, pictures, and area of interest. After data cleaning, the entire dataset includes 33,807 news data, of which 16,842 are fake.

Knowledge base "CN-DBpedia" [8] knowledge base: This knowledge base contains more than 10 million entity information and 70 million entity information semantic triples. It is a Chinese general encyclopedia knowledge graph created by the Knowledge Factory Laboratory of Fudan University through data mining and collection on encyclopedia search websites such as Chinese Wikipedia. Expanded and optimized upon the Fudan GDM Chinese knowledge graph, this knowledge base has the most entity information of all open Chinese encyclopedia knowledge graphs.

3.2 Experiment Settings

Evaluation Indicator. The classification results of the samples are sorted into the following cases: When a fake news is classified as fake, this sample is regarded as a true positive sample (TP) of this category; when a fake news is classified as real, this sample is regarded as a false negative sample (FN) of this category; when a real news is classified as real, this sample is regarded as a true negative sample (TN) of this category; when a real news is classified as fake, this sample is regarded as a false positive sample (FP) of this category.

According to the sample case, the accuracy is the ratio of the number of correct classifications by the model to the total number of news, for a given news dataset to be classified. This is indicative of the classification model's ability to classify the entire news dataset. Precision is the ratio of real fake news to the news classified as fake by the model. Recall is the ratio of fake news correctly classified by the model to the total number of fake news. F-score is the harmonic mean of precision and recall. The calculation formula is as follows:

$$Accuracy = \frac{TP+TN}{TP+FN+FP+TN} \tag{18}$$

$$Precision = \frac{TP}{TP+FP} \tag{19}$$

$$Recall = \frac{TP}{TP+FN} \tag{20}$$

$$
\begin{aligned}
F_\beta &= \left(1+\beta^2\right) \frac{Precision \times Recall}{\beta^2 \times Precision \times Recall} \\
&= \left(1+\beta^2\right) \frac{\left(1+\beta^2\right)TP}{\left(1+\beta^2\right)TP + \beta^2 FP + FN}
\end{aligned} \tag{21}
$$

When $\beta = 1$, the F-score becomes F_1 value, which is called the Balanced F-score. The formula is as follows:

$$
\begin{aligned}
F_1 &= \frac{2 \times Precision \times Recall}{Precision + Recall} \\
&= \frac{2 \times TP}{2 \times TP + FP + FN}
\end{aligned} \tag{22}
$$

Parameter Settings. Based on the experiment settings of Zhong et al. [7], this paper randomly divided the dataset into subsets of 70%, 10%, and 20% as the training set, the validation set, and the test set. The remaining parameters of the fake news detection method integrating expert knowledge proposed in this chapter are shown in Table 1.

Table 1. Parameter Setting

Training Parameter	Parameter Definition	Parameter Value
H	multi-head attention mechanism head count	12
D	KAT network layer count	2
batchsize	training batch size	16
epoch	training rounds	40
ω	similarity threshold	0.8/0.7

3.3 Comparison Methods

This section uses several classic fake news detection comparison methods that integrate expert knowledge, including previous classic methods and current mainstream novel methods. The specific comparison methods are described as follows:

1. Fake news detection method using news text features

Textual [9]: This method a basic model based solely on the news text. First, the Bert model [10] is used to convert each word into an N-dimensional feature vector representation. Then the output of the textual representation layer is passed through a single-channel text feature extractor based on a convolutional neural network, then to a fully connected layer, and finally a softmax function to make predictions for the given news.

GCN [11]: This method is based on GCN network feature fusion and classification. First, a graph structure is used to store the similarity information of news articles. The nodes store the sentences of the news, and the similarity between sentences are used to assign edge weights. Secondly, we use the graph neural network to obtain the embedding vectors of all nodes, and then the graph vector of the news text after pooling. Finally, we use the GCN network to extract news features, and feed them into the classifier for classification.

VROC [12]: This method uses a multi-task learning approach. First, a Variational Auto Encoder (VAE) is used to encode text information to obtain an embedded representation of the news text, and then the text is classified by a classifier.

2. Fake news detection method integrating expert knowledge

LOSIRD [13]: This method regards the rumor detection task as a hybrid task that includes a forensics task and a rumor detection task. It uses a pre-trained fact-checking model to search for factual evidence in an external knowledge corpus, constructs factual evidence and news content into a star graph, and uses GCN to fuse news content and factual evidence to detect fake news.

CompareNet [2]: This method uses the entity connection method to extract entity words from news texts, uses the LDA method to extract the topic words of the article, constructs a heterogeneous information network containing topic nodes, sentence nodes, and entity nodes, and uses a heterogeneous graph neural network method to fuse the semantic information of various nodes, in order to obtain a richer article representation. This work uses knowledge graph representation learning tool TransE to obtain the representation of entities in the knowledge graph, and uses the entity description information in the knowledge graph to enhance the semantic information of entities in the knowledge graph. Comparison between the entity information of the news content and that of the knowledge graph can be done by simply comparing the networks, allowing us to judge whether a news content is consistent with objective facts and common sense information. Finally, the text information of the news and the compared entity information are input into the classifier to obtain the final classification result.

MKEMN [5]: This method proposes a Multimodal Knowledge Event Memory Network (MKEMN). This method first designs a Multimodal Knowledge Network (MKN) to extract multimodal information from the news, retrieves relevant knowledge from the knowledge base based on the obtained multimodal features to supplement the news information, and then uses the attention mechanism to integrate the relevant knowledge and classify it with the classifier. Finally, the event memory network is introduced for evidence construction, which provides additional evidence and strengthens the credibility of the classification.

KAN [6]: This method proposes a multimodal fake news detection algorithm based on knowledge graphs, which uses named entity recognition technology to retrieve the corresponding entity information in the knowledge graph according to the news entity. KAN expands the original news text by introducing the corresponding entity information in the knowledge graph. The multi-head attention mechanism is used to fuse the original news text information, entity information, and entity information in the knowledge graph, thereby obtaining richer news text features, before finally being fed into a classifier. This results in a method that greatly improves the accuracy of fake news detection.

KMGCN [4]: This method proposes a Knowledge-driven Multimodal Graph Convolutional Network (KMGCN) model. First, the visual information and text content are converted into a graph, where the visual information and the disjoint phrases in the text content are used as nodes of the graph. In addition, we also lookup knowledge relevant to the news content from the real-world knowledge base, and use these entity knowledge as nodes too to supplement the news content. Through this method, text information, knowledge concepts, and visual information are jointly modeled into a unified graph structure to obtain multimodal news features with integrates external knowledge. Finally, a graph convolutional network is used to extract the structural features of these graphs, thereby improving the accuracy of fake news detection.

4 Experiment Result and Analysis

4.1 Comparative Experiment Results

Table 2 and Table 3 show the prediction results of the fake news detection method integrating expert knowledge and the comparison model on the public datasets "Weibo21" and "Covid_news". It can be seen from Table 2 and Table 3 that the fake news detection method integrating expert knowledge is superior to fake news detection methods that only use news text features. This is because expert knowledge contains important information for judging the authenticity of news. Common sense information, entity knowledge in authoritative knowledge, and official real event information are important bases for judging whether the news is true. Making full use of expert knowledge can greatly improve the accuracy and reliability of fake news detection. The fake news detection method that integrates expert knowledge proposed in this chapter has achieved overall good results on public datasets. Compared with the comparison methods, on the "Weibo21" dataset, accuracy is up by at least 1.8%. When using fake news as positive samples, accuracy is up by at least 2.5%, recall is up by at least 0.9%, and F1-index is up by at least 1.6%. When using real news as positive samples, accuracy is better than most methods, recall is up by at least 3.4%, the F1-index is up by at least 2.0%. On the Covid_news dataset, accuracy is up by at least 1.3%. When using fake news as positive samples, accuracy is up by at least 5.7%, recall is better than most methods, and F1-index is up by at least 1.9%. When using real news as positive samples, accuracy is better than most methods, recall is up by at least 4.9%, and F1 index is better than most methods.

Table 2. Comparative Experiment Results on Weibo21

Model	Accuracy	Fake News			Real News		
		Precision	Recall rate	F1	Precision	Recall rate	F1
Textual	0.641	0.687	0.707	0.697	0.573	0.549	0.561
GCN	0.682	0.668	0.771	0.716	0.703	0.588	0.640
VROC	0.718	0.701	0.805	0.750	0.745	0.623	0.679
LOSIRD	0.730	0.720	0.801	0.758	**0.745**	0.640	0.689
CompareNet	0.754	0.805	0.789	0.797	0.678	0.698	0.688
MKEMN	0.701	0.685	0.789	0.733	0.725	0.605	0.660
KAN	0.772	0.832	0.797	0.814	0.683	0.730	0.705
KMGCN	0.803	0.855	0.823	0.839	0.725	0.769	0.746
Our Model	**0.821**	**0.880**	**0.831**	**0.855**	0.733	**0.803**	**0.766**

Table 3. Comparative Experiment Results on Covid_news

Model	Accuracy	Fake News			Real News		
		Precision	Recall rate	F1	Precision	Recall rate	F1
Textual	0.625	0.612	0.721	0.662	0.645	0.525	0.579
GCN	0.658	0.632	0.758	0.689	0.698	0.558	0.620
VROC	0.685	0.663	0.779	0.716	0.718	0.587	0.646
LOSIRD	0.719	0.697	0.809	0.748	0.753	0.623	0.682
CompareNet	0.751	0.763	0.811	0.786	0.733	0.674	0.702
MKEMN	0.693	0.673	0.784	0.725	0.723	0.596	0.653
KAN	0.767	0.772	0.828	0.799	0.760	0.689	0.723
KMGCN	0.789	0.795	**0.844**	0.819	**0.780**	0.717	**0.747**
Our Model	**0.802**	**0.852**	0.824	**0.838**	0.728	**0.766**	0.746

4.2 Experiment Results

In order to verify the correctness and effectiveness of each module in the method proposed in this paper, this section conducts the following ablation experiments on the proposed method:

- R1: Only includes text feature representation and multi-layer perceptron, considered to be the- baseline model;
- R2: Adds a knowledge-enhanced transformer module to R1;
- R3: Adds a fact information fusion module to R1;
- R4: Adds a fact information fusion module to R2, i.e. the fused model of R1 and R2.

Tables 4 and 5 show the results of ablation experiments on the public datasets "Weibo21" and "Covid_news" respectively. The results show that the knowledge-enhanced transformer module and the fact information fusion module based on authoritative knowledge can both improve the performance of the classification method.

Table 4. Ablation Experiment Result on Weibo21

Model	Accuracy	Fake News			Real News		
		Precision	Recall rate	F1	Precision	Recall rate	F1
R1	0.641	0.687	0.707	0.697	0.573	0.549	0.561
R2	0.783	0.808	0.826	0.817	0.725	0.722	0.733
R3	0.717	0.728	0.785	0.755	0.700	0.632	0.664
R4	**0.821**	**0.880**	**0.831**	**0.855**	**0.733**	**0.803**	**0.766**

Table 5. Ablation Experiment Result on Covid_news

Model	Accuracy	Fake News			Real News		
		Precision	Recall rate	F1	Precision	Recall rate	F1
R1	0.625	0.612	0.721	0.662	0.645	0.525	0.579
R2	0.742	0.763	0.817	0.794	0.710	0.682	0.719
R3	0.691	0.685	0.774	0.727	0.700	0.597	0.644
R4	**0.802**	**0.852**	**0.824**	**0.838**	**0.728**	**0.766**	**0.746**

Observing the results of R1 and R2, the knowledge-enhanced transformer module can make full use of common sense information in the real world, significantly enhancing the model performance. Specifically, on the "Weibo21" dataset, accuracy is up by 14.2%. When fake news is used as positive samples, precision is up by 12.1%, recall is up by 11.9%, and F1-index is up by 12.0%; when real news is used as positive samples, precision is up by 17.2%, and recall is up by 17.3%, F1-index is up by 17.2%. On the "Covid_news" dataset, accuracy is up by 13.7%. When fake news is used as positive samples, precision is up by 15.1%, recall is up by 10.6%, and F1-index is up by 13.0%; when real news used as positive samples, precision is up by 11.5%, recall is up by 15.7%, and F1-index is up by 14.0%.

Observing the results of R1 and R3, the factual information fusion module can make full use of factual information in real events to help classify fake news. Specifically, on the "Weibo21" dataset, accuracy is up by 7.6%. When fake news is used as positive samples, precision is up by 4.1%, recall is up by 7.8%, and F1-index is up by 5.8%; when real news was used as positive samples, precision is up by 12.7%, recall is up by 8.3%, and F1-index is up by 10.3%. On the "Covid_news" dataset, accuracy is up by 6.6%. When fake news is used as positive samples, precision is up by 7.3%, recall is up by 5.3%, and F1-index is up by 6.5%; when real news is used as a positive sample, precision is up by 5.5%, recall is up by 7.2%, and F1-index is up by 6.5%.

Observing the results of R2, R3 and R4, it is found that combining the two modules can further improve the model performance. Specifically, on the "Weibo21" dataset, accuracy is up by 3.8%. When fake news is used as positive samples, accuracy is up by 7.2%, recall is up by 0.5%, and F1-index is up by 3.8%; when real news is used as positive samples, precision is up by 0.8%, recall is up by 8.1%, and F1-index is up by 3.3%. On the "Covid_news" dataset, accuracy is up by 6.0%. When fake news is used as positive samples, precision is up by 8.9%, recall is up by 0.7%, and F1-index is up by 4.4%; when using real news as positive samples, precision is up by 1.8%, recall is up by 8.4%, and F1-index is up by 2.7%.

4.3 Sensitivity Analysis Results

This paper adjusted the similarity ω in the event selection module to conduct a sensitivity analysis. The similarity threshold ranges from 0.1 to 0.9, with an interval of 0.1, resulting in 9 different values. The model in this paper is used to conduct experiments on the "Weibo21" and "Covid_news" datasets. The results are shown in Fig. 5.

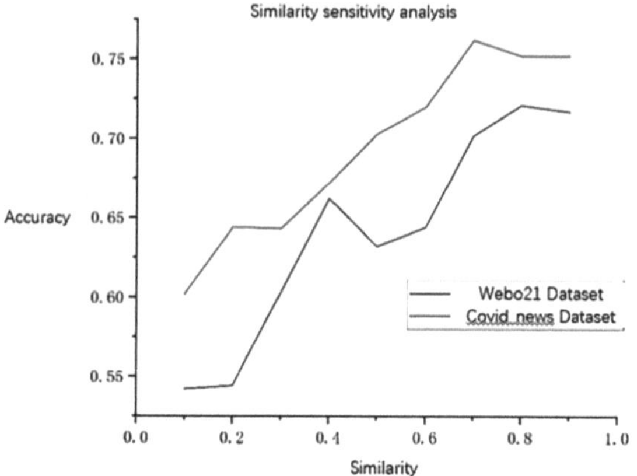

Fig.5. Similarity sensitivity analysis results

As shown in Fig. 5, on the "Weibo21" dataset, the model performs best at a similarity threshold of 0.8; on the "Covid_news" dataset, the model performs best at a similarity threshold of 0.7. We see detection performance degrading when the threshold is either too high or too low. According to experimental analysis, this phenomenon happens because when the similarity threshold is too low, many unrelated event information is regarded as authoritative knowledge through the evidence selection module, causing excessive noise to be added to the news text, which reduces its benefits to classification or even degrades it. As the threshold increases, more noise data is filtered out, and classification of the model gradually improves. The event features added to the news text are now highly relevant to the news text, thereby offering greater improvements to classification. However, when the threshold is too high, news events that can be used as authoritative knowledge are filtered out, resulting in a reduction in positive classification features. Compared to the detection model at the peak accuracy, there is now a lack of authoritative knowledge to aid in determining a news' truthfulness, which negatively affects the accuracy of the model.

5   Conclusion

In order to fully integrate common sense knowledge and authoritative factual information, this paper proposed a fake news detection method that integrates expert knowledge. First, expert knowledge is integrated into the news text representation through knowledge representation and position encoding, a masking mechanism is used to avoid information redundancy, and knowledge features are integrated through a knowledge-enhanced transformer network. Secondly, the authoritative knowledge in authoritative news is integrated into the news text information using a multi-head document attention mechanism, which can also serve as interpretability evidence for the classification results.

Finally, this paper conducted controlled experiments and ablation studies on the public datasets "Weibo21", "Covid_news", and the custom dataset "Weibo_fake24", verifying the effectiveness of this model.

Acknowledgments. The work reported herein was supported in part by the National Natural Science Foundation Foundation of China (62172324, 62272379), Key R&D in Shaanxi Province (2023-YBGY-269, 2022QCY-LL-33HZ), Xixian New Area Science and Technology Plan Project (RGZN-2023-002, 2022-ZDJS-001).

References

1. Pan, J.Z., Pavlova, S., Li, C., et al.: Content based fake news detection using knowledge graphs. In: The Semantic Web–ISWC 2018: 17th International Semantic Web Conference, Monterey, CA, USA, 8–12 October 2018, Proceedings, Part I 17. Springer International Publishing, Cham, pp. 669–683 (2018). https://doi.org/10.1007/978-3-030-00671-6_39
2. Hu, L., Yang, T., Zhang, L., et al.: Compare to the knowledge: graph neural fake news detection with external knowledge. In: Proceedings of the 59th Annual Meeting of the Association for Computational Linguistics and the 11th International Joint Conference on Natural Language Processing (Volume 1: Long Papers), pp. 754–763 (2021)
3. Yuan, C., Ma, Q., Zhou, W., et al.: Jointly embedding the local and global relations of heterogeneous graph for rumor detection. In: 2019 IEEE International Conference on Data Mining (ICDM), pp. 796–805. IEEE (2019)
4. Wang, Y., Qian, S., Hu, J., et al.: Fake news detection via knowledge-driven multimodal graph convolutional networks. In: Proceedings of the 2020 International Conference on Multimedia Retrieval, pp. 540–547 (2020)
5. Zhang, H., Fang, Q., Qian, S., et al.: Multi-modal knowledge-aware event memory network for social media rumor detection. In: Proceedings of the 27th ACM International Conference on Multimedia, pp. 1942–1951 (2019)
6. Dun, Y., Tu, K., Chen, C., et al.: KAN: knowledge-aware attention network for fake news detection. In: Proceedings of the AAAI Conference on Artificial Intelligence, vol., 35, no. 1, pp. 81–89 (2021)
7. Zhong, P., Wang, D., Miao, C.: Knowledge-enriched transformer for emotion detection in textual conversations. arxiv preprint arXiv:1909.10681 (2019)
8. Xu, B., Xu, Y., Liang, J., et al.: CN-DBpedia: a never-ending Chinese knowledge extraction system. In: International Conference on Industrial, Engineering and Other Applications of Applied Intelligent Systems. Springer International Publishing, Cham, pp. 428–438 (2017). https://doi.org/10.1007/978-3-319-60045-1_44
9. Ma, J., Gao, W., Mitra, P., et al.: Detecting rumors from microblogs with recurrent neural networks (2016)
10. Devlin, J., Chang, M.W., Lee, K., et al.: BERT: pre-training of deep bidirectional transformers for language understanding. arxiv preprint arXiv:1810.04805 (2018)
11. Yu, F., Liu, Q., Wu, S., et al.: A convolutional approach for misinformation identification. In: IJCAI, pp. 3901–3907 (2017)
12. Khattar, D., Goud, J.S., Gupta, M., et al.: MVAE: Multimodal Variational Autoencoder for fake news detection. In: The World Wide Web Conference, pp. 2915–2921 (2019)
13. Li, J., Ni, S., Kao, H.Y.: Meet the truth: leverage objective facts and subjective views for interpretable rumor detection. arxiv preprint arXiv:2107.10747 (2021)

A Novel GAN-Based DDoS Attack Detection Method for Smart Home Networks

Ismeil Ahamed[1], Abdur Rakib[1(✉)], and Mehmet Emin Aydin[2]

[1] Centre for Future Transport and Cities (CFTC), Coventry University, Coventry, UK
{ahamedi,ad9812}@coventry.ac.uk
[2] School of Computing and Creative Technologies, University of the West of England, Bristol, UK
Mehmet.Aydin@uwe.ac.uk

Abstract. Nowadays, Smart Home Systems (SHSs) have emerged as an important technology towards employing the power of the wireless media and IoT devices. Devices in SHSs interact with numerous smart applications running simultaneously with different platforms to deliver required services. Such ubiquitous systems often serve as a potential platform for escalating malicious entities to launch cyber attacks such as Distributed Denial of Service (DDoS) attacks. The expense of DDoS attacks makes it critical to develop counter-measures that can effectively stop the attack and quickly identify the attacker(s). Thus, one of the main challenges of these network monitoring is the ability to quickly and accurately detect DDoS attacks. To address this problem, we propose a Deep Learning (DL)-based method to classify smart home network traffic into two classes, namely normal and malicious. Training the proposed model with normal and DDoS attack data to classify attack instances. In order to overcome the problem of the lack of data, as is often the case, synthetic data has been generated using a Conditional Tabular Generative Adversarial Network (CTGAN). It is then used to train a DDoS attack detection model using an API functional model in order to maximise the performance and enhance detection rates. Results of experiments demonstrate that the proposed method tends to outperform existing approaches with an accuracy rate of 99.98%.

Keywords: Smart Home Systems (SSH) · Internet of Things (IoT) · Distributed Denial of Service (DDoS) attacks · Machine Learning (ML) · Deep Learning (DL) · Conditional Tabular Generative Adversarial Network (CTGAN) · Synthetic Data Generation

1 Introduction

The proliferation of Internet of Things (IoT) technologies, particularly in the realm of smart homes lack sufficient security measures, has facilitated an increase in cyberattacks, notably including Distribution Denial of Service (DDoS) attacks. DDoS attacks have emerged as one of the most prevalent forms of cyberattacks, aimed at interrupting the standard functioning of systems, networks, or infrastructures [1]. Detecting these

© ICST Institute for Computer Sciences, Social Informatics and Telecommunications Engineering 2026
Published by Springer Nature Switzerland AG 2026. All Rights Reserved
S. Li et al. (Eds.): BROADNETS 2024, LNICST 674, pp. 100–116, 2026.
https://doi.org/10.1007/978-3-032-14350-1_7

attacks in smart home networks is a challenging process due to the following reasons: (1) the variable sizes, magnitude, and frequency of the attacks; (2) the constrained nature of IoT devices in smart home networks hindered the installation of complex network security tools such as Firewall and Anti-viruses; and (3) heterogeneity and interoperability of devices in SHS have contributed in effective and efficient detection of DDoS attacks in smart home networks [2]. The lack of substantial security is made evident by a number of high-profile DDoS attacks including Mirai malware DDoS attacks, which compromised a large number of devices to form a complex botnet to orchestrate large-scale attacks, which allowed Cyber-hackers to pull sensitive data through the device to the cloud [3].

Machine learning (ML) algorithms offer intelligence capabilities for detecting DDoS attacks on smart home networks. ML systems demonstrate the ability to learn from a specific problem, automating the detection process and developing a model to solve the task [4]. The concept of DL is a set of ML algorithms used to solve complex tasks. These systems have brought remarkable success with sophisticated and efficient data pre-processing techniques in recent years. DL models often outperform their shallow ML models; however, training DL models often requires a large amount of data. The lack of such a dataset has become one of the most critical challenges in the development of DL models [5]. In this paper, we use Conditional Tabular Generative Adversarial Network (CTGAN) architecture to generate new synthetic data, which is used to train the DL model for detecting DDoS attacks in smart home Networks [6].

IoT exhibits significant heterogeneity, which complicates the establishment of uniform communication standards across various networks. As mentioned before, one of the predominant threats to Smart Home Networks (SHNs) associated with IoT is DDoS attacks, recognized as a critical security concern [7]. These attacks typically inundate a network with fraudulent requests, making the rapid and precise detection of DDoS incidents a primary focus of network surveillance. However, the intricate and advanced nature of these attacks often renders current detection solutions ineffective [8] [9]. Therefore, this paper aims to propose a novel DDoS attack detection model using DL algorithms with a functional API. The objectives include investigating ML and DL techniques for detecting DDoS attacks in smart home networks, examining their limitations, assessing benchmark datasets with recent DDoS records, generating synthetic data, and developing an efficient detection method for comparison with similar studies.

The rest of the paper is organised as follows: Sect. 2 presents a review of the literature on DDoS attack detection approaches proposed for IoT-based smart home networks. Section 3 discusses synthetic data generation methods and uses the CTGAN network to generate new data. Section 4 describes the proposed DDoS attack detection method. Section 5 discusses the results of the performance evaluation. Finally, Sect. 6 concludes the paper with final remarks and future directions.

2   Related Work

This section discusses the application of ML and DL techniques for DDoS attacks in SHSs and critically evaluates the literature to identify the key criteria influencing the detection of DDoS attacks in smart home networks. In recent years, several ML and DL solutions have been proposed to detect DDoS attacks in SHN. These techniques aim to analyse network traffic patterns and identify abnormal behaviour that may indicate a DDoS attack [10] [11]. Mishra et al. [12] investigated the application of the Generative Adversarial Network (GAN) to detect DDoS attacks in SHS. The proposed solution uses generate synthetic data that mimic the characteristics of real DDoS attacks. However, the success of GANs in this context depends on the quality and quantity of data available for training, evaluation, and testing.

Xuanqing et al. [13] presented Two Timescale Updated Rules (TTUR), proposed to improve the stability and convergence of GAN-based approaches for detecting DDoS attacks in SHSs. TTUR involves a separate learning rate for the discriminator model, which allows for faster learning of the discriminator than the generator. The rationale behind this approach is that the discriminator needs to be able to distinguish between real and generated data accurately before the generator can learn to produce more realistic data.

The TTUR method also involves updating the generator and discriminator at different timescales, with the generator being updated less frequently than the discriminator. This can help prevent oscillations and instability during training, which can occur when the generator and discriminator are updated simultaneously. The TTUR method has shown promise in improving the stability and convergence of GAN-based approaches for detecting DDoS attacks in SHSs. However, this technique requires a large amount of data.

Yilmaz et al. [14] proposed a method that involves using a DCGAN model to sample the minority class distributions in an imbalanced dataset for improving the performance of the classification model. The imbalanced dataset in the context of DDoS attack detection refers to the situation where the positive class (DDoS attack traffic) is significantly smaller than the negative class (legitimate traffic). The minority class samples are often difficult to collect, and this can result in poor performance, particularly in terms of false-positive rates. The DCGAN model is used to generate synthetic data that mimics the characteristics of the minority class samples. The synthetic data generated by the DCGAN model is then used to augment the training data, which helps improve the performance of the classification model. Experimental results have shown that using the DCGAN model for sampling the minority class distributions can significantly reduce the false-positive rate and improve the overall performance of the classification model for DDoS attack detection. This approach has shown promising results in improving the performance of DDoS attack detection models by addressing the challenges of imbalanced data.

The work by [15, 16] have investigated the use of GANs for detecting DDoS attacks in SHSs. These studies have shown that GANs can improve DDoS attack detection by generating high-quality synthetic data, which can be used to augment the limited and imbalanced training data. However, one of the challenges with using GANs for DDoS attack detection is the requirement for a large amount of data to train, evaluate, and test the performance of the model. This can be a significant challenge, particularly in SHSs, where the amount of data available for training may be limited due to privacy concerns.

Similarly, Tanvir et al. [17] proposed two heuristic approaches to improve performance and enhance training stability: 1) conduct feature matching of the generator to minimise statistical differences between real data features and generated features, and 2) use minibatch on the discriminator to isolate samples to help prevent the mode collapse problem. During training, the generator model is trained to generate synthetic data that is as similar as possible to the real data. The discriminator model is trained to distinguish between real and synthetic data. The goal of the generator model is to fool the discriminator model by generating synthetic data that are indistinguishable from real data. In the case of DDoS attack detection in SHSs, the generator model would be trained to generate synthetic data that mimics the traffic patterns of both normal and malicious traffic. The discriminator model would then be used to classify the traffic as normal or malicious.

According to [18], GAN-based DDoS attacks often mislead the ML model detection system by generating new traffic data. Most of these studies focused on the Internet infrastructure, which is not suitable for smart home networks. A possible explanation for these results may be the lack of adequate data, which appears to be the main challenge. Some existing solutions for detecting DDoS attacks on smart home networks include network-based approaches such as traffic analysis and anomaly detection, as well as host-based approaches such as behaviour analysis and machine learning-based techniques. However, these solutions often have limitations in terms of accuracy, scalability, and applicability to different types of attacks.

The above discussed literature evaluates the application of ML and DL techniques for detecting DDoS attacks in smart home systems (SHSs) and identifies key criteria influencing the efficacy of the detection. GAN-based approaches have shown promise in generating synthetic data to enhance DDoS attack detection. This paper addresses the issue of the lack of data using a Conditional Tabular Generative Adversarial Network (CTGAN). This synthetic data is then utilized to train a DDoS attack detection method with an API functional model, aiming to maximize performance and improve detection rates.

3   Synthetic Data Generation

Nowadays, Data has become a valuable commodity and its critical for the development of cutting-edge applications, including DDoS attack detection [19]. Addressing problems such as incomplete observations, data imbalance, and small dataset sizes is cumbersome [20]. Generative models such as generative adversarial networks (GANs) and variational auto-encoders (VAEs) are DL models that can generate new samples that are similar to the training data. These models can be trained on small datasets and can be used to generate large amounts of synthetic data for various applications [21].

3.1   Constraints of Existing Datasets

In order to detect DDoS attacks effectively, it is imperative to carefully evaluate and select a suitable dataset. This selection process involves considering various criteria that are vital for the successful implementation of ML and DL-based applications. This section focuses on discussing the constraints associated with existing datasets that are commonly identified in the current literature.

Size: the dataset size should be sufficiently large to offer a comprehensive representation of DDoS attacks. A larger dataset can aid in constructing more precise and resilient models, particularly for deep learning models that demand more data due to the intricate nature and numerous parameters in deep neural networks. Resource limitations are a crucial factor to consider when working with large and potentially complex datasets. This encompasses the capability to load such data into memory as well as the computational resources required to process and analyse it efficiently, thus the size presence of resource limitations.

Authenticity: the authenticity of the dataset used for training and evaluating machine learning models that identify DDoS attacks is of utmost importance. It is imperative that this dataset accurately represents real-world scenarios to ensure the effectiveness of these models. To achieve this, the dataset must be derived from actual instances of DDoS attacks and should encompass the techniques, mechanisms, and objectives employed by genuine attackers. It is essential that the dataset includes data from real scenarios where DDoS attacks have occurred, and these attacks should have been executed by real perpetrators. By incorporating such data, a more precise understanding of the types of attacks that can be launched in the real world, as well as the patterns and nature of these attacks, can be attained. Ultimately, the utilisation of an authentic dataset that holds the potential to facilitate the development of more accurate DL models that possess enhanced capabilities to detect and mitigate DDoS attacks in SHN.

Diversity: the construction of models aimed at detecting and mitigating DDoS attacks requires meticulous consideration of comprehensive and diverse datasets during the training and evaluation phases. This diversity encompasses a wide range of elements, including the incorporation of different types of attack, diverse attack vectors, and varying levels of attack intensity. By integrating various forms of DDoS attacks into the training data, the resultant models acquire the capacity to recognise and respond to a broader spectrum of attack types. This enhancement significantly improves their accuracy and generalisability, thus bolstering their resilience against different types of attacks. Furthermore, it is crucial to ensure that the data set includes contemporary and sophisticated forms of attacks in SHN systems.

3.2   GAN Networks Architecture

The concept of the GAN network is based on a game theory, a scenario in which both networks, The Generator G and Discriminator D models, compete against each other to improve the training outcome [22]. Each network can be trained with any neural network algorithm, such as an artificial neural network (ANN), a convolution neural network (CNN), a recurrent neural network (RNN), and long- and short-term memory (LSTM).

Generator network (G): The generator network uses random noise data to generate fake data. For example, it uses a random noise vector to create unique data points. G is constantly learning to trick D to improve results and generate more realistic data on each epoch or iteration.

Discriminator Network (D): In contrast, the main aim of the Discriminator D model is to use probability functions to classify whether G observations are real or fake data.

The accuracy of the D network improves on each iteration for generated or actual predictions. In addition, the Discriminator network tries to differentiate between the actual data and the data generated by the G network.

Although GANs have shown tremendous success in various applications including synthetic data generation. However, training GANs is notoriously challenging [23]. One common problem in GAN training is mode collapse, where the generator produces a limited variety of outputs, ignoring some modes in the data distribution [24].

3.3   Conditional Generative Adversarial Network (CGAN)

CGAN is a variant of the original GAN architecture that uses condition vectors to guide the generation process. The generator of the CGAN model takes in both a random latent vector z and a condition vector c as inputs and produces G(c, z) to generate fake data points [25]. The discriminator in the CGAN model, on the other hand, takes in both real data points (x, c) and fake data points G(z, c) and tries to distinguish between them. By doing so, it provides feedback to the generator on how to improve its generated outputs. To address these challenges introduced a new techniques Conditional Tabular Generative Adversarial Network (CTGAN) has been proposed. Figure 1 depicts the architecture of the integrated functional API model, whereas Fig. 4 depicts the architecture of the functional API model.

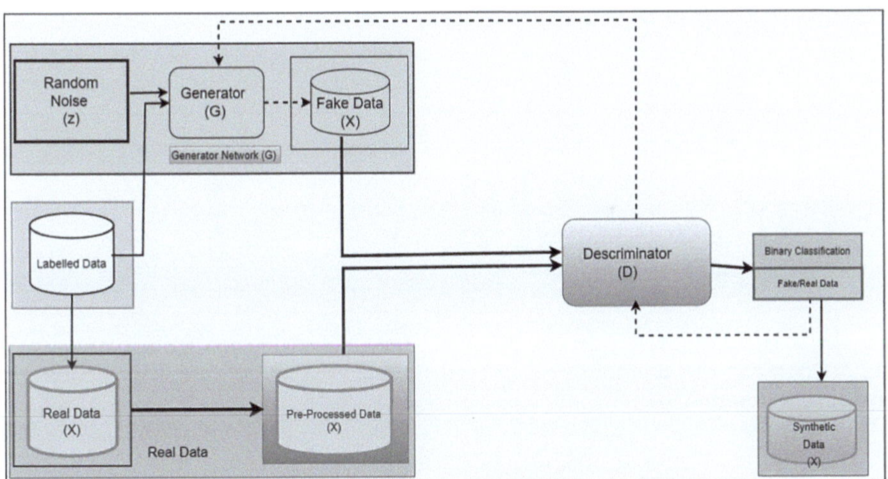

Fig. 1. Architecture of integrated functional API model

3.4   Synthetic Data Validation

The CTGAN model made substantial progress to stabilise the training of the model performance, subsequently improving the quality of the synthetic data. The Generative data produce synthetic data that contain a statistical representative of actual data.

Evaluation methods of the CTGAN model have often been categorised into two main classes, namely Statistical measures and Machine Learning techniques [26]. The Statistical measures such as Correlations Coefficient (SCC), probability mass functions, Cumulative distribution and probability density functions are used to validate the quality of the synthetic data [27]. Moreover, the visualisation tools such as the Area Under the Curve (AU-curve), and Receiver Operating Characteristic (ROC) are useful to evaluate the performance of the CTGAN model [28]. In addition, visualisation analysis can also be produced by plotting the distribution and correlation functions of both real and synthetic data. Figures 2 and 3 depict the distribution results of real and synthetic data.

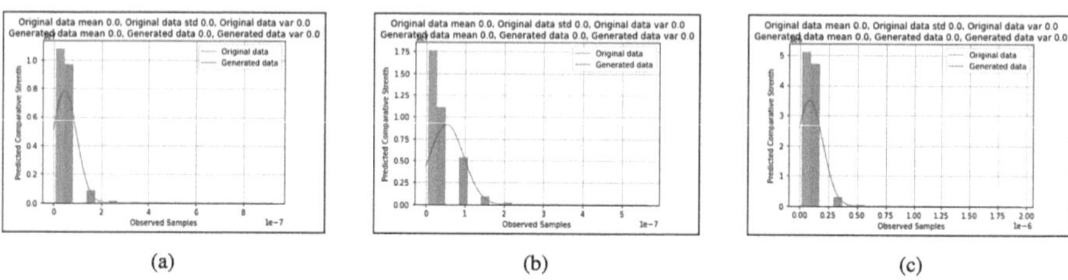

Fig. 2. Comparison of the distribution of futures such as packet sizes, Total packet size and Packet Length (a, b, c) of real-world and synthetic data

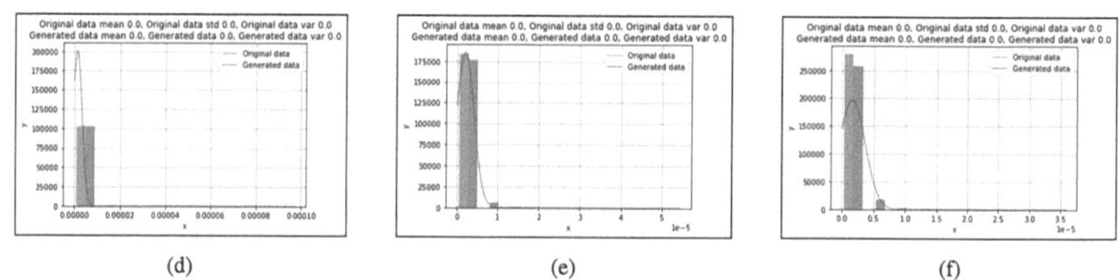

Fig. 3. Dimension-wise results between real and synthetic data (d), standard deviations (e), and prediction performance (f).

4   Proposed System Architecture

This section outlines the suggested DL framework, which utilizes synthetic data for the purpose of identifying DDoS attacks within smart home networks. The architecture is designed to effectively detect and mitigate DDoS attacks by leveraging advanced machine learning techniques, ensuring the security and reliability of smart home devices.

4.1 Train Neural Network Model

The primary purpose of training a neural network is to reduce the weight vector to reach the optimal point. Optimisation algorithms are a set of instructions that allow DL to reduce the error, during training using many parameters such as weight vector and a number of hidden layers are used to improve the performance of the actual and predicted output by calculating the loss. Gradient descent optimisation is the main mechanism used to map the input value to the corresponding target output. Activation functions are mathematical models that enable the model to map input data to predict the output [29].

4.2 Dataset Description and Experiments

This section presents a description of the benchmark dataset that is used to generate synthetic data. Obtaining a high-quality IoT-based botnet dataset is extremely difficult, due to the aforementioned reasons. This paper uses the IoT-Botnet a new IoT security network traffic dataset captured in 2020 by the Cyber-Range lab at UNSW Canberra [30]. The lab environment incorporates a combination of malware-infected and IoT-benign traffic to develop ML models to detect DDoS attacks. The dataset contains various malicious activities, such as HTTP-DDoS, TCP-DDoS, UDP-DDoS attacks, Data exfiltration, OS Fingerprinting, and Keylogging attacks. It contains 83 network features and three label features categories, subcategories, and binary.

4.3 Activation Functions

Activation functions are mathematical functions that are applied to the target of a neuron or a set of neurons in a neural network. The main purpose of these functions is to introduce non-linearity into the output of a neuron, which allows the network to learn complex patterns and relationships in the input data. The following points discuss the main activation functions used in this paper.

- **Sigmoid:** The sigmoid is a non-linear activation function, it is one of the most common types of activation used to construct binary classes in neural networks. Both sigmoid and tanh functions squash values into the ranges [0,1] and [-1, 1], respectively [31].

$$Sigmoid = \sigma(z) = \frac{1}{1 + e^{-z}} \qquad (1)$$

- **SoftMax:** SoftMax activation or normalised experimental is a function that takes a vector of input values and normalises it into a probability distribution by calculating proportionally of input vectors. The SoftMax function is often used in multi-class classification algorithms to assign decimal probabilities to each class [32].

$$SoftMax : \sigma(z_i) = \frac{e^{z_i}}{\sum_{j=1}^{K} e^{z_j}} \quad for\ i = 1, 2, \ldots, K \qquad (2)$$

- **ReLU:** ReLU is one of the widely used activation functions [33]. The ReLU function uses a derivative of one for any positive input value, thus improving the vanishing gradient problem.

$$Relu(z) = max(0, z) \qquad (3)$$

– **Leaky ReLU:** Leaky ReLU is a variant of the ReLU function used to solve the problem of dying gradient by assigning a non-zero slope to the negative value [34]. The mathematical equation of leaky ReLU is defined as follows:

$$LeakyReLU : f(x) = \begin{cases} 0.01x, & \text{if } x < 0 \\ x, & \text{otherwise} \end{cases} \tag{4}$$

4.4 Data Pre-processing

Data pre-processing is a crucial stage in training the DL model. It helps improve the quality of data and promotes meaningful insights [35]. The Gini index and chi-square are the most common data pre-processing techniques. The Gini index is one of the widely used techniques in the data pre-processing field, this technique uses information theory and entropy of random variables for feature selection. The Gini index or Gini is a technique used to calculate the amount of probability for each feature, which is determined by the deduction of the squared sum of probabilities of each class. Chi-square is a non-parametric method used to compare more than two variables for a random feature selection. Chi-square is the most common correlation measure suitable for categorical output [36].

4.5 Test System Specifications

This section presents detailed information on the experimental system setup. The hardware and software properties listed are actually two different systems - one is a Windows 10 system with an Intel Core i7-6700HQ CPU and 8 GB RAM, while the other is a Google Collab instance with a Tesla K80 GPU. It is important to note that while the Windows 10 system can be used for running software and conducting experiments, the Google Collab instance with the Tesla K80 GPU is better suited for training tasks. Further to the experimental system specifications, different software tools and techniques have been utilised to create DL models. To train the model, the proposed DDoS attacks method was developed using various technologies. Specifically, NumPy version 1.1.9.5, Pandas version 1.1.1, Sklearn version $0.22.2.post1$, Seaborn version 0.1.1.1, Keras version 2.4.3, and TensorFlow version 2.4.1 were utilized. The development platform was Linux-4.19.112+ running on an Intel(R) Xeon(R) CPU at 2.20 GHz.

4.6 Performance Evaluation Metrics

Performance evaluation metrics are instrumental in measuring the efficiency and effectiveness of a system or process. The selection of appropriate performance evaluation metrics depends on the specific system or process being assessed. In the context of this model, its performance has been meticulously evaluated using a diverse set of metrics, including Accuracy, Precision, Recall, ROC, confusion matrix and execution time [2].

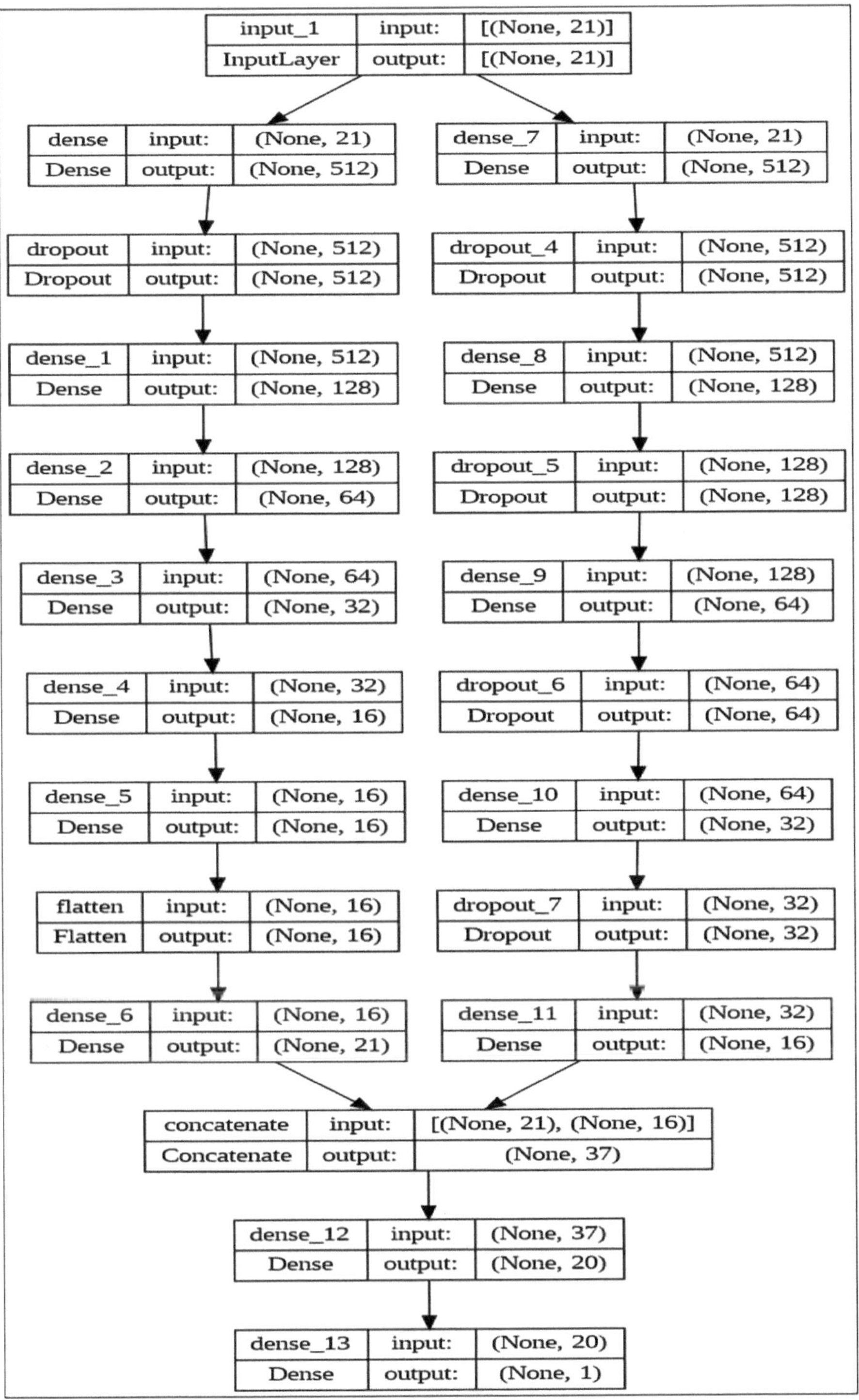

Fig. 4. Architecture of functional API model

4.7   Proposed Model Configuration

This section describes the components of a functional API model, consisting of two MLP models, each with a unique input node representing 21 input features. The first MLP model has 4 hidden layers with 128, 64, and 32 neurons, and a ReLU activation function. The output layer has 11 classes, and the softmax activation function is used for multi-class classification. The model also includes three dropout layers with a dropout ratio of 0.2 and flattened layers. The second MLP model has 7 hidden layers with 128, 64, and 32 neurons, also with a ReLU activation function. The output layer has a softmax activation function and is used for multi-class classification. Like the first model, it includes three dropout layers with a ratio of 0.2 and a flattened layer. The two MLP models are integrated using the Model node, which accepts 21 input features and produces a binary output. Table 3 shows the configuration setup of the API model. It's worth noting that the configuration of a machine-learning model depends on the specific problem being addressed and the data used to train the model. While the proposed model configuration might work well for a particular use case, it's always essential to evaluate the model's performance and adjust the configuration as needed. Table 1 shows the configuration metrics of the API model. Figure 4 depicts the architecture of the functional API model.

Table 1. Proposed model configuration information

No	Hyperparameter	Value
1	Number Of Batches	128
2	Number Of Training Steps (Epochs)	20
3	Input activation function	ReLU
4	Input Dim	21
5	Output Optimiser	Sigmoid
6	Number of hidden layers	11
7	Dropout ratio	0.05
8	Targets	1
9	Loss function	binary cross-entropy loss
10	Target Encoder	Label Encoder
11	Feature Encoded	Dummies Encoder

5   Results and Discussion

We conducted experiments to evaluate the performance of our proposed DDoS detection method. We used a data set of network traffic that included both normal and DDoS attack traffic. Our proposed method was able to accurately detect DDoS attacks with

Table 2. Execution time of the proposed model

Training	Testing	Ex time	Epoch	Batch Size	Metrics	Results
884630	221158	24 s	20	128	Accuracy	99.83%
884630	221158	19 s	20	128	Precision	99.83%
884630	221158	19 s	20	128	Recall	99.81%
884630	221158	23 s	20	128	F1_score	99.94%

Table 3. Comparison of the results of the proposed approach with similar other approaches in Smart Homes domain

Ref	Year	Dataset	Task	Exec Time	Results
[37]	2021	IoT-Bot	Multi-Class	191 sec	97.96 %
[38]	2022	IoT-Bot	Multi-Class	121 sec	99.14%
[39]	2022	CIC-DDoS2019	Multi-Class	43 sec	98.97%
[40]	2022	CIC-DDoS2019	Multi-Class	36 sec	98.97%
Proposed Method	2023	Synthetic Data	Binary-Class	19 sec	99.94%

a high degree of accuracy. Specifically, our method achieved an accuracy rate of 98% and a false positive rate of less than 1%. In addition, we compared the performance of our method with several existing DDoS detection methods. Our method outperformed all these existing methods in terms of accuracy and false-positive rate. Experimental results demonstrate that our proposed DDoS detection method is highly effective in detecting DDoS attacks. The high accuracy rate and low false positive rate indicate that our method can reliably detect DDoS attacks without generating a large number of false alarms. Furthermore, the comparison with existing methods shows that our method is superior in terms of performance. This suggests that our method has the potential to be a valuable tool for detecting and mitigating DDoS attacks on real-world networks. Table 2 shows the results of the proposed model.

It is important to note that our experiments were conducted using a synthetic dataset of smart home network traffic. It is possible that our method may not perform as well on different types of traffic or in different network environments. In addition, our method may require further testing and optimisation before it can be implemented in real-world networks. In general, our results and discussion highlight the effectiveness of our proposed DDoS detection method and its potential to improve the security of computer networks. Table 3 shows the performance of the two most prominent types of DDoS attacks in the smart home domain. Figure 5 depicts the evaluation results (Loss, Accuracy, Confusion matrix, and ROC) of the proposed model.

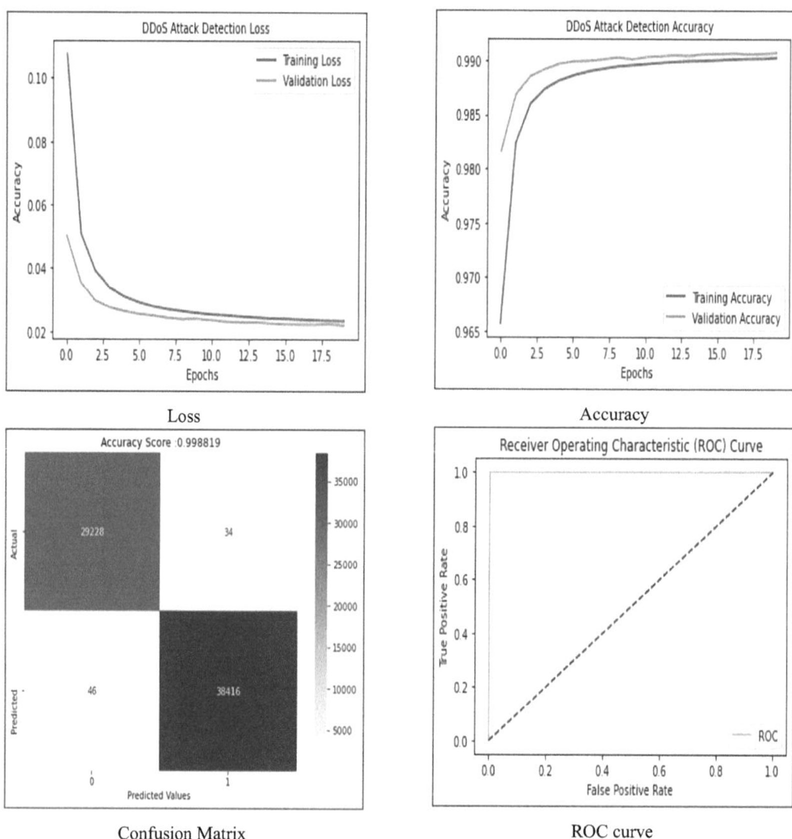

Fig. 5. Evaluation results of the proposed model

5.1   Limitations of Synthetic Data

Synthetic data can inherit and propagate biases present in the original dataset or the algorithms used for its generation. A biased data generator might not only amplify existing biases but also introduce new ones, potentially compromising the fairness of models developed from such data [41]. Moreover, synthetic data may fail to capture the full complexity and variability of real-world data. When generated data does not accurately represent the true distributions of the original dataset, models trained on it may underperform in real-world scenarios. Models trained on synthetic datasets may become overly fitted to the specific characteristics of that data, leading to poor performance when these models are applied to real-world data.

Producing high-quality synthetic data can also be computationally intensive, particularly for complex or high-dimensional datasets [42]. In large-scale environments like smart homes, actual user behavior often exhibits intricate patterns, such as correlated failures or cascading effects, which may not be well-represented in synthetic data. Advanced techniques like Generative Adversarial Networks (GANs) require substantial resources to generate reliable outputs. As datasets grow in size, scaling up synthetic data generation poses additional challenges in terms of storage and processing capacity [43].

6 Conclusions and Future Work

The DDoS attack is one of the most prominent threats to smart home networks. The main aim of these attacks are to shut down normal operations and render the system or network unavailable to legitimate users. Therefore, successful detection of these attacks in an early stage is paramount to maintaining the availability and stability of service in smart home networks.

Our investigation highlights significant advancements in identifying DDoS attacks within smart home networks using DL models. These models demonstrate high precision in distinguishing between legitimate and malicious traffic, outperforming traditional detection methods. This suggests that incorporating DL into smart home security can provide real-time protection, reduce false alarms, and adapt to evolving cyber threats, ensuring reliable performance of smart home devices. The novelty of our study lies in the application of advanced DL techniques tailored to the specific characteristics of smart home networks (SHN). Unlike previous methods that relied on rule-based systems or traditional machine learning, our research utilizes neural networks to effectively identify complex attack patterns. This marks a significant advancement in IoT Cyber Security.

The efficacy of DL models is evident in accuracy, significantly reducing false positives and improving detection rates. These models are adaptable, continuously training with new data to stay updated on the latest attack patterns and strategies. Moreover, our DL-based DDoS detection method is designed to integrate seamlessly with various IoT devices, ensuring comprehensive security coverage across the entire network. The significance of our study on DDoS attack detection in SHN using DL is multifaceted. By leveraging DL-based techniques, our approach significantly enhances the security of SHN against increasingly sophisticated and frequent DDoS attacks. The accuracy of our model reduces false positives, ensuring the continuity of legitimate traffic. Additionally, using a functional API model trained with synthesized data, our approach is scalable and adaptable, regularly updating with new data to respond effectively to evolving DDoS attacks, thereby ensuring the long-term viability of smart home security.

There are a number of interesting directions in this area for future research. First, the proposed method can be improved to evaluate the effectiveness of existing DDoS attack detection systems. This could involve testing different algorithms on real-world datasets, comparing the performance of different systems, or exploring the impact of different types of attacks. Second, to explore the use of alternative data sources for DDoS attack detection, analysing patterns of smart home network behaviour. Finally, the proposed approach can be extended to other IoT areas, such as smart cities, transportation systems, and industrial IoT, to help protect these critical systems from cyber attacks.

References

1. Vishwakarma, R., Jain, A.K.: A survey of DDOS attacking techniques and defence mechanisms in the IoT network. Telecommun. Syst. **73**(1), 3–25 (2020)
2. Anthi, E., Williams, L., Słowińska, M., Theodorakopoulos, G., Burnap, P.: A supervised intrusion detection system for smart home IoT devices. IEEE Internet Things J. **6**(5), 9042–9053 (2019). https://doi.org/10.1109/JIOT.2019.2926365
3. Paudel, R., Muncy, T., Eberle, W.: Detecting dos attack in smart home IoT devices using a graph-based approach. In: 2019 IEEE International Conference on Big Data (Big Data), pp. 5249–5258. IEEE (2019)
4. Xin, Y., et al.: Machine learning and deep learning methods for cybersecurity. IEEE Access **6**, 35365–35381 (2018). https://doi.org/10.1109/ACCESS.2018.2836950
5. Perez, L., Wang, J.: The effectiveness of data augmentation in image classification using deep learning. CoRR abs/1712.04621. arXiv:1712.04621
6. Kumar, V., Sinha, D.: Synthetic attack data generation model applying generative adversarial network for intrusion detection. Comput. Secur. **125**, 103054 (2023). https://doi.org/10.1016/j.cose.2022.103054, https://www.sciencedirect.com/science/article/pii/S0167404822004461
7. Al Mtawa, Y., Singh, H., Haque, A., Refaey, A.: In: Smart Home Networks: Security Perspective and Ml-based DDOS Detection, pp. 1–8. (2020). https://doi.org/10.1109/CCECE47787.2020.9255756
8. Djenna, A., Harous, S., Saidouni, D.E.: Internet of things meet internet of threats: new concern cyber security issues of critical cyber infrastructure. Appl. Sci. **11**(10). https://doi.org/10.3390/app11104580, https://www.mdpi.com/2076-3417/11/10/4580
9. Marvi, M., Arfeen, A., Uddin, R.: A generalized machine learning-based model for the detection of DDOS attacks. Int. J. Netw. Manage **31**(6), e2152 (2021)
10. Schiller, E., Aidoo, A., Fuhrer, J., Stahl, J., Ziörjen, M., Stiller, B.: Landscape of IoT security. Comput. Sci. Rev. **44**, 100467 (2022). https://doi.org/10.1016/j.cosrev.2022.100467
11. Mustapha, A., et al.: Detecting DDOS attacks using adversarial neural network. Comput. Secur. **127**, 103117 (2023)
12. Mishra, N., Pandya, S.: Internet of things applications, security challenges, attacks, intrusion detection, and future visions: a systematic review. IEEE Access **9**, 59353–59377 (2021). https://doi.org/10.1109/ACCESS.2021.3073408
13. Shieh, C.-S., et al.: Detection of adversarial DDOS attacks using generative adversarial networks with dual discriminators. Symmetry **14**(1)
14. Yilmaz, I., Masum, R., Siraj, A.: Addressing imbalanced data problem with generative adversarial network for intrusion detection. In: 2020 IEEE 21st International Conference on Information Reuse and Integration for Data Science (IRI), pp. 25–30 (2020). https://doi.org/10.1109/IRI49571.2020.00012
15. Anthi, E., Williams, L., Javed, A., Burnap, P.: Hardening machine learning Denial of Service (dos) defences against adversarial attacks in IoT smart home networks. Comput. Secur. **108** 102352 (2021). https://doi.org/10.1016/j.cose.2021.102352. https://www.sciencedirect.com/science/article/pii/S0167404821001760
16. Gümüşbaş, D., Yıldırım, T., Genovese, A., Scotti, F.: A comprehensive survey of databases and deep learning methods for cybersecurity and intrusion detection systems. IEEE Syst. J. **15**(2), 1717–1731 (2021). https://doi.org/10.1109/JSYST.2020.2992966
17. Ahamed, T., Zou, B., Farazi, N.P., Tulabandhula, T.: Deep reinforcement learning for crowdsourced urban delivery: system states characterization, heuristics-guided action choice, and rule-interposing integration. arXiv:2011.14430
18. Shahriar, M.H., Haque, N.I., Rahman, M.A., Alonso, M.: G-IDS: generative adversarial networks assisted intrusion detection system. In: 2020 IEEE 44th Annual Computers, Software, and Applications Conference (COMPSAC), pp. 376–385. IEEE (2020)

19. Bzai, J., et al.: Machine learning-enabled internet of things (IoT): data, applications, and industry perspective. Electronics **11**(17), 2676 (2022)
20. Figueira, A., Vaz, B.: Survey on synthetic data generation, evaluation methods and GANs. Mathematics **10**(15), 2733 (2022)
21. Wang, X., Wang, K., Lian, S.: A survey on face data augmentation for the training of deep neural networks. Neural Comput. Appl. **32**(19), 15503–15531 (2020). https://doi.org/10.1007/s00521-020-04748-3
22. Zhong, Z., Li, J., Clausi, D.A., Wong, A.: Generative adversarial networks and conditional random fields for hyperspectral image classification. IEEE Trans. Cybern. **50**(7), 3318–3329 (2019)
23. Karnewar, A., Wang, O.: MSG-GAN: multi-scale gradients for generative adversarial networks. In: Proceedings of the IEEE/CVF Conference on Computer Vision and Pattern Recognition, pp. 7799–7808 (2020)
24. Lata, K., Dave, M., Nishanth, K.: Image-to-image translation using generative adversarial network. In: 2019 3rd International Conference on Electronics, Communication and Aerospace Technology (ICECA), pp. 186–189. IEEE (2019)
25. Chai, P., Hou, L., Zhang, G., Tushar, Q., Zou, Y.: Generative adversarial networks in construction applications. Autom. Construct. **159** 105265 (2024). https://doi.org/10.1016/j.autcon.2024.105265, https://www.sciencedirect.com/science/article/pii/S0926580524000013
26. Genovese, A., Piuri, V., Scotti, F.: Towards explainable face aging with generative adversarial networks. In: 2019 IEEE International Conference on Image Processing (ICIP), pp. 3806–3810. IEEE (2019)
27. Sundell, K.E., Saylor, J.E.: Unmixing detrital geochronology age distributions. Geochem. Geophys. Geosyst. **18**(8), 2872–2886 (2017)
28. Shao, C., Yang, Y., Juneja, S., GSeetharam, T.: IoT data visualization for business intelligence in corporate finance. Inf. Process. Manage. **59**(1) 102736 (2022)
29. Ren, L., Dong, J., Wang, X., Meng, Z., Zhao, L., Deen, M.J.: A data-driven auto-CNN-LSTM prediction model for lithium-ion battery remaining useful life. IEEE Trans. Industr. Inf. **17**(5), 3478–3487 (2020)
30. Sriram, S., Vinayakumar, R., Alazab, M., Soman, K.: Network flow based IoT botnet attack detection using deep learning. In: IEEE INFOCOM 2020-IEEE Conference on Computer Communications Workshops (INFOCOM WKSHPS), pp. 189–194. IEEE (2020)
31. Apicella, A., Donnarumma, F., Isgrò, F., Prevete, R.: A survey on modern trainable activation functions. Neural Netw. **138**, 14–32 (2021)
32. Gong, W., et al.: A novel deep learning method for intelligent fault diagnosis of rotating machinery based on improved CNN-SVM and multichannel data fusion. Sensors **19**(7), 1693 (2019)
33. Yu, Y., Adu, K., Tashi, N., Anokye, P., Wang, X., Ayidzoe, M.A.: RMAF: RELU-memristor-like activation function for deep learning. IEEE Access **8**, 72727–72741 (2020)
34. Xu, J., Li, Z., Du, B., Zhang, M., Liu, J.: RELUplex made more practical: leaky RELU. In: 2020 IEEE Symposium on Computers and Communications (ISCC), pp. 1–7. IEEE (2020)
35. ul Haq, A., et al.: A survey of deep learning techniques based Parkinson's disease recognition methods employing clinical data. Expert Syst. Appl. **208** 118045 (2022)
36. Albezzawy, M.N., Nassef, M.G., Sawalhi, N.: Rolling element bearing fault identification using a novel three-step adaptive and automated filtration scheme based on GINI index. ISA Trans. **101**, 453–460 (2020)
37. Alatwi, H.A., Morisset, C.: Adversarial machine learning in network intrusion detection domain: a systematic review. arXiv:2112.03315
38. Samy, A., Yu, H., Zhang, H.: Fog-based attack detection framework for internet of things using deep learning. IEEE Access **8**, 74571–74585 (2020)

39. Ismaeel, H., Elmedany, W.: Anomaly-based detection technique using deep learning for internet of things: a survey. In: 2022 International Conference on Innovation and Intelligence for Informatics, Computing, and Technologies (3ICT), pp. 278–284. IEEE (2022)
40. Lysenko, S., Bobrovnikova, K., Kharchenko, V., Savenko, O.: IoT multi-vector cyberattack detection based on machine learning algorithms: traffic features analysis, experiments, and efficiency. Algorithms **15**(7), 239 (2022)
41. Beery, S., et al.: Synthetic examples improve generalization for rare classes. In. IEEE Winter Conference on Applications of Computer Vision (WACV), vol. 2020, pp. 852–862 (2020)
42. Pezoulas, V.C., et al.: Synthetic data generation methods in healthcare: a review on open-source tools and methods. Comput. Struct. Biotechnol. J. **23**, 2892–2910 (2024)
43. Safonova, A., Ghazaryan, G., Stiller, S., Main-Knorn, M., Nendel, C., Ryo, M.: Ten deep learning techniques to address small data problems with remote sensing. Int. J. Appl. Earth Observ. Geoinf. **125** 103569 (2023). https://doi.org/10.1016/j.jag.2023.103569, https://www.sciencedirect.com/science/article/pii/S156984322300393X

Optimization of Image Binarization Threshold Based on Gaussian Weighted Averaging and Machine Learning

Tao Li[1], Shuyu Fan[2], Kui Lu[1], and Baopeng Ye[3]($\boxtimes$)

[1] School of Computer Science, Qufu Normal University, Rizhao 276827, China
[2] College of Artificial Intelligence, China University of Petroleum, Beijing 102249, China
[3] Guizhou Science and Technology Innovation Center Co., Ltd., Guiyang 550002, Guizhou, China
yebaopeng@yeah.net

Abstract. The process of image binarization is widely utilized in image processing, however, in embedded systems, yet traditional algorithms exhibit output instability. To address this issue, a method for optimizing the image binarization threshold based on Gaussian weighted averaging and machine learning is proposed in this paper. In contrast to traditional algorithms, the classic Otsu method is employed to determine the binarization threshold, and Gaussian weighted averaging and machine learning techniques are introduced to smooth, denoise, and limit the threshold, thereby enhancing the stability of the binarization algorithm in embedded systems. To validate the effectiveness of the algorithm, threshold data collection was conducted on an embedded system using the TC264 chip, and a detailed comparative analysis of the results from various binarization algorithms was performed. The experimental results demonstrate a significant improvement in both stability and accuracy of the algorithm.

Keywords: Otsu Method · machine learning · Gaussian weighted average

1 Introduction

Image binarization (threshold selection) refers to the conversion of a gray-scale image into a binary image. It is the initial step of most document image analysis and understanding systems [1]. Image binarization simplifies the pixel values of an image into two levels (usually 0 and 255, representing black and white), significantly reducing the data volume of the image and enabling more efficient subsequent image processing tasks. Additionally, binarization can emphasize key information in the image, such as contours, textures, etc., making the features of the target area more prominent. This process also helps to remove noise and redundant information from the image, thus improving image quality. In document processing, pattern recognition, feature extraction, and various other fields, image binarization plays a crucial role and is an indispensable step in the image processing workflow.

S. Li et al. (Eds.): BROADNETS 2024, LNICST 674, pp. 117–125, 2026.
https://doi.org/10.1007/978-3-032-14350-1_8

In the field of binarization, previous work has laid a solid foundation for the development of image processing techniques. Approaches that deal with image binarization are either global or local. In a global approach, threshold selection leads to a single threshold value for the entire image. Global thresholding [2–5] has a good performance in the case that there is a good separation between the foreground and the background. However, images are exposed to degradations that weaken any guaranty for such a separation. Unlike globalapproaches, local area information may guide the threshold value for each pixel in local (adaptive) thresholding techniques [6–15]. The global and local threshold algorithms for image binarization designed by predecessors have been widely applied in the field of image processing.

However, in embedded systems, threshold calculation is required for each frame of grayscale images, and both global and local thresholding methods often lack fine optimization of the output threshold when processing images. To address this issue, a method is proposed in this paper that combines the advantages of Gaussian weighted averaging and machine learning, providing a new approach for optimizing threshold selection in the field of binarization.

The method effectively reduces the impact of noise and outliers on threshold selection through the use of Gaussian weighted averaging techniques. Furthermore, the utilization of machine learning models for prediction sets reasonable upper and lower limits for threshold variation, ensuring the stability and reliability of the thresholds. This approach not only addresses the issue of insufficient optimization in traditional binarization methods, but also enhances the clarity and stability of binarized images.

In this paper, a new method for optimizing the output of image binarization is proposed, which combines Gaussian weighted averaging and machine learning to optimize the continuous threshold output of the threshold algorithm. The remainder of this paper is organized as follows: Sect. 2 provides a detailed explanation of the application process of Gaussian weighted averaging and machine learning. Section 3 showcases and discusses the experimental results. Finally, Sect. 4 presents the conclusions and limitations.

2   Method

This section focuses on the algorithm process that combines Gaussian weighted averaging with machine learning, as proposed in this paper.

2.1   Framework of the Optimization Method Based on Gaussian Weighted Averaging and Machine Learning

Upon the grayscale image, the classic Otsu method is used to calculate the binarization threshold. In embedded systems, the continuous thresholds output by the Otsu method are subjected to Gaussian weighted averaging, and predictive machine learning is employed to determine the range of threshold variations. The combination of Gaussian weighted averaging and machine learning results in stabilized threshold data, enhancing the clarity and stability of the binarized images. Figure 1 illustrates the framework diagram of the optimization method based on Gaussian weighted averaging and machine learning.

Upon the grayscale image, the classic Otsu method is used to calculate the binarization threshold. In embedded systems, the continuous thresholds output by the Otsu method are subjected to Gaussian weighted averaging, and predictive machine learning is employed to determine the range of threshold variations. The combination of Gaussian weighted averaging and machine learning results in stabilized threshold data, enhancing the clarity and stability of the binarized images. Figure 1 illustrates the framework diagram of the optimization method based on Gaussian weighted averaging and machine learning.

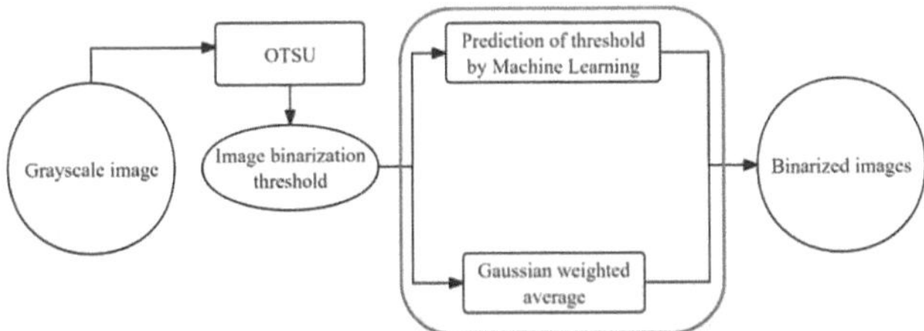

Fig. 1. Flowchart of ECG signal preprocessing

1) *Grayscale image:* Grayscale image is an image in which each pixel is represented by a single value ranging from 0 to 255, indicating the intensity of brightness or darkness.

2) *OTSU:* The OTSU method is an adaptive threshold selection technique used for image segmentation, which determines the optimal threshold by maximizing inter-class variance to separate the image into foreground and background.

3) *Image Binarization Threshold:* The threshold is determined by the OTSU algorithm. After applying the thresholding algorithm to determine the threshold, each data element in the two-dimensional array representing the grayscale image is compared. If a data element's value is greater than the threshold, it is assigned a value of 255; otherwise, it is assigned a value of 0.

4) *Prediction in Machine Learning:* The threshold for binarizing images was calculated using Otsu's method, but further calibration of the threshold size is required. Therefore, this study has enhanced the algorithm design based on a machine learning model. The model learns patterns from the collected thresholds and predicts the range of threshold variations.

5) *Gaussian Weighted Averaging:* The Gaussian weighted averaging algorithm is a method used for smoothing data, and it finds wide application in fields such as signal processing, image processing, and statistics. This algorithm utilizes the Gaussian function (normal distribution) to perform weighted averaging on the data, thereby reducing noise and highlighting the overall trend of the data.

6) *Binarized Image:* A binarized image is a simplified representation where the grayscale value of each pixel is converted to either 0 (black) or 1 (white), resulting in an image with only two colors.

2.2 Gauss-Weighted Average and Machine Learning Applications

Gaussian weighted average is a method that assigns weights to data points based on their distance from a central point, with closer points receiving higher weights. This technique is commonly used in signal processing, image processing, and data analysis to smooth out noise and emphasize important features.

The Gaussian weighted average algorithm first defines a Gaussian function, which takes the form:

$$f(x) = \frac{1}{\sqrt{2\pi}} e^{-\frac{(x-\mu)^2}{2\sigma^2}} \tag{1}$$

where μ represents the mean of the Gaussian function, which controls the center point of the function. And σ represents the standard deviation, which controls the width of the function.

In this paper, Gaussian weighted averaging is employed to process the threshold data continuously output by the threshold algorithm through weighted averaging, aiming to enhance the stability of threshold output and improve the performance of image binarization in embedded systems. To better highlight the advantages of Gaussian weighted averaging, during the experiment, this algorithm is compared with non-weighted processing, median processing, and mean processing, respectively, to underscore its superiority in Sect. 3.

Additonally, Machine learning is a field of computer science that gives computers the ability to learn without being explicitly programmed [16]. Linear regression is a linear approach to modeling the relationship between a dependent variable and one or more independent variables [17].

Furthermore, in this paper, linear regression prediction from machine learning is utilized to predict the variation range of continuously output threshold data, aiming to mitigate the occurrence of threshold anomalies.

3 Experiment Results and Discussion

This section primarily delineates the experiments conducted using Gaussian weighted averaging and machine learning prediction, followed by a thorough analysis of the experimental outcomes.

3.1 Gaussian Weighted Average

After conducting an experimental comparison of unweighted processing, mean processing, median processing, and Gaussian-weighted averaging, it was discovered that Gaussian-weighted averaging offers adjustable and optimal performance. Unweighted processing typically refers to the direct manipulation of raw data without any form of weight allocation. This method, though straightforward, is limited in its effectiveness when dealing with noisy data. Mean processing involves averaging consecutive threshold data values, which stabilizes the thresholds but yields suboptimal output results. Median processing, on the other hand, sorts consecutive threshold data and selects the median value as the processed output, yet it is susceptible to the impact of continuous noise.

In experiments, we utilized an identical dataset and evaluation criteria to compare the four processing methods. The results indicate that Gaussian-weighted averaging effectively removes noise while preserving image details, maintaining stable threshold performance across different noise levels. In contrast, unweighted and mean processing exhibit inferior performance in handling noisy data, while median processing, though outstanding in certain scenarios, may falter when dealing with continuous noise.

Figure 2 illustrates the experimental results. It clearly demonstrates the comparative effects of the different processing methods on image quality. Through comparison, we can observe that Gaussian-weighted averaging removes noise while retaining image details and edge information, resulting in clearer and more natural processed images. Additionally, the adjustable standard deviation of the Gaussian function allows for catering to the needs of diverse application scenarios.

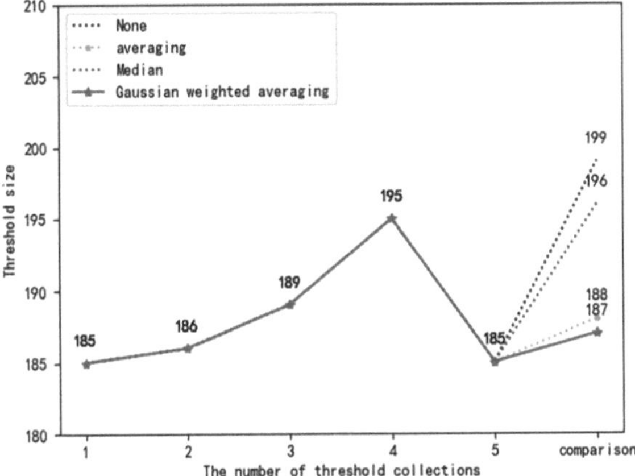

Fig. 2. The predictive graph of the linear regression model

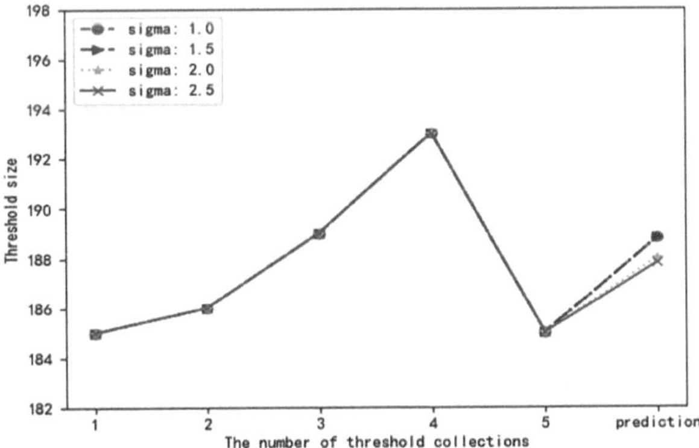

Fig. 3. Output of Gaussian weighted averages

In this paper, the Gaussian kernel function is initially selected to generate weights, and subsequently, weighted averaging is performed on continuous threshold data to ensure its stability. To enhance the data fitting effect, experiments were conducted using the same dataset with Gaussian functions of varying standard deviations, and a comparative analysis of their variance effects was performed. Figure 3 demonstrates the effectiveness of Gaussian weighted averaging in resolving threshold fluctuations (Fig. 4).

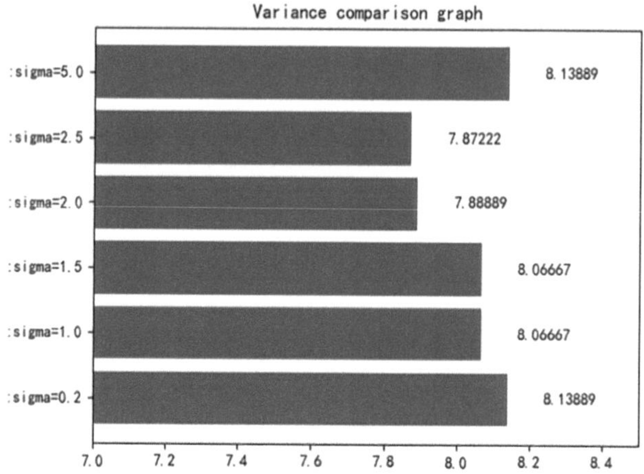

Fig. 4. Variance comparison graph

3.2 Prediction in Machine Learning

The Python-based linear regression method is suitable for datasets with linear relationships and is considered reliable. During the data processing stage, preprocessing operations are conducted for batches of binarization thresholds, followed by data visualization to observe the linear relationships in the threshold outputs. Subsequently, a linear regression model is created and trained to accurately fit the linear relationships within the threshold data. Upon completing the model training, predictions for the binarization thresholds can be made. Figure 5 illustrates the visualization of threshold data, showcasing the collection of thresholds in three different environments. Figure 6 depicts the linear fitting relationship of the threshold output data.

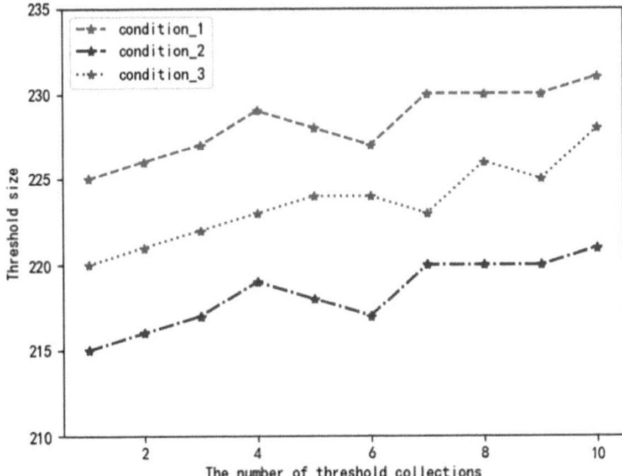

Fig. 5. Visualization of continuous threshold data

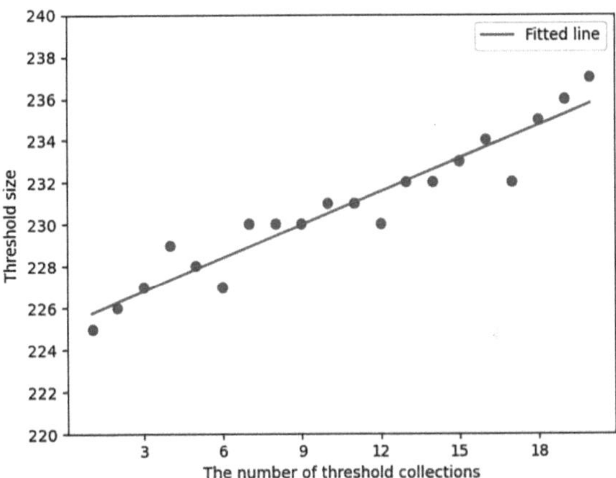

Fig. 6. The linear fitting relationship of threshold output data

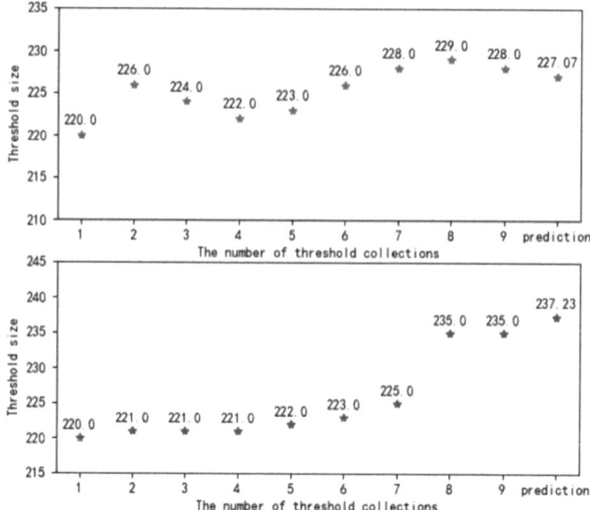

Fig. 7. The predictive graph of linear regression model

By collecting binary threshold data multiple times and conducting predictions, the gradual determination of the range of binary threshold variations can be achieved, thereby providing support for subsequent image processing and analysis. This process not only enhances the accuracy of predictions but also contributes to optimizing the performance and stability of the image processing system. Following the completion of model training, this system conducts predictions using data from every fifth round and then statistically organizes the predicted values to establish the range of threshold variation limits. Figure 7 depicts the predictive graph of the linear regression model, demonstrating that the predicted threshold values adhere primarily to a linear pattern.

4   Conclusion and Outlook

Based on the utilization of the OTSU method to generate continuous threshold values for image binarization, this paper proposes a combined approach of Gaussian weighted averaging and machine learning prediction. This method leverages the Gaussian kernel function to optimize the threshold data and employs machine learning to predict and determine the range of threshold variations, thereby optimizing the threshold output. Ultimately, this approach aims to stabilize the binarized images in embedded systems and achieve optimal binarization. However, there is still room for improvement. As the Gaussian kernel weight parameters are variable and selected through numerous comparative experiments, they may only achieve local optimality. Therefore, the next step will involve the adoption of machine learning techniques to train and select the optimal parameters.

Acknowledgment. Thanks for Professor Wang Yilei for the guidance on the paper.

References

1. Gatos, B., et al.: Adaptive degraded document image binarization. Pattern Recognition (2006)
2. Rosenfeld, A., Kak, A.C.: Digital Picture Processing, 2nd edn. Academic Press, New York (1982)
3. Otsu, N.: A threshold selection method from gray-level histograms. IEEE Trans. Syst. Man Cybernet. **9**(1), 62–66 (1979)
4. Kittler, J., Illingworth, J.: On threshold selection using clustering criteria. IEEE Trans. Systems Man Cybernet. **15**, 652–655 (1985)
5. Brink, A.D.: Thresholding of digital images using two-dimensional entropies. Pattern Recogn. **25**(8), 803–808 (1992)
6. Yan, H.: Unified formulation of a class of image thresholding techniques. Pattern Recogn. **29**(12), 2025–2032 (1996)
7. Sahoo, P.K., Soltani, S., Wong, A.K.C.: A survey of thresholding techniques. Comput. Vis. Graph. Image Process. **41**(2), 233–260 (1988)
8. Kim, I.-K., Jung, D.-W., Park, R.-H.: Document image binarization based on topographic analysis using a water flow model. Pattern Recogn. **35**, 265–277 (2002)
9. Niblack, W.: An introduction to digital image processing. Prentice Hall, Englewood Cliffs, NJ, pp. 115–116 (1986)
10. Yang, J., Chen, Y., Hsu, W.: Adaptive thresholding algorithm and its hardware implementation. Pattern Recognit. Lett. **15**(2), 141–150 (1994)
11. Parker, J.R., Jennings, C., Salkauskas, A.G.: Thresholding using an illumination model. ICDAR 1993, pp. 270–273 (1993)
12. Sauvola, J., Pietikainen, M.: Adaptive document image binarization. Pattern Recogn. **33**, 225–236 (2000)
13. Chang, M., Kang, S., Rho, W., Kim, H., Kim, D.: Improved binarization algorithm for document image by histogram and edge detection. ICDAR 1995, pp. 636–643 (1993)
14. Trier, O.D., Jain, A.K.: Goal-directed evaluation of binarization methods. IEEE Trans. Pattern Anal. Mach. Intell. **17**(12), 1191–1201 (1995)
15. Eikvil, L., Taxt, T., Moen, K.: A fast adaptive method for binarization of document images. In: International Conference on Document Analysis and Recognition, France, pp. 435–443 (1991)
16. Samuel, A.L.: Some studies in machine learning using the game of checkers. II—Recent progress. IBM J. Res. Dev. (1988)
17. Neter, J., Wassermann, W.: Applied linear statistical models. In: Regression, Analysis of Variance, and Experimental Designs. 4th printing. R.D. Irwin (1974)

A Hierarchical Lattice-Based Distributed Identity Authentication Scheme

Xinqi Dong, Yijia Wang, Xu Zhang, and Yilei Wang[✉]

School of Computer Science, Qufu Normal University, Rizhao 276827, China
wang_yilei2019@qfnu.edu.cn

Abstract. With the rapid development of blockchain technology, the hierarchical distributed authentication system has been widely adopted due to its efficient authentication and flexible authorization among multi-level nodes, but the traditional hierarchical authentication mechanism is based on classical cryptography, which is not able to resist the attack of quantum computers. Constructing an authentication mechanism using post-quantum cryptography is a reliable solution, such as lattice-based cryptography, etc. However, most of these approaches, while capable of providing quantum-resistant security, lack a hierarchical structure to efficiently support the need for authentication between multi-level nodes in a blockchain environment. In this paper, a Hierarchical distributed authentication scheme based on lattice cryptography is proposed. Specifically, the counter quantum property of lattice cryptography is utilized in conjunction with optimized non-interactive zero-knowledge proofs to design a multi-layer authentication process that guarantees the integrity of authentication information while reducing the communication overhead. The results show that the proposed method not only has significant advantages in resisting quantum attacks, but also effectively reduces the authentication delay and improves the overall efficiency of the system.

Keywords: Hierarchical Authentication · Lattice Cryptography · Blockchain

1 Introduction

With the development of blockchain technology and quantum computing, the security problem of distributed systems becomes increasingly serious. In particular, the strong computational power of quantum computers will break traditional cryptography-based authentication methods, such as RSA and ECC, which poses a great threat to current authentication systems using these algorithms [1]. However, most of the existing Hierarchical distributed authentication systems are based on classical cryptographic schemes, e.g., blockchain-based Hierarchical authentication frameworks rely on classical public key infrastructures and symmetric cryptography to realize authentication [10]. Similarly, blockchain-based multi-server hierarchical authentication relies on the classical elliptic curve algorithm for authentication [11]. In addition, Consortium Blockchain-Based Hierarchical Identity Authentication (CBHIA) proposes a hierarchical identity authentication

S. Li et al. (Eds.): BROADNETS 2024, LNICST 674, pp. 126–135, 2026.
https://doi.org/10.1007/978-3-032-14350-1_9

mechanism in a consortium chain environment, which utilizes the multi-layered structure of the blockchain to enhance the system's decentralization and scalability. Although the system enables cross-organizational authentication through blockchain technology, it relies on classical cryptographic algorithms [12]. Overall, these traditional schemes have significant shortcomings in terms of resistance to quantum computing.

To address this challenge, post-quantum cryptography offers several possible directions for quantum-computing-resistant authentication. Lattice-based cryptography is one of the most mature and widely researched post-quantum cryptography methods, and is considered to be highly resistant to quantum computation because it is based on mathematical puzzles such as LWE (Learning With Errors) and SIS (Short Integer Solution). Lyubashevsky proposed a lattice-based zero-knowledge proof scheme that generates commitment values via random vectors and implements non-interactive zero-knowledge proofs in conjunction with the Fiat-Shamir transform. This approach is widely used in subsequent lattice signature and authentication protocols [2]. Peikert's research further develops LWE-based Non-Interactive Zero-Knowledge (NIZK) proofs, optimizing the efficiency and security of the proofs and providing feasibility for larger scale applications [3]. Ducas and Micciancio, on the other hand, improved the short lattice signature scheme under the standard model, which provides shorter signature lengths and higher computational efficiency, providing a more practical solution for lattice-based authentication systems [4]. In addition, Xu et al. proposed a lattice-based lightweight authentication protocol for Internet of Things (IoT) devices, demonstrating its efficiency and security in resource-constrained environments [5]. Hossain et al. designed a lattice-based authentication framework for edge computing and cloud computing environments to defend against quantum attacks by combining signature and authentication techniques of lattice cryptography [6].

Although these lattice-based zero-knowledge proof and authentication schemes are superior in terms of resistance to quantum computing, most of the existing schemes lack a hierarchical design to support the authentication requirements among multi-level nodes in a blockchain environment. Specifically, these schemes are usually designed for flat network structures and do not adequately take into account the trust relationships and authentication needs of nodes at different levels. In a system with a Hierarchical structure, authentication between different levels requires more efficient and secure mechanisms to maintain the overall chain of trust of the system, and these traditional solutions cannot effectively deal with this complex scenario. To address this problem, this paper introduces the LATTE encryption scheme and improves it so that it is combined with lattice-based Non-Interactive Zero Knowledge Proof (NIZK) to propose a Hierarchical Distributed Identity Authentication Mechanism for Blockchain. The LATTE encryption solution provides a secure, efficient and flexible way to manage authentication and authorization between nodes at different tiers through identity-based encryption and key delegation capabilities. In a multi-level system, the LATTE scheme not only simplifies the complex key management, but also enables efficient cryptographic delegation between different levels, which allows the authentication process to be dynamically adjusted, and enhances the flexibility and security of the system in a multi-level chain of trust environment [7]. In addition to lattice-based research, other post-quantum cryptography directions have proposed quantum-resistant authentication schemes. The McEliece public key cryptosystem based on code cryptography and the Rainbow signature scheme based on multivariate polynomial cryptography, among others, provide quantum-resistant security using their respective mathematical puzzles. However, these schemes generally face the problems of large key size and high computational complexity, which limit their wide adoption in practical applications [8, 9]. More importantly, these schemes are mainly designed for single-layer authentication scenarios, and similarly lack support and optimization for Hierarchical structures.

In order to solve the above problems, this paper proposes a new identity authentication scheme by introducing a lattice cryptography-based anti-quantum authentication mechanism combined with the optimized design of the Hierarchical structure, which can better support the identity authentication requirements between multi-level nodes in the blockchain environment.

The architecture of this paper utilizes a Hierarchical framework as shown in Fig. 1, which includes the Root Level, Intermediate Level, and User Level. By using an improved LATTE encryption scheme and lattice-based NIZK, the authentication mechanism designed in this paper is able to achieve efficient authentication between nodes at different levels while reducing communication overhead and improving security. The introduction of LATTE further solves the problem of complex and inflexible key management in the Hierarchical structure, making the authentication mechanism more suitable for quantum security and multi-level trust management in large-scale blockchain networks. In Sect. 2, it is shown how nodes of different levels can authenticate each other and how cross- level authentication can be achieved using non-interactive zero-knowledge proofs with the involvement of the parent node. This mechanism ensures efficient authentication in a Hierarchical structure while optimizing communication overhead and improving security by reducing direct interaction.

The main contribution of this paper is to propose a Hierarchical distributed authentication mechanism based on lattice cryptography, which is suitable for quantum computing environments and blockchain with high security requirements. The mechanism combines lattice-based NIZK and an improved LATTE encryption scheme to enable the authentication process to achieve efficient authentication between nodes at different levels. The LATTE cryptographic scheme enhances the quantum-resistant security of the authentication mechanism through secure key generation and delegation operations. Meanwhile, the design of Hierarchical structure makes the authentication process with good scalability and decentralization characteristics, which is adapted to multi-level trust management in large-scale blockchain networks.

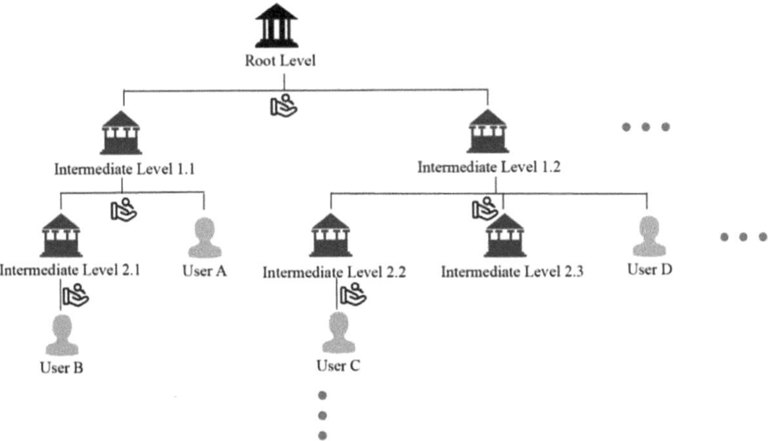

Fig. 1. Hierarchical structure framework

2 Design of the Protocol

In this part, a hierarchical lattice-based distributed identity authentication protocol is designed. The protocol design adopts LATTE, a HIBE scheme proposed by the UK's National Cyber Security Center (NCSC) in 2017 and endorsed by the European Telecommunications Standards Institute (ETSI), and the meanings of some of the symbols are shown in Table 1. The LATTE algorithm in [7] optimizes the key operations KeyGen, Delegate and Extract. The Delegate algorithm uses the private key matrix of the parent node to generate the private key matrix of the subordinate node for subsequent delegation operations, and the Extract algorithm uses the private key matrix of the parent node to generate the private key of the subordinate node. To ensure that the LATTE scheme can be combined with lattice-based non-interactive zero-knowledge proofs, we improve its Extract algorithm as shown in Algorithm 1.

Table 1. Meanings of symbols

symbols	Meanings
ℓ	Lever
σ_ℓ	Standard deviation of a discrete Gaussian distribution
$S_{\ell-1}$	Level ℓ-1 private key matrix
$S_{\ell-1}^*$	The transpose of matrix $S_{\ell-1}$
R_q	polynomial ring of integers mod q
$\lfloor f \rceil$	Polynomial $\mathbf{f}$ coefficients rounded

2.1 Program Processes

The whole process of the Hierarchical lattice-based distributed authentication mechanism designed in this paper can be divided into the following phases: (1) system initialization, (2) registration, and (3) verification. The detailed process of these phases is as follows.

System Initialization Phase.   In this phase, the KGC prepares the global parameters for subsequent phases.

Algorithm 1: Improved LATTE.Extract algorithm

Input: N, q, σ_ℓ, $S_{\ell-1}$, H: $\{0, 1\}^\star \to \mathbb{Z}_q^N$, G: $\{0, 1\}^\star \to \{0, 1\}^{256}$, ID_ℓ
Output: t_1, ..., $t_\ell \in R_q$, y
function LATTE.Extract
     $A_\ell' \leftarrow H("E" || ID_1 || ... || ID_\ell)$ *in NTT domain*
//"E" *is to distinguish it from the* A_ℓ *generated in the*
LATTE.Delegate algorithm
    seed $\leftarrow G(ID_1 || ... || ID_\ell)$
    $y \leftarrow H(ID_\ell) \cdot A_\ell \bmod q$
    $T_{\ell-1} \leftarrow$ ffLDL(FFT($S_{\ell-1} \cdot S_{\ell-1}^*$))
    For each leaf of $T_{\ell-1}$, leaf.value $\leftarrow \sigma_\ell / \sqrt{\text{leaf.value}}$
    $t \leftarrow (A_\ell', 0, ..., 0) \cdot S_{l-1}^{-1}$
    $t \leftarrow t - (A_\ell' \cdot t - y) \cdot S_{l-1}^{-1} \bmod q$
    $z \leftarrow$ FFT^{-1}(ffSampling(t, $T_{\ell-1}$, seed))
    $(t_0, t_1, ..., t_\ell) \leftarrow \lfloor \bar{z} \rceil$, where $\lfloor \bar{z} \rceil \leftarrow (t - z) \cdot S_{\ell-1}$
    return t_1, ..., $t_\ell \in R_q$ in NTT domain, y
end function

Step1. The key generation center KGC (root node) is chosen to be a large integer N, an integer polynomial ring $R_q := Z_q[x]/\langle x^N + 1 \rangle$ of mode q, and a discrete Gaussian distribution D_σ with center 0 standard deviation σ.

Step2. KGC runs the LATTE.KeyGen algorithm to generate the master public key h and master private key matrix S_0.

Step3. Making the master public key and selected global parameters public and uploading them to the blockchain ensures that all nodes and users can access them and work in the same secure environment.

Registration Phase. A new user has to send a registration request to a node before joining and that node will become the parent node of the new user.

Step1. The new user node selects a unique identity ID_{new} and generates the current timestamp T, which is sent to the parent node along with the ID_{new} to submit the registration request.

Step2. When the parent node receives the application, it first verifies whether the timestamp T is within the allowed range, if T is within the allowed time then it verifies whether ID_{new} exists on the blockchain, otherwise it rejects it. If ID_{new} already exists, it means that it has already been registered, it will also be rejected and return an error message to the user node.

Step3. The parent node uses its private key matrix and LATTE.Delegate algorithm to generate the new node's private key matrix S_{new}, and uses LATTE.Extract algorithm to generate the new node's private key sk_{new} and identity matrix A_{new}, which is passed to the new node over a secured channel to prevent key leakage.

Step4. The parent node uploads the identity matrix of the new node, A_{new}, and the proof of registration to the blockchain to ensure the transparency and verifiability of the registration process.

Verification Phase. In Hierarchical distributed authentication, the authentication is divided into two parts: cross-hierarchical authentication and same-hierarchical authentication, both of which are implemented using lattice-based non-interactive zero-knowledge proofs, and the authentication results are uploaded to the blockchain. In this scheme, key generation is passed down level by level. Therefore, there is a close relationship between the key of each user and the key of its parent node. In order to ensure the security and correctness of authentication, cross-level authentication must be realized through the parent node. In contrast, authentication at the same level does not involve a hierarchical relationship, so authentication is simpler and is accomplished directly between nodes at the same level without the intervention of an intermediate level. In addition, the passing of the key makes a trust chain between the parent node and the child nodes, and the authentication on the same trust chain requires only one-way authentication.

The cross-level authentication process is described here using the authentication of user B and user D in Fig. 1 as an example. Since user B and user D are not in the same level, their parent nodes need to be involved in auxiliary authentication to ensure the validity and integrity of user B and user D's identity information in their respective trust chains. And user B and user D are not in the same trust chain, serial mutual authentication is required to ensure the trustworthiness and legitimacy of both identities.

Step1. User B sends an authentication request to the parent node (intermediate level 2.1) indicating that it needs to authenticate with user D. The request information contains the identity ID_B of user B, the identity ID_D of the target user D, and the current timestamp T_B. Upon receipt of user B's request, parent node 2.1 forwards the request to the parent node (intermediate level 1.2) of user D. Upon receipt of the request, parent node 1.2 notifies user D of the authentication.

Step2. User B proves identity to user D. User B generates a random vector vB and computes the commitment value c_B (see Eq. (1)), and then submits the commitment value c_B and the timestamp T_B to its parent node.

$$c_B = A_B \cdot v_B \bmod q \tag{1}$$

A_B is the identity matrix of user B.

Step3. The parent node 2.1 generates the challenge e_B (see Eq. (2)) using Fiat-Shamir transformation, sends the challenge value e_B to the user B and the parent node 1.2, which forwards e_B to the user D.

$$e_B = H (c_B, T_B, block\_hash, A_B) \qquad (2)$$

The block_hash is the latest block hash on the blockchain.

Step4. After receiving e_B user B computes a response value r_B with his private key sk_B (see Eq. (3)) and sends r_B to the parent node.

$$r_B = v_B + e_B \cdot sk_B \qquad (3)$$

Step5. Parent node 2.1 sends the proof (c_B, r_B, T_B) of user B to parent node 1.2, who sends the received (c_B, r_B, T_B) to user D.

Step6. User D receives the proof (c_B, r_B, T_B) from parent node 1.2 and verifies the validity of T_B and block hash. Then recalculate the challenge value $e_{B'} = H (c_B, T_B, block\_hash, A_B)$ to verify that Eq. 4 holds. If it holds, the verification passes and the identity of user B had been confirmed.

$$A_B \cdot r_B = c_B + e_{B'} \cdot y_B \bmod q \qquad (4)$$

Step7. Repeat the above steps to verify the identity of user D. If the identity of user D is also verified successfully, the authentication process is complete. The authentication result and timestamp are uploaded to the blockchain to ensure that the result is open and transparent for auditing.

For same-level authentication, it only needs to be done directly between two nodes without involving the participation of other parent nodes or higher-level nodes. The user initiates the authentication application on user's own, and in step 3 the user generates the challenge e alone, which will not be repeated here.

3 Security Analysis

In this section, we provide a comprehensive security analysis of the proposed Hierarchical lattice-based distributed authentication scheme to evaluate its robustness and security under various potential attacks. The main analyses include the quantum attack resistance, the effectiveness of resisting traditional attacks (e.g., replay attacks, man-in-the-middle attacks, etc.), and the advantages in terms of privacy protection and trust management in the blockchain environment.

3.1 Quantum Attack Resistance Analysis

The proposed authentication scheme is based on lattice cryptography and utilizes LWE and SIS mathematical puzzles with significant resistance to quantum computation. Unlike traditional RSA and ECC algorithms, these lattice problems prove difficult under known models of quantum computing. Specifically, the scheme employs lattice-based

NIZK, a proof method that provides zero-knowledge authentication without the need to interact with each other, thus avoiding correlation and direct attacks that may be performed by quantum computers.

In addition, the improved LATTE encryption scheme introduced in this paper enhances the resistance to quantum attacks through encrypted delegation and key management functions between nodes at different levels. The optimized design of the LATTE scheme makes the key transfer process between different levels more secure, especially in the quantum-resistant computing environment, and effectively prevents possible key-breaking attempts of quantum algorithms.

3.2 Resistance to Traditional Attack Analysis

Each communication during the authentication process contains a timestamp and the latest block hash of the blockchain to ensure that the authentication request is current. Any attempt to replay an old authentication request is rejected due to a failure of the timestamp validation and is therefore resistant to replay attacks; by introducing NIZK into the authentication process, no third party can forge a legitimate authentication response without revealing the private key, and furthermore, since the authentication results and proofs are kept on the chain, any attempts of tampering or forgery are recorded and exposed by the blockchain, and thus can be protected against man-in-the-middle (MITM) attacks; the key and identity information used in the authentication process are based on the difficult construction of lattice cryptography, and it is difficult for an attacker to obtain useful information from the communication data even if it is intercepted, in addition, the key delegation mechanism in the LATTE encryption scheme ensures key independence between nodes of different tiers, which further reduces the risk of a single point of leakage and therefore prevents information leakage.

3.3 Privacy Protection in Blockchain Environments

Due to the transparency of blockchain, all authentication results and related information are saved on the chain, and how to protect users' privacy in the public ledger becomes an important challenge. In this paper, NIZK is used, and the authentication process does not need to expose the user's private key or specific identity information, which ensures the security of the user's privacy. At the same time, the LATTE encryption scheme makes it difficult for an attacker to map the information actually transmitted during the authentication process back to the real identity, even if it is exposed on the blockchain, through the use of identity-based encryption and key delegation functions that make the information actually transmitted during the authentication process go through multiple obfuscations. In addition, the decentralized architecture using blockchain does not rely on a single trust center, and all nodes verify each other in the authentication process, eliminating the privacy risk of centralized identity management.

3.4 Balancing Security and Performance

This scheme achieves a better balance between security and authentication efficiency. By optimizing the LATTE scheme and the NIZK process, the authentication process not only provides sufficient security in a quantum computing environment, but also effectively reduces computational complexity and communication overhead. This is particularly important for multi-level trust management in large-scale blockchain networks.

Table 2 compares the performance of this paper's scheme with existing schemes in terms of security features. The results show that the scheme in this paper has obvious advantages in key aspects such as quantum attack resistance and Hierarchical authentication support, especially in dealing with multi-level node authentication in complex blockchain environments.

Table 2. Comparison of security analysis

Security features	quantum attack resistance	replay attack resistance	MITM attack resistance	Data privacy protection	Balancing security and efficiency	Hierarchical authentication support
Ducas [4]	✓	✗	✓	✗	✓	✗
Xu [5]	✓	✓	✓	✓	✓	✗
Hossain [6]	✓	✓	✓	✓	✓	✗
Feng [10]	✗	✓	✓	✓	✓	✓
Wu [11]	✗	✓	✓	✓	✓	✓
Zyskind [12]	✗	✓	✓	✓	✗	✗
Ours	✓	✓	✓	✓	✓	✓

4   Conclusion

This thesis proposes a hierarchical lattice-based distributed identity authentication scheme to cope with the security threats posed by quantum computing. The scheme combines lattice-based NIZK and lattice-based encryption methods to design an authentication process applicable to multilevel nodes, which can realize secure and efficient authentication and key management among different levels. By introducing the Hierarchical structure and optimized authentication process, the method in this paper not only reduces the communication overhead, but also improves the overall system's anti-attack capability, especially in the context of quantum computing. Security analysis shows that the scheme can effectively defend against multiple types of attacks and ensure the reliability and privacy of the authentication process, providing a new security solution for Hierarchical authentication in blockchain and other distributed systems.

References

1. Schärer, K., Comuzzi, M.: The quantum threat to blockchain: summary and timeline analysis. Quantum Mach. Intell. **5**(1), 19 (2023)
2. Lyubashevsky, V.: Fiat-Shamir with aborts: applications to lattice and factoring-based signatures. In: International Conference on the Theory and Application of Cryptology and Information Security. Springer, Heidelberg (2009)
3. Peikert, C.: A decade of lattice cryptography. Found. Trends® Theor. Comput. Sci. **10**(4), 283–424 (2016)
4. Ducas, L., Micciancio, D.: Improved short lattice signatures in the standard model. In: International Cryptology Conference. Springer, Heidelberg (2015)
5. Xu C., Ai, X., Wang, S., Zhao, G., Han, Z.: A lightweight lattice-based group signcryption authentication scheme for Internet of things. Telecommun. Sci. **40**(4), 88–106 (2024)
6. Hossain, M.J., Xu, C., Zhang, Y., et al.: LAMA: a secure lattice-based authentication scheme for cloud storage against misbehaved private key generator. J. Ambient Intell. Hum. Comput. **14**, 8613–8629 (2023). https://doi.org/10.1007/s12652-021-03620-z
7. Zhao, R.K., et al.: Quantum-safe HIBE: does it cost a Latte? IEEE Trans. Inf. Forensics Secur. (2023)
8. Baldi, M., et al.: Enhanced public key security for the McEliece cryptosystem. J. Cryptol. **29**, 1–27 (2016)
9. Ding, J., Schmidt, D.: Rainbow, a new multivariable polynomial signature scheme. In: International Conference on Applied Cryptography and Network Security. Springer, Heidelberg (2005)
10. Feng, Q., et al.: A survey on privacy protection in blockchain system. J. Netw. Comput. Appl. **126**, 45–58 (2019)
11. Wu, M., You, L, Hu, G., Li, L., Cao, C.: A blockchain-based hierarchical authentication scheme for multiserver architecture. Secur. Commun. Netw. **5592119**, 20 (2021). https://doi.org/10.1155/2021/5592119
12. Zyskind, G., Nathan, O.: Decentralizing privacy: using blockchain to protect personal data. In: 2015 IEEE Security and Privacy Workshops. IEEE (2015)

OST: An AI Enabled One-Stop Station Platform for Cyber Security Incident Reporting

Alwaleed Al Rashdi and Shancang Li[✉] [iD]

Cardiff University, Cardiff CF24 4AG, UK
`shancang.li@ieee.org`

Abstract. This paper proposes a "One Stop Station" (OST) with an AI-powered "CyberBot" to streamline incident reporting and management. The OST tackles inefficiencies by offering a unified platform that streamlines threat reporting, delivers real-time threat intelligence, and enhances user interaction with an intuitive interface. Leveraging AI like GPT-3.5 and Rasa, the OST automates responses, generates detailed reports, and integrates with existing tools like VirusTotal. This demonstrably improves response speed and accuracy. Testing results show a potential 600% reduction in reporting time. The OST empowers both cyber security professionals and less technical users, reducing workload and enhancing overall incident management. This project highlights the potential of AI in cyber security and positions the OST as a pioneer. It reinforces discussions on leveraging AI to fortify digital defences and integrate AI into daily life.

Keywords: Cyber security · Incident Reporting · Generative AI

1 Introduction

1.1 Background

Cybercrime has become a pervasive global threat, affecting over one in five people worldwide [1]. As cyber-attacks grow increasingly sophisticated, traditional security measures are proving inadequate. The OST was developed to address this critical challenge by offering a proactive and intelligent solution. Recognizing the urgent need to safeguard sensitive data, the OST's integrated approach streamlines incident reporting and accelerates threat hunting, enabling organizations to minimize the impact of cyber-attacks.

The proposed OST acts as a comprehensive system that provides users with a single point for all cyber security-related matters, in addition to having access to the tools required to investigate cyber security incidents, the platform is equipped with a password cracking software and a word list of 14,341,564 unique elements, which should be capable of tackling even the hardest passwords. Tying

S. Li et al. (Eds.): BROADNETS 2024, LNICST 674, pp. 136–147, 2026.
https://doi.org/10.1007/978-3-032-14350-1_10

all this together is the CyberBot, which is a virtual assistant that can access all the tools using a single text field, and is integrated to a database to store all the case information.

The main purpose of the OST is to allow the first responders to quickly create an incident report, and log information for future reference. The development of the OST is particularly relevant in sectors possessing dedicated Security Operations Centers (SOCs). By streamlining incident reporting, the OST can enhance operational efficiency and enable SOC teams to focus on higher-level threat analysis and response. This research aims to pioneer a new era of AI specialization, where chatbots can be tailored to provide direct benefits to organizations.

The main contributions of this work can be summarized as:

- A centralized incident management platform (OST) has been developed that automates incident report generation. Leveraging advanced threat intelligence, the OST provides tailored cyber recommendations based on user-supplied incident details.
- Standardization of incident reports is achieved through a unified template, ensuring consistency across all records.
- By integrating AI capabilities, the OST offers a comprehensive suite of tools for enhanced incident management. The OST chatbot can access real-time data and conduct intelligent analysis to support incident response efforts.
- Adherence to National Cyber Security Centre (NCSC) guidelines is a core feature of the OST, with additional provisions for risk mitigation. Sensitive information is securely stored in a local SQL database fortified with robust security measures.

2   Related Works

Unlike most existing cyber security platforms that predominantly focus on specific facets of the security life-cycle, this work aims to develop an AI-empowered comprehensive one-stop solution, which integrates multiple tools excelling in threat detection, incident response, or vulnerability management but often lack a holistic approach.

Security Operations Centres (SOCs) have emerged as centralized hubs [2], they often rely on multiple disparate systems for effective operation. Some platforms have begun integrating multiple security functions, such as SIEM (Security Information and Event Management) and SOAR (Security Orchestration, Automation, and Response) solutions [3,4]. These platforms offer centralized logging, analysis, and response capabilities.

Since the project deals with GPT3.5, custom instructions enable training the model with data and setting limitations on specific functions that can make the model more secure, for example ChatGPT is usually accused of spurring responses. created by its "hallucinations", meaning that it is just generated and not true. Fine-tuning the model and hardcoding prompts such as tell the model to "Answer the question as truthfully as possible, and if you're unsure of the answer, say "Sorry, I don't know"." [5] eliminates the risk of hallucinations by 100%, which avoids the detrimental risk that can be caused in cyber security, especially if it mislabels a malicious link to be safe.

In the past few years, several OST platforms have been developed to provide a centralized hub for managing and coordinating incident response activities, but most of these works focus on tracking and managing incidents (e.g., Rapid 7 InsightDR) [6,7]. Palo Alto Networks developed Cortex XSOAR to help organizations automate and streamline incident response processes [8,9]. IBM developed security QRadar to focus on security information and event management (SIEM) for incident response and threat detection, while Splunk also specializes in incident response and threat detection [10].

In recent, deep learning, specific GPT models are increasingly used to help users to generate incident management insights. Fine-tuning the ChatGPT model was used in biomedicine and health research [12], showing the increasing accuracy of these models after they have been fed information in a specific domain. This is the main reason that a custom GPT-3.5 model was used in this paper to summarize the incident report and generate recommendations.

Some companies have attempted to reduce human intervention in Security Operations Centres (SOC) usually by implementing a chatbot, but significant technical gaps remain, particularly in the integration with existing systems and scalability of the system.

For example **Onyoursix** claims to have a fully customizable bot that is active "24/7, 365", but the lack of access, detailed technical documentation raises questions about the product's maturity and readiness for official launch, especially at an enterprise level.

Similarly, **Cisco's Securex platform**, integrated Extended Detection and Response (XDR) with chatbot functionality to enhance SOC operations. However, despite Cisco's reputation and extensive resources (£182.61 Billion market cap) [11] Cisco has announced the platforms decommission as of July 2024.

The examples above underscore the broader technical gaps within current chatbot solutions in cyber security. While implementing AI into cyber security seems very promising, the issues with integration and scalability cause current solutions to fail.

The extent to which a cyber threat can be neutralized depends mainly on the incident response team and how well they capture the full scope of the attack [13]. During the research, it became clear that there is no full cyber security incident report platform that uses a chatbot. However, by combining the knowledge of past researchers, this papers focuses on creating a revolutionary step in the cyber industry and emphasizes the seamless integration with diverse cyber security ecosystems.

3   Methodology

3.1   Problem

SOC teams face significant challenges due to understaffing, with over 70% of cyber security professionals reporting that their organizations are understaffed

[8], meaning that some cases are either not properly documented or ignored using the discretion of the first responders, harming the companies infrastructure and putting data at risk, the OST supplements human work with automation thus reducing the effects of understaffing, ensuring the report is as detailed as possible, and includes a well written summary.

Additionally, a discussion on a Reddit forum about the use of AI in cyber security highlighted that threat intelligence report standardization remains underdeveloped [14], especially as countries like Saudi Arabia are investing \$ 40 billion into artificial intelligence [15]. This government support highlights the necessity to implement solutions that leverage computational power and AI. This aligns with the goal of the OST, which is why AI was chosen as the main focus of this project

3.2   Solution

Developing a cyber platform that -theoretically- simplifies hours of investigation into a few minutes requires multiple steps. The foundation of the chatbot application is built on a custom flask server that integrates with existing systems through APIs, such as SIEM (Security Information and Event Management) systems. The system boasts a modular design that allows for simple implementation of systems like VirusTotal for threat scanning, SQL databases for incident logging, email servers for automated reporting, and includes proper API documentation and webhook configurations to enable real-time data transmission. Currently, the data is being manually inputted from the SIEM system into the OST. The key functionalities provided by the OST include:

- **AI empowered Incident Management**. Having all the tools required in one place and having a chatbot that can access real-time data and perform intelligence gathering.
- **Advanced Threat Analysis**. Integration with VirusTotal and other tools for scanning and analysing malicious files and URLs.
- **Automatic creation of incident reports**. The OST will also generate cyber recommendations for the incident, using the threat intelligence it has been fed and the case information inputted by the user.
- **Standardization of incident reports**. Each report will be the exact same since a single template will be used, this will ensure that there will be consistency between the reports.
- **Compliance and Risk Management**. The incident report will be compliant with the National Cyber Security Centre guidelines, and will also have an extra section relating to risk mitigation.
- **Centralized storage location**. A local SQL database will be used in the development on the OST, the database will be developed to a high standard of safety to secure the confidential information being transmitted.
- **Scalability and Customization**. The project will use Rasa for the chatbot making the information gathering scalable by simply adding more intents, and the website is built using a Flask template meaning that new tools can be added by creating a div container and inserting the code into it.

The OST leverages several AI models to enhance its capabilities:

1) **GPT-3.5 (Generative AI)**: GPT3.5 is a Generative AI model developed by OpenAI, that excels in processing and generating human-like text. In the OST platform, ChatGPT is used for generating SQL queries and detailed summaries of incidents, while also answering questions and providing recommendations. However, due to the studies highlighting the risks associated with the availability of AI services like ChatGPT [16], the development of the OST will limit the use of third-party services as much as possible, and it will also offer a redundancy mechanism to maintain the chatbot's operational period.

   Another major fear for companies of their staff using services like ChatGPT with business data was not only caused by the security issue of sharing confidential information with a third-party company, but also due to an understanding that unauthorized access to users account would also cause the data to be jeopardized, which influenced the OST to use a secure API call and encrypting the data sent to and from the server. All data passed to Chat-GPT is encrypted on the backend of the flask server using the post method (methods=['POST']) and access by need-to-know basis only.

2) **RasaNLU Model**: Rasa was selected to be the interface for the chatbot in conjunction with GPT3.5 to supplement the shortcomings of using Chat-GPT highlighted above. Additionally, using Rasa will allow for more control over the training data which can eliminate the "hallucination" effect that is common in ChatGPT, and flexibility in fine-tuning with APIs rather than datasets, Rasa can also be run locally which can be seen as a method of reducing security threats by keeping all data offline until it is necessary. Above all Rasa stands out due to its ability to integrate seamlessly with spaCy for the entity recognition, which demonstrated its ability to extract information from the users input with a high level of accuracy and speed in parsing. Rasa was selected for the core of the NLU because it is specifically designed for creating chatbots, offering advanced features for conversation management, it also has great integration abilities, making it a valuable tool for the chat interface, it is used to develop the core functionality of the chatbot, enabling it to understand and process natural language, manage dialogues, and preform custom actions based on user input.

3) **Hugging Face**, Hugging Face was proposed to be the main source for machine learning algorithms along with datasets, but due to the recent discovery of a vulnerability in the platform [19], this work will use the GPT-3.5 model and pass custom prompts to achieve the report generation functionality.

3.3   Key Techniques

The OST integrates all the tools mentioned below in symphony to form a comprehensive, centralized platform. Having a large number of tools working independently yet being able to communicate with each other means that the data transfer model must be meticulously designed, this ensures efficient and secure data flow and processing.

After the user logs in and begins a chat with the CyberBot, the Flask server will display a text field in which the user will type their prompt. The prompt is then sent to the Rasa server via a secure AJAX request. The Rasa chatbot will then process the input, and run a function depending on the user's intent. For instance, if the user wanted to create an incident report, the Rasa server will send a response to the user through the AJAX server and enabling the user to reply to the answer which will trigger the Rasa server to start the information gathering process, subsequently storing this data in an SQL database.

Following the information collection and storage, data is securely read by Python code that filters the data; the information undergoes data cleansing to remove irrelevant information, and prepares it for analysis, the data fields like IP address and domain name are passed through a Python function that takes the information as an input and returns the sanity of the input using an API call, the response is then saved into the SQL database for the next step which is report generation.

After the database is fully populated with as much case information as possible and the sanity checks for all data fields have been completed, another Python function then packages the details for the case and concatenates it with an engineered prompt to send to the ChatGPT model via an API call. The code then waits for a response from the model stating that the report generation has been completed; after receiving the final report in text format, the data is then parsed by another Python function which formats the data and saves it in a PDF format on the user's machine using an OS command. This data transfer model is designed with scalability in mind. Using SQL allows larger volumes of data to be transferred without compromising on processing efficiency. A simplified model of the data flow between the various services of OST can be seen in Fig. 1.

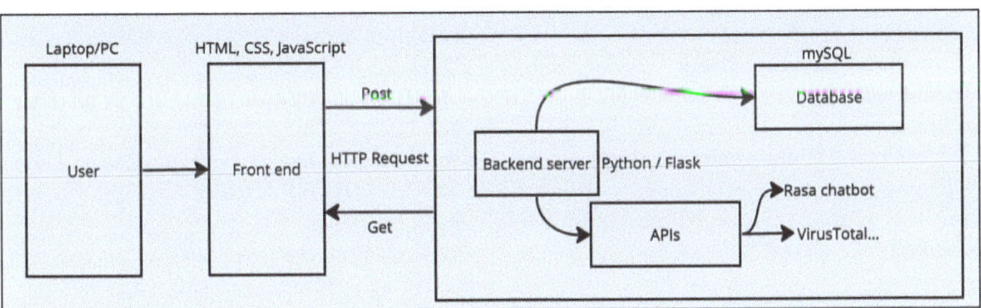

Fig. 1. OST workflow.

The OST ensures no information is missed by storing all data that was mentioned in the existing frameworks, including National Institute of Standards and Technology, NASA, and SANS Framework, etc., covering the basic information, affected clients, assessed secrecy, report to the stakeholders, description of the event, time, incident category, extent of the consequences, and the mitigation strategy.

The above frameworks were chosen due to the high success rate and standardisation in many countries [17], the report also covers all stages from containment, eradication, to recovery, and ensures that the issue is reflected on, to avoid the likelihood of it happening again. Using pre-existing frameworks to generate the report maintains the uniform information that creates a standardised report.

The final step after gathering the information is to analyse the data, the level of advancement the cyber security industry has achieved is unmatchable in a short time frame, for that reason the OST incorporates existing systems such as VirusTotal and Hashcat, these system's ability to enhance the chatbot's threat detection was a key consideration driven by the literature reviewed, due to their high success rate and wide ability to customize them. One of the biggest issues encountered was the availability of thousands of intelligence gathering tools, but the OST selected the best performing options and implement them so the results can be trusted, forming the research question:

"Can a chatbot help cyber security teams create incident reports faster and with more accuracy?"

3.4   Integrating Cyber Security Tools and Types of Cyber Incidents

To ensure effective functionality for the OST, research was conducted to find the top tools required by members of the SOC team, which will then be incorporated into the platform. Table. 1 summarises the tools and type of cyber incidents that OST can provide.

Table 1. Tools and Types of Cyber Incidents in OST

Required Cyber Security Tools	Types of Cyber Incidents
– VirusTotal IP address check – VirusTotal Website Check – Email scanner – Threat map – Access to GPT for general queries – File password cracker: (hash extracted with john the reaper, password cracking using Hashcat)	– Phishing Attacks – Malware Infections – Unsafe website (user opened a website that is not safe) – Denial of Service (DoS)/Distributed Denial of Service (DDoS) Attacks – Data Breaches – Social Engineering Attacks – Man-in-the-Middle (MitM) Attacks – Unsafe file name (like having a file called password.txt) – Brute Force Attacks – Zero-Day Exploits

3.5   Website Design

The OST provides a website portal with several webpages, each dedicated to a specific function of the system. This structure allows for a clear development plan. The first step is to log into/register to the website, after that the user will be presented with all the tools required to create an incident report. The hierarchical structure created for the site map ensures that the user does not find it difficult to navigate through the site, as the tools are positioned in a logical way [18]. The arrow in the sitemap simply demonstrates the way that a user can flow through the interface and are bidirectional (Fig. 2)

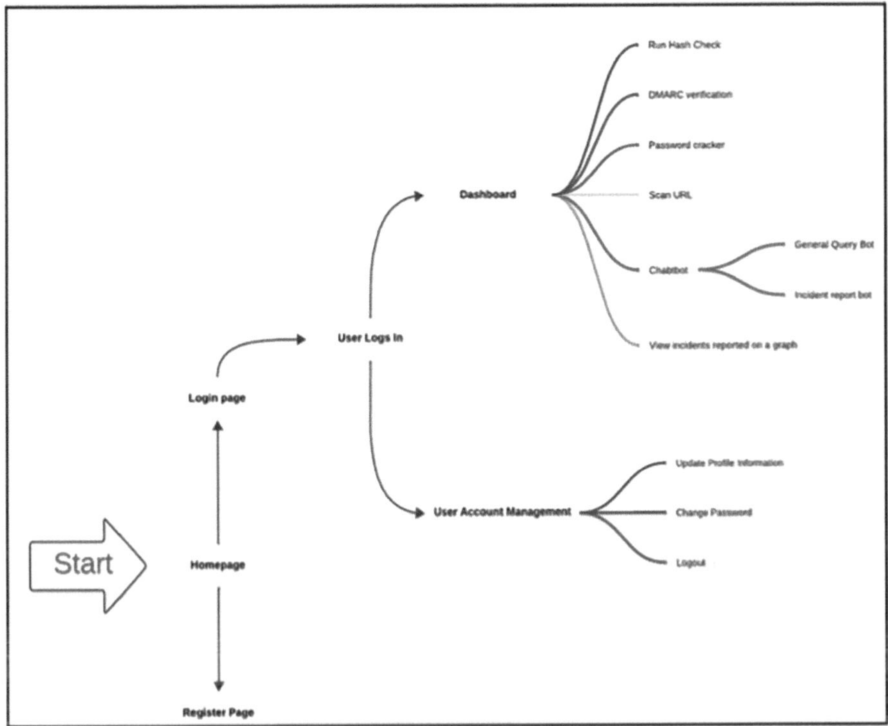

Fig. 2. Website Flowchart.

4   Validation

4.1   Implementation

Creating the brain of the chatbot begins with a deep understanding of user interactions and ends with a functional model capable of engaging in meaningful dialogues, the development stages aim to solve the inefficiencies of manual information gathering and report writing. A simplified diagram addressing the chatbot architecture can be seen in the figure below, showing the intents that the user can request, and how the bot responds to them. Where the squares are actions completed by the chatbot and the diamond-shapes represent a decision to be made by the user, the oval is the termination step (Fig. 3).

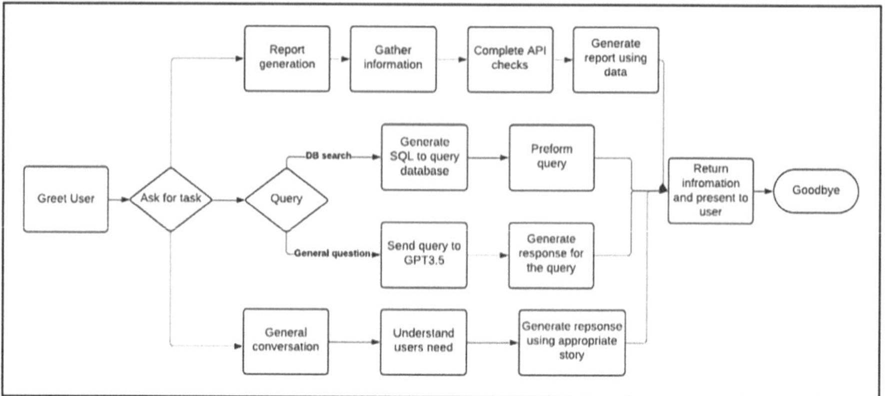

Fig. 3. Rasa Flowchart.

Creating the above design in the Rasa model through intents and entities, the chatbot can now understand the user's needs and manage user dialogue. The last step is to combine all the information created and involves feeding the bot all the defined entities, stories, and domain data. To test the model an interactive test using extra dialogue is employed, this allows the machine learning algorithm to make the chatbot predictions more accurate by correcting any misclassified information where necessary.

Custom actions allow the chatbot to surpass the basic conversational capabilities, and give it the ability to fetch real-time data from external APIs and interact with databases, which is required for cases where the chatbot is not general, rather aims to solve a specific task. The tasks which rely on third parties are:

1. Information extraction: To collect the case details by asking the user questions incrementally, each time the user is asked a question the chatbot back-end opens a listening server and waits for the user's response, for example the listener action is used to log the name of the person creating the report.
2. Database management: After collecting all the information and temporarily holding it, the next task is to store the data in a more permanent way, this is done by creating an integration between the chatbot and the SQL database. Another intent of the chatbot is to be able to retrieve information from the database, this is very complex as the user will be inputting data in plain English, but database retrieval uses Structured Query Language (SQL).

3. GPT AI Model Integration: Since the CyberBot leverages some of its capabilities to extract entities, answer questions, generate reports and SQL queries using the GPT-3.5 turbo model, to use OpenAI's model an API must be called.
4. Security and Analysis Features: One of the threat intelligence providers in the OST is VirusTotal, their services are being utilized to scan IP addresses, websites, domains, and file hashes (Fig. 4).

4.2   Experiments

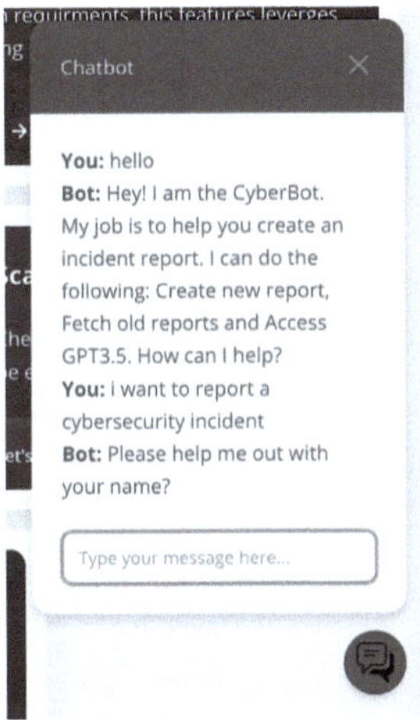

Fig. 4. Operating the chatbot from the OST website.

Overall, the speed of writing a traditional case report with a summary and information gathering took me 24 minutes and 30 s. However, when using the OST with the same information it took 4 minutes, this is much faster at about **600% time reduction**, (when manually timed by myself) highlighting the time saved by using an AI chatbot to complete all the checks and using the Cyber-Bot to write the summary of the report, in terms of mistakes both the manual and the OST generated report had the exact same details and information intelligence, the major difference was that in the manual report had some typos, while **the OST report had 100% grammatically correct English**. In conclusion, the system works as intended and I am confident that the project is a success. However, testing with real participants will be required to gain further confidence, but it is not possible due to the difficulty to deploying the chatbot along within the timeframe for this project and might have shown less promising results. However, current testing passed with outstanding results (Fig. 5).

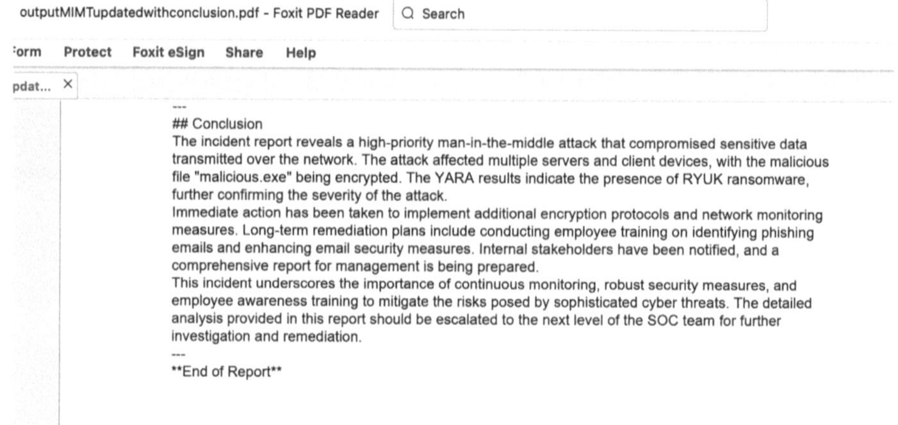

Fig. 5. Demo report automatically generated by OST.

5   Conclusion

In this work, the OST was developed to streamline cyber incident reporting by leveraging a chatbot-driven platform. We designed and implemented a solution to address the understaffing challenges faced by SOC teams. The OST's success demonstrates its potential to revolutionize the cyber security industry. By conducting thorough validation and user testing, the OST successfully consolidated essential tools into a single platform, enabling efficient incident reporting.

References

1. Liu, Y., Li, S.: Hybrid cyber threats detection using explainable AI in industrial IoT. In: 2023 International Conference on Human-Centered Cognitive Systems (HCCS), pp. 1–6 (2023). https://doi.org/10.1109/HCCS59561.2023.10452621
2. Mughal, A.A.: Building and Securing the Modern Security Operations Center (SOC). Int. J. Bus. Intell. Big Data Analyt. 5(1), 1–15 (2022)
3. Li, S., Zhao, S., Yang, P., Andriotis, P., Xu, L., Sun, Q.: Distributed consensus algorithm for events detection in cyber-physical systems. IEEE Internet Things J. 6(2), 2299–2308 (2019). https://doi.org/10.1109/JIOT.2019.2900242
4. Hulayyil, S.B., Li, S., Xu, L.: Machine-learning-based vulnerability detection and classification in internet of things device security. Electronics 12(18), 3927 (2023). https://doi.org/10.3390/electronics12183927
5. Dibia, V.: Practical Steps to Reduce Hallucination and Improve Performance of Systems Built with Large Language Models (2023). https://newsletter.victordibia.com/p/practical-steps-to-reduce-hallucination. Accessed 12 July 2024
6. Binhulayyil, S., Li, S.: Ripple20 vulnerabilities detection using a featureless deep learning model. In: 2023 IEEE 22nd International Conference on Trust, Security and Privacy in Computing and Communications (TrustCom), pp. 1236–1240 (2023). https://doi.org/10.1109/TrustCom60117.2023.00168

7. Brewer, R.: Could SOAR Save Skills-Short SOCs? Computer Fraud & Security **2019**(10), 8–11 (2019)
8. (ISC)2: (ISC)2 Cybersecurity Workforce Study (2022). https://www.isc2.org/-/media/Project/ISC2/Main/Media/documents/research/ISC2-Cybersecurity-Workforce-Study.pdf
9. Accenture: Accenture | New Insights. Tangible Outcomes. New Applied Now. https://www.accenture.com. Accessed 26 May 2025
10. Williams, C., Chaturvedi, R., Chakravarthy, K.: Cybersecurity Risks in a Pandemic. J. Med. Internet Res. **22**(9), e23692 (2020). https://doi.org/10.2196/23692
11. Companies Market Cap: Cisco (CSCO) - Market Capitalization (2024). https://companiesmarketcap.com/eur/cisco/marketcap/. Accessed 24 Aug 2024
12. Tian, S., et al.: Opportunities and Challenges for ChatGPT and Large Language Models in Biomedicine and Health. Briefings Bioinform. **25**(1), bbad493 (2024). https://doi.org/10.1093/bib/bbad493
13. O'Neill, A., Ahmad, A., Maynard, S.: Cybersecurity Incident Response in Organisations: A Meta-level Framework for Scenario-Based Training. Cybersecurity Incident Response in Organisations: A Meta-level Framework for Scenario-Based Training, pp. 11, August 2021
14. Reddit: AI in Cybersecurity (2024). https://www.reddit.com/r/cybersecurity/comments/. Accessed 15 April 2024
15. Reuters: Saudi Arabia Plans 40 Bln Push into Artificial Intelligence. Reuters, vol. 1, no. 1 (2024). https://www.reuters.com/world/middle-east/saudi-arabia-plans-40-bln-push-into-artificial-intelligence-nyt-reports-2024-03-19/. Accessed 15 April 2024
16. Tran, T.H.: OpenAI's ChatGPT Went Completely off the Rails for Hours. The Daily Beast, 21 February 2024. https://www.thedailybeast.com/openais-chatgpt-went-completely-off-the-rails-for-hours. Accessed 15 April 2024
17. Kashmer, K.: A Step-by-Step Guide to Creating a Cyber Security Incident Report (2022). https://techsevenpartners.com/a-step-by-step-guide-to-creating-a-cyber-security-incident-report/
18. Usability.gov: User-Centered Design Basics. (2019). https://www.usability.gov/what-and-why/user-centered-design.html
19. Vulnera: Hugging Face Vulnerability Could Lead to AI Model Supply Chain Attacks (2024). https://vulnera.com/newswire/hugging-face-vulnerability-could-lead-to-ai-model-supply-chain-attacks/. Accessed 15 April 2024

Performance Evaluation of SARQ in LLNs

Manel Chahed[1(✉)], Aref Meddeb[2], and Amine Boufaied[3]

[1] NOCCS Research Laboratory, Higher Institute of Computer Science and
Communication Technologies of Sousse, University of Sousse, Sousse, Tunisia
`chahedmanel07@gmail.com`
[2] Faculty of Engineering, University of Sherbrooke, Sherbrooke, Canada
`Aref.Meddeb@Usherbrooke.ca`
[3] MARS Research Laboratory, Higher Institute of Computer Science and
Communication Technologies of Sousse, University of Sousse, Sousse, Tunisia
`Amine.boufaied@isitc.u-sousse.tn`

Abstract. In today's interconnected world, Lossy and Low Power Networks (LLNs) have become increasingly prevalent across a wide range of Internet of Things (IoT) applications. As these networks continue to expand and evolve, reliability has emerged as a critical requirement that must be prioritized and addressed. In fact, to function effectively and fulfill their intended purpose, LLNs must be reliable. The reliability of LLNs includes factors such as consistent data delivery and durability. When reliability is compromised, the entire IoT system can be affected, leading to data loss and delayed decision-making. In this paper, we evaluate the performance of the Simple ARQ protocol (SARQ) in LLNs. Through a realistic simulation setup using Contiki motes in the Cooja Simulator, we show that SAQR demonstrates better performance in terms of reliability compared to UDP, as well as improved energy consumption relative to TCP. We analyze the impact of the number of nodes on the performance of SARQ compared to TCP and UDP. We show that SARQ maintains good performance across all configurations, demonstrating reliable packet delivery and efficient energy consumption. Furthermore, SARQ's performance consistently falls between that of TCP and UDP in terms of Packet Delivery Ratio (PDR) and Energy Consumption (EC), making it a very effective compromise and effective choice in various LLN scenarios.

Keywords: IoT Networks · Transport Layer Protocols · Reliability · Simple ARQ Protocol

1 Introduction

Reliability is a critical requirement for the successful operation of Low Power and Lossy Networks (LLNs). As these networks continue to expand and power a growing number of Internet of Things (IoT) applications, ensuring reliable data

S. Li et al. (Eds.): BROADNETS 2024, LNICST 674, pp. 148–161, 2026.
https://doi.org/10.1007/978-3-032-14350-1_11

delivery, uninterrupted connectivity, and resilience against failures has become paramount.

Traditional transport layer protocols like TCP (Transmission Control Protocol) and UDP (User Datagram Protocol), while widely used, may not always be sufficient to meet the unique needs of LLNs. TCP is designed for reliable, ordered, and error-checked data delivery. It establishes a connection between devices, retransmits lost packets, and ensures that data arrives in the correct sequence. However, TCP's overhead and connection-oriented nature can be inefficient for many IoT use cases that require low-power, low-bandwidth, and connectionless communication. UDP, on the other hand, offers a lightweight, connectionless alternative. It prioritizes speed over reliability, sending data packets without waiting for acknowledgments or re-transmissions. While this makes UDP faster, it also means that data loss can occur, and there is no guarantee of delivery.

As the IoT ecosystem continues to evolve, the development and adoption of reliable transport layer protocols will remain a key focus area. To address this need, we have recently introduced a novel protocol referred to as Simple ARQ (SARQ) [1]. This protocol utilizes an acknowledgment and re-transmission mechanism to ensure the reliable transport of packets in IoT devices.

In this paper, we analyze the performance of the Simple ARQ protocol (SARQ) in IoT networks. The paper is structured as follows: In Sect. 2, we present standard IETF transport protocols, including detailed descriptions of UDP, TCP, QUIC, DCCP, and SCTP. Section 3 discusses IoT application domains and the need for reliable data transfer. In Sect. 4, we review related works focusing on adaptations of transport protocols for IoT and Low-Power and Lossy Networks (LLNs). Section 5 describes our SARQ protocol. Section 6 presents our experimental evaluation, including network performance metrics, experimental setup, results and analysis, and a discussion of our findings. Finally, in Sect. 7, we conclude the paper by summarizing our results and suggesting future work directions.

2   Standard IETF Transport Protocols

The most widely so far used transport protocols are the streamlined UDP and TCP. Other commonly used transport layer protocols include Datagram Congestion Control Protocol (DCCP), Stream Control Transmission Protocol (SCTP), and Quick UDP Interconnections (QUIC) [2]. In this Section, we describe the principal features of these protocols. We emphasize on their pros and cons in IoT environments. Figure 1 illustrates the IoT Transport Layer Protocols.

2.1   User Datagram Protocol

UDP is a connectionless non-reliable protocol. It supports a basic error control feature through a 16-bit checksum. It is recommended for real-time delay-sensitive applications. UDP does not provide any reliability whatsoever. If

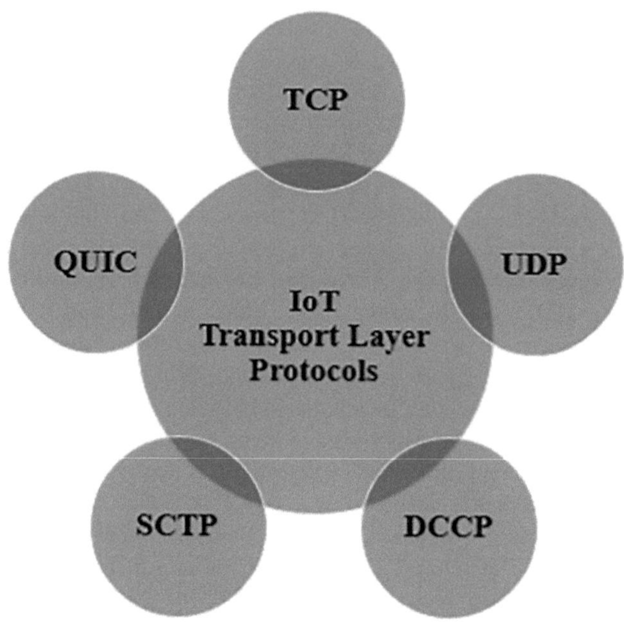

Fig. 1. IoT Transport Layer Protocols.

required, the upper layer protocol, primarily the application, may provide segment reordering and loss of data recovery. UDP has been adopted by one of the most popular IETF standards for IoT, namely the IPv6 low-power wireless personal area networks (6LowPAN for short with various choices of letter combinations), with very aggressive compression schemes.

2.2   Transmission Control Protocol

TCP is connection-oriented and a complex but reliable transport layer protocol. It uses cumulative acknowledgments of data segments, re-transmission, as well as window-based flow control. It implements implicit congestion control and checksum error detection. It combines several features. TCP uses as Round Trip Time (RTT) estimation mechanisms and a Retransmit Time Out (RTO) linked to the RTT. The RTO is used to determine whether a segment (or a set of segments) needs to be re-transmitted in the absence of acknowledgment within the RTO period. TCP cumulative acknowledgments allow a set of transmitted segments to be acknowledged by a single response. TCP also implements an exponentially increasing flow control window, expressed in several segments. This flow control mechanism, referred to as Slow Start, comes with various flavors, wherein the initial window size is set to one segment and is then duplicated at each RTT with a positive acknowledgment.

TCP also supports a Congestion Avoidance mechanism that limits the increments of the flow control window size in case of congestion. With this mechanism, the window size is incremented by one segment at each RTT during congestion periods. This is an implicit congestion control wherein the absence (or delay) of the acknowledgment of previous segments is assumed to be caused by a congested network.

In addition, TCP supports another flow control mechanism based on a window expressed in bytes, which sets the maximum number of bytes that can be accepted on a given TCP connection. The size of this window depends on the available resources, primarily memory, and is set by the network administrator. TCP connection setup operates in three phases referred to as the three-way handshake. TCP supports sequence numbers, expressed in bytes, which do not identify segments themselves, but rather the data fragment carried within the segments. The Initial Sequence Number (ISN) is randomly generated and is not set to zero to prevent zombie packets from emerging following inappropriate old connection closures. Other TCP mechanisms include Urgent Data delivery, Restart, and Push mechanisms. Urgent data means that TCP can interrupt the operating system by pointing to urgent information that must be treated without delay. The Reset feature gives TCP the ability to reinitialize the values of the sequence numbers of an active TCP connection. The Push mechanism refers to the ability to request a fragment transmission even though the amount of data in not large enough to fill a packet. This can be the case where only a few bytes need to be sent.

Furthermore, TCP requires at least a twenty-byte header, which is deemed too large for the Maximum Transfer Unit (MTU) defined by most IoT standards such as the IEEE 802.15.4 frame, which has a size of only 127 bytes. As such, several proposals have been made to perform TCP header compression. Back in 2010, a TCP header compressions for 6LowPAN was proposed [3], but with no further development.

2.3 Quick UDP Interconnections

Quick UDP Interconnections, or QUIC [3], is a transport layer protocol commonly used by most well-known Web browsers. It establishes a set of independent multiplexed connections between two endpoints over UDP. QUIC connections are composed of streams, which are ordered sequences of bytes. These latter can be bidirectional or unidirectional. QUIC uses a credit-based flow control scheme to limit the total number of bytes of all streams and the amount of data that can be exchanged over each stream. It also implements a handshake scheme that combines the negotiation of transport and cryptographic parameters. QUIC allows the immediate transmission of data at connection setup i.e. in 0-RTT. This aims to improve the performance, primarily latency, of connection-oriented web applications that currently use TCP but that may want to run on UDP. QUIC allows bandwidth estimation to avoid congestion. Congestion control is implemented at the connection endpoints. Optionally, QUIC also supports Forward Error Correction (FEC). QUIC was not originally designed for IoT. Nevertheless, since streamlined IoT standards such as 6LowPAN uses UDP, QUIC can be adapted to provide reliable transport for IoT applications. This has yet to be investigated. A recent study shows that a QUIC client requires about 60KB of flash, 4 KB of stack, and can retrieve 5 KB of data in 4.2 to 5.1 s over 0-RTT or 1-RTT connections, using less than 16 KB of heap memory, less than 4 KB of stack memory and less than 1.09 J of energy per transaction. These findings are rather interesting as they may pave the way towards implementing QUIC in IoT systems.

2.4 Datagram Congestion Control Protocol

Datagram Congestion Control Protocol (DCCP) (RFC 4340 and RFC 4336) is a message-oriented transport layer protocol that supports connection setup, teardown, Explicit Congestion Notification (ECN) (RFC 3168), and feature negotiation. It provides congestion-controlled unreliable datagram delivery. DCCP supports flow-based semantics like TCP but does not guarantee in-order fragment delivery i.e., these can be received out of sequence. Nonetheless, DCCP supports acknowledgments for segment delivery. Reliable acknowledgments delivery may be configured as needed. DCCP is suitable for applications that transfer large amounts of data with a tradeoff between delay and reliability such as streaming, video games, and VoIP.

In reality, such applications have often used TCP or UDP and implemented their congestion-control mechanisms, if any. In such applications, old data messages quickly become obsolete making their re-transmission irrelevant. DCCP supports different, but TCP-friendly congestion-control mechanisms. DCCP optionally uses 24 or 48-bit long sequence numbers, corresponding to a message ID, rather than byte sequence numbers as in TCP. It also supports a configurable checksum-based error control. DCCP is not optimized for constrained devices. Its usage to deliver multimedia streams in IoT is needed and has yet to be investigated. Future IoT applications may include video and real-time multimedia delivery with embedded cameras and video/audio sensors that can be used in firefighting, military reconnaissance, health care (COVID-19 patient tracking for instance), remote site monitoring, etc.

2.5 Stream Control Transmission Protocol

SCTP (RFC 4960) is a reliable, in-sequence, message-oriented transport layer protocol. SCTP uses the same flow and congestion control mechanisms as TCP, with slightly different implementations. SCTP uses a 12-byte header and a secured four-way handshake procedure to establish an association of data streams. SCTP supports multi-homing and redundant paths between the same endpoints to increase resilience and reliability. The congestion control applies to the association of data streams, not to an individual stream. For instance, stream association multi-homing allows the setup of a voice call on one stream, the related signaling on another stream, and video transfer on a third stream, simultaneously between two endpoints. In such cases, if errors occur in one stream, this will not impact the data transfer of the other streams. The feasibility of SCTP in IoT has yet to be demonstrated. In [4], the authors claim that SCTP is a valid candidate for industrial IoT scenarios in a fog-computing environment. Further, ref. [5] claims that switching between TCP and SCTP according to the network traffic could improve network throughput and reduce packet loss rate. The authors propose a dynamic multipath handover method for SCTP, which selects the transmission path according to the packet error rate and the packet re-transmission ratio in the senders' buffer.

3   IoT Applications Domain and the Need for Reliable Data Transfer

This section looks at the wide range of IoT applications and highlights the important need for reliable data transfer in these connected systems.

3.1   IoT Applications Domain

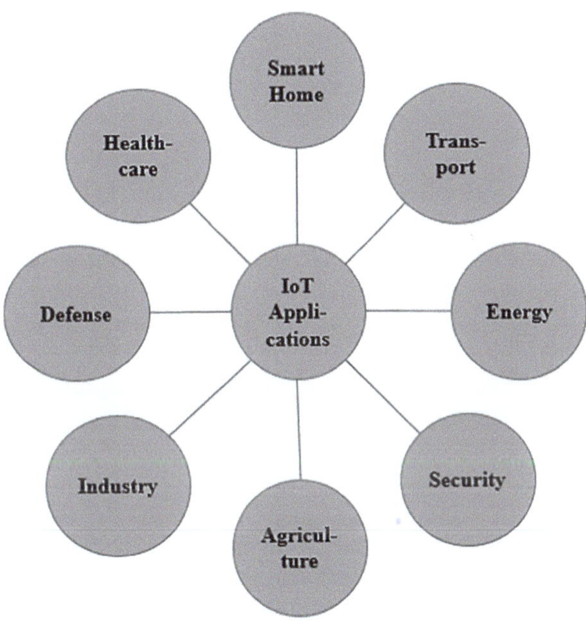

Fig. 2. IoT Applications Domain.

The Internet of Things (IoT) has applications spanning a wide range of domains, each leveraging connectivity and data exchange to enhance efficiency, safety, and user experience. In healthcare, IoT enables remote monitoring and telemedicine through wearable devices and smart medical equipment; in smart homes, it improves convenience and security via interconnected devices for automation and energy management; in industrial settings, IoT focuses on predictive maintenance, supply chain optimization, and smart manufacturing; in smart cities, it enhances urban management and quality of life through traffic optimization, waste management, and public safety systems; in agriculture, IoT transforms precision farming with smart greenhouses, soil monitoring, and livestock tracking; in transportation, it improves safety and efficiency with connected vehicles, fleet management, and smart parking solutions; and in defense, IoT enhances operational efficiency and situational awareness through surveillance systems, equipment management, and soldier health monitoring. Figure 2 illustrates the IoT applications domain [6].

3.2 Importance of Reliable Transfer Protocols

The risk of severe consequences from data loss or corruption in the aforementioned IoT domains highlights the importance of reliable data transfer protocols. These protocols are crucial for maintaining data integrity and security in IoT networks, ensuring accurate transmission, error handling, and providing authentication and encryption. Researchers [7] explore their reliability mechanisms, emphasizing their critical role in IoT systems. The following Section overviews key protocols currently in use.

4 Related Work

The evolution of transport protocols for Low-power and Lossy Networks (LLNs) and Internet of Things (IoT) environments has been driven by the unique challenges these networks pose, such as limited energy resources, lossy links, and constrained computational capabilities. This section discusses various adaptations of TCP and UDP for IoT, highlighting the need for protocols that can effectively manage the trade-offs between reliability and resource efficiency. While TCP was initially designed in the 1980s for limited-resource computers, its adaptations for modern IoT systems still present challenges in LLN contexts. The IETF has established working groups like Light-Weight Implementation Guidance (LWIG), Constrained RESTful Environments (CoRE), and TCP Maintenance and Minor Extensions (TCPM) [8] to address these evolving needs. However, despite various adaptations of TCP and UDP for IoT, many implementations remain inadequate for LLNs. For instance, implementations such as μIP [9], lwIP [9], and RIOT (GNRC TCP) [10] cater to devices with 8- to 32-bit processors but often struggle with the inherent limitations of LLNs. μIP, while simple, has limited TCP functions and a stop-and-wait flow control mechanism, which can lead to poor performance on unreliable links. Similarly, lwIP supports advanced features but lacks extensive testing in congestion scenarios, potentially compromising reliability under heavy load. GNRC TCP, designed for Class 1 devices, is resource-limited, rendering it unsuitable for more demanding applications. BLIP offers basic congestion control but is constrained by its single Maximum Segment Size (MSS) window and constant Retransmission Timeout (RTO), reducing its adaptability. FreeRTOS TCP [11], while balancing memory allocation and performance, may slow down data transmission in its flexible memory usage mode. μC/OS [12] TCP employs a deterministic scheduler for faster processing but sacrifices flexibility in application design. TCPlp [13], based on FreeBSD, is designed for resource-constrained IoT hardware but faces challenges with header compression and may not be implementable on devices with extremely limited memory. These limitations highlight the inadequacy of traditional transport protocols for the specific demands of LLNs, necessitating the development of more suitable solutions.

On the other hand, UDP is considered a lightweight, connectionless protocol commonly used in IoT networks due to its low overhead and suitability for low-latency communications. However, its lack of reliability, congestion control, and standardized security can be problematic for IoT applications. To address these issues, researchers [14] have proposed modified versions like UDP-Lite, which allows partial checksum coverage, enabling the delivery of partially damaged packets. This can reduce energy consumption as partially damaged packets may still be useful in certain applications. Despite its advantages, UDP-Lite also suffers from a lack of congestion control, which can lead to higher packet drops in congested networks, negatively impacting reliability. This is particularly critical in environments requiring timely and accurate data transmission, such as industrial automation and healthcare monitoring. Overall, the limitations of UDP and its adaptations highlight their inadequacy for LLNs, where packet loss and transmission delays can severely affect application performance. The absence of mechanisms for ensuring data integrity and managing network congestion makes these protocols less suitable for mission-critical IoT applications that demand reliable communication.

The ongoing evolution of transport protocols for LLNs reflects the critical need for solutions that can effectively balance reliability and resource constraints in IoT environments. As the number of IoT devices continues to grow, the development of lightweight and reliable transport protocols will be essential to support the diverse range of applications that rely on these networks.

5   SARQ Protocol

The choice between UDP and TCP for IoT applications depends on specific needs, such as reliability and security versus low latency and battery life. To meet these diverse requirements, we developed a new transport protocol called SARQ (Simple ARQ Protocol). SARQ addresses the limitations of existing protocols by using acknowledgments and retransmission mechanisms to ensure reliable data delivery. Designed specifically for IoT challenges, SARQ enhances reliability, efficiency, and adaptability with a lightweight design that minimizes overhead, making it suitable for resource-constrained devices. Additionally, SARQ's flexible architecture allows customization for various IoT use cases, from low-power sensor networks to critical industrial applications. Moreover, SARQ is particularly effective for Low-Power and Lossy Networks (LLNs), as it addresses challenges noted in this study [15] such as Round-Trip Delay Time (RTT) and Packet Loss

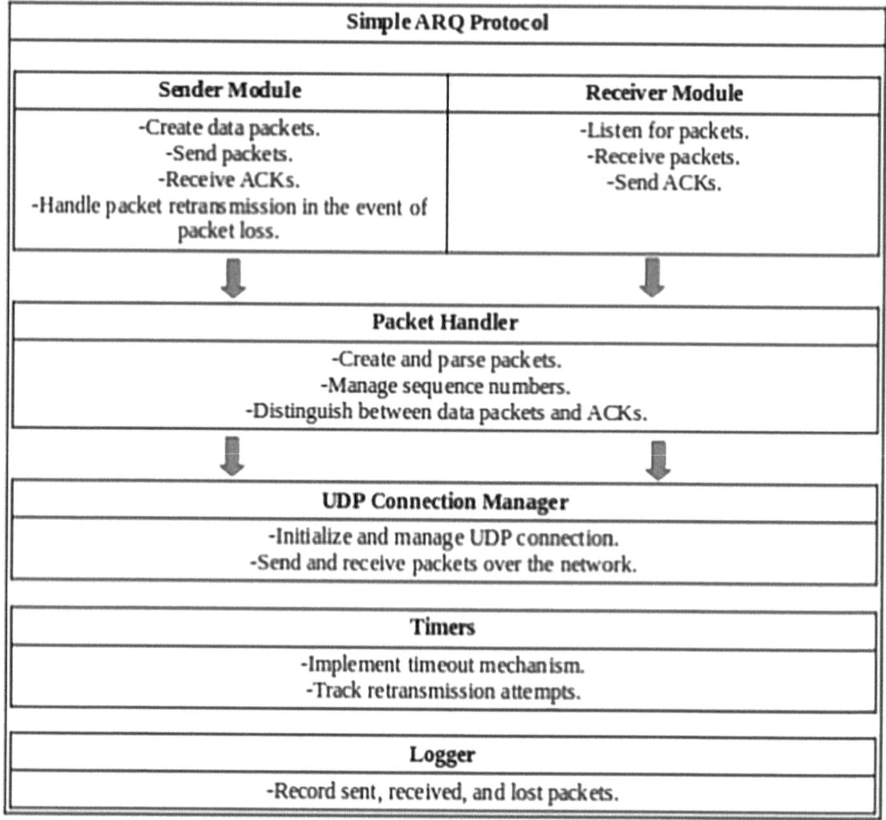

Fig. 3. Architecture of Simple ARQ Protocol.

Ratio (PLR) that affect LLN performance. Key features of SARQ include an adaptive acknowledgment mechanism that employs selective acknowledgments to reduce unnecessary retransmissions, a resource-optimized design with a minimal header size of only 2 bytes compared to TCP's 20 bytes when no options are included, and IoT-specific optimizations like built-in support for sleep modes and adaptive retransmission timing based on network conditions. These characteristics make SARQ a robust solution for IoT applications, providing higher reliability than UDP while outperforming TCP in energy consumption and overall efficiency. Figure 3 illustrates the architecture of Simple ARQ Protocol.

6   Experimental Evaluation

In this section, we provide a comprehensive overview of the experimental evaluation conducted to assess the performance of TCP, UDP, and SARQ protocols. The evaluation focuses on key network performance metrics, specifically the

Packet Delivery Ratio (PDR) and Energy Consumption (EC), under varying network conditions influenced by the number of nodes.

6.1   Network Performance Metrics

The chosen metrics for this evaluation are critical in understanding how different protocols behave in a network environment.

- **Packet Delivery Ratio (PDR):** This metric is calculated as [16]:

$$\text{PDR} = \frac{\text{Number of packets received}}{\text{Number of packets sent}} \times 100\% \tag{1}$$

  PDR provides insight into the reliability and efficiency of data transmission.
- **Energy Consumption (EC):** This metric measures the amount of energy used by the network nodes during operation. It can be expressed as [17]:

$$\text{EC} = \sum_{i=1}^{n} E_i \tag{2}$$

Where E_i is the energy consumed by node i, and n is the total number of nodes in the network, which is 100 nodes. This metric helps evaluate the energy efficiency of the network.

It is important to note that these protocols exhibit different performance characteristics as the number of nodes in the network changes.

6.2   Experimental Setup

The experimental setup was implemented using the Contiki-NG platform and the primary objective of this investigation is to evaluate the performance of TCP, UDP, and SARQ protocols under specific network conditions, with a focus on varying the number of nodes. Table 1 presents the key parameters used in our simulation setup.

Table 1. Simulation Parameters

Parameter	Value	Unit
Number of Server nodes	1	Node
Number of client nodes	3–15 (step 3)	Nodes
Packet Size	10	Bytes
Number of Packets Sent	100	Packets
Protocols	TCP, UDP, SARQ	–
Mobility Model	Random Waypoint	–
Communication Type	Unicast	–

Our simulation environment is designed to evaluate the performance of the protocols under varying network densities. We adjust the number of client nodes from 3 to 15 in increments of 3, while maintaining a single server node due to the RAM size constraints of the Z1 mote in Contiki-NG. As a result, the maximum number of client nodes is limited to 15. Each client node is set up to send 100 packets, with each packet having a size of 10 bytes.

This setup allows us to observe how the protocols behave as the network becomes more complex and congested. The Random Waypoint mobility model [18] is employed to simulate realistic movement patterns of nodes within the network. However, this model is widely used in ad-hoc network simulations and provides a good representation of unpredictable node movement. All communications in our simulation are unicast, meaning data is sent from a single sender to a single receiver. This choice allows us to evaluate the protocols' performance in direct, point-to-point communications within the network.

6.3   Results and Analysis

This part presents the results of our simulations and provides an in-depth analysis of the performance of TCP, UDP, and SARQ protocols under varying network conditions.

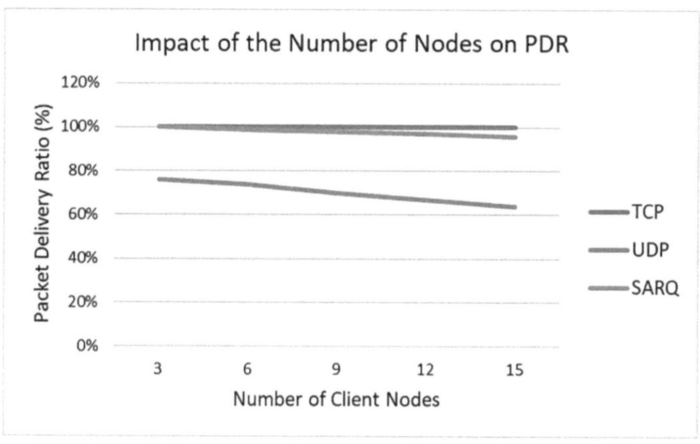

Fig. 4. Impact of the Number of Nodes on PDR.

Packet Delivery Ratio (PDR) Analysis: Figure 4 shows that TCP maintains a consistently high PDR, with a constant PDR of 100% across all node counts. However, UDP starts with a lower PDR than TCP, around 76% with 3 nodes and declines gradually with the increase in the number of nodes; at 15 nodes, UDP's PDR drops to about 64%. In contrast, we find that SARQ stays close to 100% across all node counts. It outperforms UDP in terms of consistency. With 3 nodes, SARQ achieves a PDR of 100%, and even at the highest node count of 15, its PDR remains high at 96%.

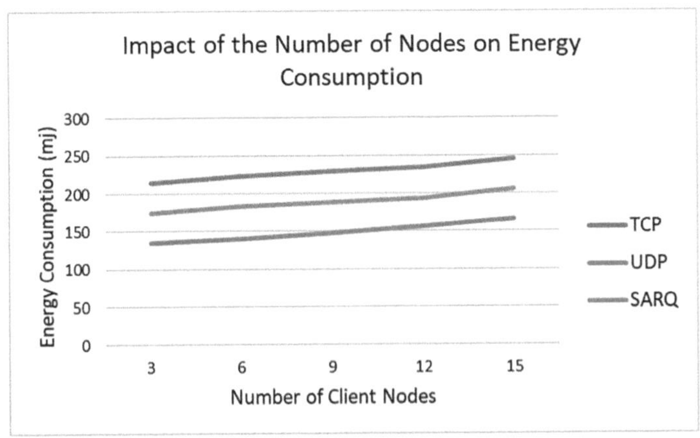

Fig. 5. Impact of the Number of Nodes on Energy Consumption.

Energy Consumption (EC) Analysis: Figure 5 illustrates that for all three protocols (TCP, UDP, and SARQ), the energy consumption increases as the number of client nodes increases from 3 to 15. However, the TCP protocol consistently shows the highest energy consumption across all node counts. It starts at about 214 mJ for 3 nodes and increases to about 245 mJ for 15 nodes. In contrast, UDP protocol demonstrates the lowest energy consumption among the three protocols. It starts at approximately 134 mJ for 3 nodes and increases to about 165 mJ for 15 nodes. On the other hand, we find that SARQ's energy consumption falls between TCP and UDP. It begins around 174 mJ for 3 nodes and increases to about 205 mJ for 15 nodes. These results reveal that all protocols show increased energy consumption with more nodes. In addition, we observe that SARQ's performance is consistent and falls between the performance of TCP and UDP.

6.4   Discussion

If we compare the PDR analysis from the graph of Fig. 4 with the graph of the energy consumption in Fig. 5, we can see a trade-off between energy consumption and packet delivery ratio. Moreover, we observe that TCP and SARQ are more reliable for packet delivery compared to UDP. UDP's performance degrades more significantly with increased network size. In addition, these results show also that TCP and SARQ consume more energy but offer better PDR, while UDP is more energy-efficient but has lower PDR. Thus, we can conclude that SARQ and TCP protocols are more suitable for applications requiring high reliability in packet delivery, especially in larger networks. UDP might be preferred in scenarios where some packet loss is acceptable, and lower overhead is desired.

7   Conclusion

In this paper, we illustrated the effectiveness of the Simple ARQ (SARQ) protocol in attaining reliable and efficient communication, with low energy consumption and high PDR, regardless size of the LLN. The SARQ protocol represents an effective alternative to UDP and TCP and a reasonable compromise between reliability and energy efficiency. This makes it a suitable option for scenarios where both low energy consumption and high PDR are essential at the transport layer.

In addition, the simplicity and robustness of SARQ make it an attractive choice for IoT applications that require reliable data transfer without the overhead of more complex protocols. Thus, LLN designers may prefer the SARQ protocol in applications that require a balance between energy usage and reliable data transfer.

As a continuation of this work, we envision the development of advanced features for the SARQ protocol that may enhance its adaptability and scalability in diverse IoT environments. This includes exploring integration with emerging technologies, such as machine learning and edge computing, to further enhance transport layer energy efficiency and reliability.

References

1. Chahed, M., Meddeb, A., Boufaied, A.: Simple ARQ protocol for reliable transport in LowPANs. In: The ACS/IEEE 21st International Conference on Computer Systems and Applications (AICCSA) (2024)
2. Polese, M., Chiariotti, F., Bonetto, E., Rigotto, F., Zanella, A., Zorzi, M.: A survey on recent advances in transport layer protocols. IEEE Commun. Surv. Tutorials **21**(4), (2019)
3. Iyengar, J., Thomson, M.: QUIC: a UDP-based multiplexed and secure transport. Internet Engineering Task Force, RFC 9000 (2020)
4. Wiss, T., Forsström, S.: Feasibility and performance evaluation of SCTP for the industrial internet of things. In: IECON 2017 - 43rd Annual Conference of the IEEE Industrial Electronics Society (2017)
5. Sun, W., Yu, S., Xing, Y., Qin, Z.: Parallel transmission of distributed sensor based on SCTP and TCP for heterogeneous wireless networks in IoT. Sensors **19**(9), 2005 (2019)
6. Rehman, H.U., Asif, M., Ahmad, M.: Future applications and research challenges of IoT. In: IEEE International Conference on Internet of Things (2017)
7. Pillai, S.E.V.S., Gopal, S.K.: Performance evaluation of transport layer protocols in mobile networks. In: IEEE 13th International Conference on Communication Systems and Network Technologies (CSNT) (2024)

8. Gomez, C., Arcia-Moret, A., Crowcroft, J.: TCP in the internet of things: from ostracism to prominence. IEEE Internet Comput. **22**(1), 29–37 (2018)
9. Dunkels, A.: Full TCP/IP for 8-Bit architectures. In: Proceedings of the 1st International Conference on Mobile Systems, Applications and Services (MobiSys 2003), pp. 85–98 (2003)
10. Baccelli, E., et al.: RIOT: an open source operating system for low-end embedded devices in the IoT. IEEE Internet Things J. **5**(6), 4428–4440 (2018)
11. Guan, F., Peng, L., Perneel, L., Timmerman, M.: Open source FreeRTOS as a case study in real-time operating system evolution. J. Syst. Softw. **118**, 19–35 (2016)
12. Labrosse, J.J., Torres, F.: The Real-Time Kernel and the NXP LPC1700. Micrium Press (2010)
13. Forouzan, B.A., Fegan, S.C.: TCP/IP Protocol Suite. McGraw-Hill Higher Education (2002)
14. Chai, L., Reine, R.: Performance of UDP-Lite for IoT network. In: IOP Conference Series: Materials Science and Engineering, vol. 495, no. 1 (2019)
15. Cai, L.Z., Zuhairi, M.F.: Performance evaluation of low-power and lossy networks. In: Proceedings of the 12th International Conference on Ubiquitous Information Management and Communication (IMCOM 2018) (2018)
16. Haglan, H.M., et al.: Analyzing the impact of the number of nodes on the performance of the routing protocols in MANET environment. Bull. Electr. Eng. Inf. **9**(6), 2516–2527 (2020)
17. Ramli, A.F., Shabry, M.I., Abu, M.A., Basarudin, H.: A study on the impact of nodes density on the energy consumption of LoRa. Int. J. Interact. Mob. Technol. **15**(7), (2021)
18. Bettstetter, C., Wagner, C.: The spatial node distribution of the random waypoint mobility model. In: German Workshop on Mobile Ad-Hoc Networks (WMAN) (2002)

Evaluating DMM Based Handover Solutions Towards Serving uRLLc in Heterogeneous Networks

Krati Rastogi[ID], K. B. Megha, Shankar K. Ghosh[✉][ID], and Rajeev K. Singh[ID]

Department of Computer Science and Engineering, Shiv Nadar Institution of Eminence, Delhi, NCR 201314, India
kr777@snu.edu.in, mk197@snu.edu.in, shankar.ghosh@snu.edu.in,
rajeev.kumar@snu.edu.in

Abstract. Distributed mobility management (DMM) has emerged as a promising solution to manage mobility in heterogeneous networks consisting of both Long term evolution advanced (LTE-A) and New radio (NR) systems. While switching from one kind of access network to another, satisfying the quality of service requirement for ultra reliable low latency communication (uRLLc) is particularly challenging. This is due to the delay introduced by the handover algorithms operating from Layer 2 (L2) and Layer 3 (L3). Minimum L2 handover latency in NR system is known to be 50 ms, which is higher than the permissible range for uRLLc services. To reduce handover latency, different L2 (e.g., semisoft handover) and L3 (IP Preregistration) enhancements have been proposed. However, performance analysis of DMM protocol in conjunction with these enhancements is quiet limited in the existing literature. Moreover the existing works on DMM do not focus on the delay and reliability requirements of uRLLc applications. In this work, through analysis and simulation, effectiveness of different DMM based handover solutions in minimizing handover latency and packet loss have been investigated. Our analysis show that DMM with semisoft handover at L2 and IP preregistration at L3 can reduce the handover latency upto 7 ms, and therefore reducing the packet loss per handover upto 1.5 packets for uRLLc services.

Keywords: Distributed mobility management (DMM) · Ultra reliable low latency communication (uRLLc) · handover latency · Handover packet loss · Heterogeneous network

1 Introduction

One of the major goals in fifth-generation (5G) mobile network is to satisfy the quality of service requirements for ultra-reliable low-latency communication (uRLLc) services [1]. Ideally, uRLLc services require ultra-low latency (<1 ms) and exceptionally high reliability ($>99.999\%$) [2]. Examples of uRLLc services

S. Li et al. (Eds.): BROADNETS 2024, LNICST 674, pp. 162–176, 2026.
https://doi.org/10.1007/978-3-032-14350-1_12

include time-sensitive applications such as industrial automation, autonomous vehicles and remote surgery. The reliability of uRLLc is critically dependent on delay and packet loss.

In this work, we particularly focus on non standalone (NSA) deployment [3] of 5G network, which consists of both Long term evolution advances (LTE-A) and New radio (NR) base stations. Such heterogeneous nature of 5G networks imposes significant challenges in handover management, the process of transferring an ongoing session of a user equipment (UE) from one type of base station to another (e.g., LTE-A to NR) [4]. To ensure minimized delay and packet loss, designing efficient handover algorithms for heterogeneous networks (HetNet) are extremely important. Higher handover latency causes higher packet loss in downlink, leading to reduced reliability which is not acceptable for uRLLc services.

In HetNet, the handover mechanisms across different kinds of access networks involve operations at both Layer 2 (L2) and Layer 3 (L3). At L2, handover is initiated based on *A3 condition* [6], i.e., reference signal received power (RSRP) from the neighboring network surpasses the RSRP from the serving network by a threshold called hysteresis (Hys) for time-to-trigger (TTT) period of time. Once the L2 handover is successful, L3 handover is initiated. The L3 handover is associated with IP connectivity and routing. Distributed mobility management (DMM) has evolved as a promising solution to handle IP connectivity at L3 in 5G systems [7]. DMM reduces latency by placing mobility anchors closer to the UE, thus enabling reduced signaling overhead and latency [8,9].

To support uRLLc services, the cumulative handover latency (including both L2 and L3) has to be less than 1 ms [1]. On the other hand, the minimum L2 handover latency in NR system is known to be around 50 ms [2]. To reduce handover latency, different enhancements at L2 and L3 have been proposed. For example, the *semisoft* handover (at L2) [9] allows the UE to remain connected with both serving and target access networks simultaneously during the handover process, thereby reducing handover latency [8]. The *IP preregistration* technique (at L3) [7] enables the UE to configure and obtain IP address from the target network while connected with the serving network itself, thereby reducing the time needed for IP configuration, context transfer and routing updates from handover latency. **The effectiveness of these techniques have not been investigated in conjunction with DMM towards minimizing handover latency.**

DMM offers significant advantages in terms of handover latency and signalling overhead in contrast to Centralized mobility management schemes [7], which imposes significant delay due to redirection of traffic through the anchor points. Software defined networking (SDN) has gained attention for optimizing DMM through load-balanced handover decisions, predictive handovers and intelligent cell selection [10]. However, challenges remain in efficient new access point selection and predictive handover triggering. The Named Data Networking [11] uses anchor-based and anchor-less approaches in order to minimize packet loss and delay during handover. However, this approach suffer from limitations in latency, scalability and resource utilization. In [12], the Zero handover failure with unforced and automatic time-to-execute scaling (ZEUS) algorithm has been proposed to minimize handover failure by eliminating the need for a fixed TTT and enabling dynamic handover decisions. In [2], a conditional handover algorithm has been proposed to minimize mobility interruption time and handover failure rate for uRLLc services. In these existing works, [10,11] focuses on L3 handover only, whereas [12] and [2] focuses on only L2 handovers. Therefore these algorithms are not directly applicable to the considered HetNet scenario which involves both L2 and L3. In [5], analytic model to evaluate handover packet loss in DMM has been proposed and further validated assuming IEEE 802.11 as underlying access technology. In [7], analytic model to evaluate handover latency and packet loss in DMM have been proposed assuming LTE-A as underlying radio access technology. These existing works [5,7] focus on specific access technology and therefore are not directly applicable to the considered HetNet scenario.

In this work, our *objective* is to investigate the effectiveness of different DMM-based handover solutions towards minimizing handover latency in HetNet scenario. A semi-analytic framework has been proposed to investigate four distinct DMM based handover options: DMM (at L3) + A3 (at L2), DMM with IP pre-registration (at L3) + A3 handover (at L2), DMM (at L3) + semisoft handover (at L2) and DMM with IP preregistration (at L3) + semisoft handover (at L2). The semi-analytic framework evaluates handover latency and handover packet loss as a function of underlying L2 and L3 handover mechanisms. We assume that the uRLLc UEs generate small bursts of data packets following the FTP3 model [15]. Our *contributions* are summarized below:

- Considering HetNet scenario, analytic model have been developed to characterize handover latency and handover packet loss for four possible DMM based handover options, i.e., DMM (at L3) + A3 (at L2), DMM with IP preregistration (at L3) + A3 handover (at L2), DMM (at L3) + semisoft (at L2), DMM with IP preregistration (at L3) + semisoft (at L2). The proposed analytic model considers the effect of handover failure.
- Through system level simulation, handover failure probability (p) has been evaluated for LTE-A $\rightarrow$ NR and NR $\rightarrow$ LTE-A handovers considering UE velocity, UE mobility pattern and L2 handover parameters such as TTT and Hys. Then, p has been given as input to the equations characterizing handover latency and handover packet loss.

Our analysis show that DMM with IP Preregistration (at L3) and semisoft (at L2) exhibits superior performance compared to the other handover strategies. This particular combination reduces the handover latency to 7 ms (approx.), while the minimum L2 handover latency in NR systems is known to be 50 ms. **Accordingly, it has been shown that the packet loss per handover is** 1.54 **for uRLLc services (attained at UE velocity** 16.8 **m/s).**

The rest of the manuscript is organized as follows: In Sect. 2, the considered system model has been described. In Sect. 3, analytic models to evaluate different DMM based handover options have been presented. In Sect. 4, semi-analytic expression for handover latency and packet loss have been derived for different

DMM based handover solutions. Both analytic and simulation results have been presented and discussed in Sect. 5. Finally, Sect. 6 concludes the work. Important abbreviations are summarized in Table 1.

Table 1. Table of abbreviations

Abbreviation	Description
LTE	Long Term Evolution
NR	New Radio
HetNet	Heterogeneous Network
DMM	Distributed Mobility Management
uRLLc	Ultra-Reliable Low-Latency Communication
5G	Fifth Generation
UE	User Equipment
MAG	Mobile Access Gateway
eNB	Evolved Node B
gNB	Next-Generation Node B
LMA	Local Mobility Anchor
L2	Layer 2
L3	Layer 3
CN	Core Network
AMF	Access and mobility management function
CoA	Care-of-address
TTT	Time-to-trigger
Hys	Hysteresis
RSRP	Reference Signal Received Power

2 System Model

We consider a HetNet scenario consisting of N LTE-A evolved node Bs (eNBs) and M New radio next generation node Bs (gNBs), providing ubiquitous network coverage to U UEs. The eNBs, gNBs and UEs are indexed using the sets of integers $\mathcal{N} = \{1, 2 \cdots N\}$, $\mathcal{M} = \{1, 2 \cdots M\}$ and $\mathcal{U} = \{1, 2 \cdots U\}$ respectively. The LTE eNBs and NR gNBs are providing ubiquitous coverage to the UEs. We assume that all eNBs are connected to LMA 1 and all gNBs are connected to LMA 2. Handovers within LMAs (LTE-A $\rightarrow$ LTE-A and NR $\rightarrow$ NR handovers) involve only L2, whereas handovers between LMA 1 and LMA 2 (LTE-A $\rightarrow$ NR and NR $\rightarrow$ LTE-A handovers) involve both L2 and L3 (depicted in Fig. 1).

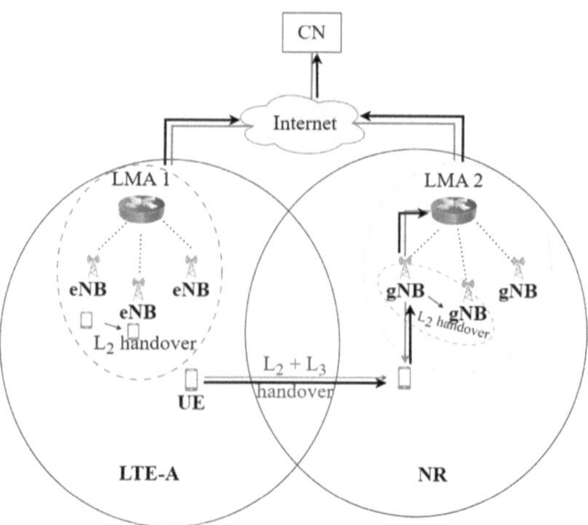

Fig. 1. Considered HetNet scenario.

Power received at UE i from gNB c at time t is measured as follows [13]:

$$P_{ci}^r(t) = |h_{ci}\sqrt{d_{ci}^{-\alpha}}|^2 P_c^T,\tag{1}$$

where P_c^T denotes power transmitted by the gNB c, d_{ci} denotes the distance between the UE i and the gNB c, h_{ci} is channel coefficient vector modeled using a complex Gaussian distribution. Here the severity of fading is determined by the Rician factor (k) with mean $\mu = \sqrt{\frac{k(k+1)}{2}}$ and variance $\sigma = \sqrt{\frac{(k+1)}{2}}$. Here k = 0 corresponds to Rayleigh fading where no dominant line-of-sight path is present between the UE i and gNB c. We assume that eNBs and gNBs are connected via non-ideal X2 interface, facilitating data forwarding between LTE-A and NR. Additionally, all eNBs and gNBs are connected to the core network (CN) via the Internet.

In our considered scenario, there are two Local mobility anchors namely LMA 1 and LMA 2. Local mobility anchors are mobile access gateways (MAGs) which control UE mobility by managing data forwarding and control signalling during handovers. The MAGs assist in distributing mobility management tasks and thereby reducing latency and signalling overhead.

The LTE-A $\rightarrow$ NR handover process is triggered based on the A3 event i.e., RSRP from NR is greater than RSRP from LTE-A by a Hys amount for a TTT period of time [6], i.e.,

$$\text{RSRP}_{\text{NR}}(t) > \text{RSRP}_{\text{LTE}}(t) + \text{Hys}\tag{2}$$

$\forall t \in [t_0, t_0 + \text{TTT}]$. Here t_0 is the starting time when the RSRP condition is first met.

3   DMM Based Handover Options

In this section, we briefly describe the steps of different DMM based handover solutions for LTE-NR HetNet (depicted in Fig. 2).

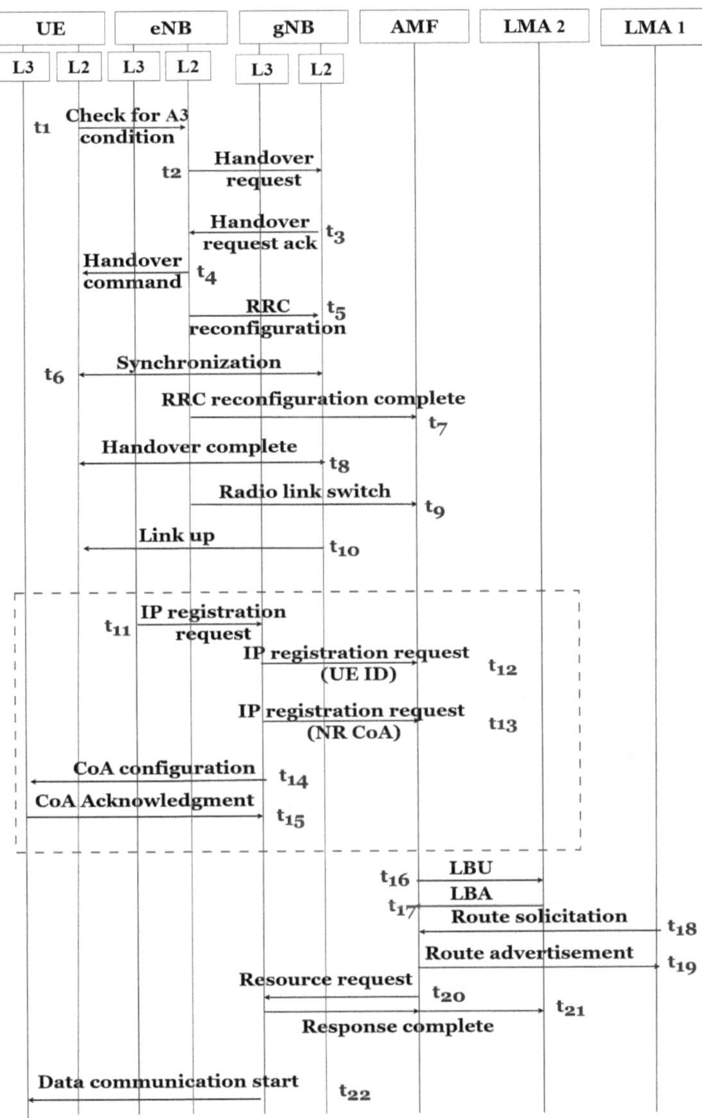

Fig. 2. Signalling diagram of DMM based handover mechanism in HetNet. Using IP preregistration, the duration $t_{15} - t_{11}$ (shown in dotted box) can be eliminated.

3.1   DMM (at L3) + A3 (at L2)

This DMM-based handover solution consists of four phases namely L2 handover, IP configuration and path switch. The L2 handover begins as soon as the A3 condition is satisfied at time t_1. Afterwards a handover request is sent from eNB to gNB at t_2, and the eNB receive handover request acknowledgement at time t_3. The handover command is sent by the eNB to UE at time t_4. RRC connection reconfiguration is initiated at t_5 by the gNB and completed at t_7, ensuring further synchronization. The UE performs the L2 radio link switch at t_9, and the L2 handover process is completed at t_{10}. The next phase is IP configuration (t_{15} - t_{11}). The eNB sends an IP registration request to gNB at t_{11}. Subsequently, the gNB informs the UE ID and the care-of-address (CoA) to the access and mobility management function (AMF) at t_{12} and t_{13} respectively. The AMF is responsible for managing user registration, mobility, session management and authentication. Further, the gNB informs the configured CoA to the UE during $t_{15} - t_{14}$. The last phase is path switch (t_{22} - t_{16}). This phase involves signalling between the AMF, LMA 1 and LMA 2 for local binding updates (t_{17}-t_{16}), route solicitation and advertisement (t_{19}-t_{18}), resource requests and responses (t_{21}-t_{20}) and resuming data communication in down-link (at t_{22}). Therefore, the total handover latency in this handover option is t_{22}-t_1.

3.2   DMM with IP Preregistration (at L3) + A3 Handover (at L2)

In this handover option, delay associated with IP configuration (t_{15} - t_{11}) is eliminated, because the IP address to be used at gNB is configured before the L2 handover is started. Therefore, the total handover latency in this option is (t_{22}-t_1)- (t_{15}-t_{11}).

3.3   DMM (at L3) + Semisoft (at L2)

In this handover option, the L2 handover latency (t_{10}-t_1) is not present. This is because, the semisoft handover enables the UE to remain connected with the eNB and gNB simultaneously. During handover, the L2 handover signalling is performed using eNB while data is received from gNB. Accordingly, total handover latency in this handover option is $t_{22} - t_{11}$.

3.4   DMM with IP Preregistration (at L3) + Semisoft (at L2)

In this handover option, IP configuration delay is eliminated by the IP preregistration technique, whereas the L2 handover latency is eliminated by the semisoft handover. Accordingly, the total handover latency is t_{22}-t_{16}.

4   Performance Analysis

In this section, semi-analytic models have been developed to characterize handover latency and handover packet loss for all possible DMM based handover options. In the subsequent subsection, first we derive the expressions for handover latency and handover packet loss. In both of the expressions, handover failure probability (p) has been given as input. Here p has been computed using system level simulation considering UE velocity, eNB/gNB configuration and T_{L2} handover parameters such as Hys and TTT. Schematic representation of the proposed semi-analytic model has been shown in Fig. 3. Important parameters used in this study is summarized in Table 2.

Table 2. Parameter table

Notation	Description
T_{HO}	Total handover latency
T_{L2}	Layer 2 handover latency
T_{A3cond}	Time to trigger for A3 event
T_{HOreq}	Time to send handover request
T_{HOack}	Time to acknowledge handover request
T_{HOcmd}	Time to send handover command
T_{RRC}	Time to RRC connection reconfiguration
$T_{RRCcomp}$	Time to confirm RRC connection reconfiguration
T_{HOcomp}	Time to complete handover process
T_{linkup}	Time to establish new radio link
T_{RLS}	Time required for radio link setup
T_{IPreg}	Time required for IP registration
$T_{CoAconfig}$	Time required for CoA configuration
T_{CoAack}	Time to receive CoA acknowledgment
T_{LBU}	Time to send LBU
T_{LBA}	Time to receive LBA
T_{RS}	Time required for route setup
T_{route}	Time for routing update
λ	Mean packet arrival rate
P_d	Size of data packet size
p	Handover failure probability

4.1 Modelling Handover Latency

Handover latency is defined as the time between beginning of T_{L2} handover at the eNB and resuming data communication with gNB. Handover packet loss is defined as the number of packets send to the UE during handover process in down-link and thereby lost.

Preliminary Derivations: The total handover latency in the DMM-based handover procedure for HetNet comprises of both L2 and L3 components. The L2 handover comprises of signalling delays for exchanging measurement report to evaluate A3 condition, handover request, handover acknowledgment, handover command, RRC reconfiguration and link switch. Thus, the total time T_{L2} required for all of the steps (t_{10}-t_1 in Fig. 2) is computed as:

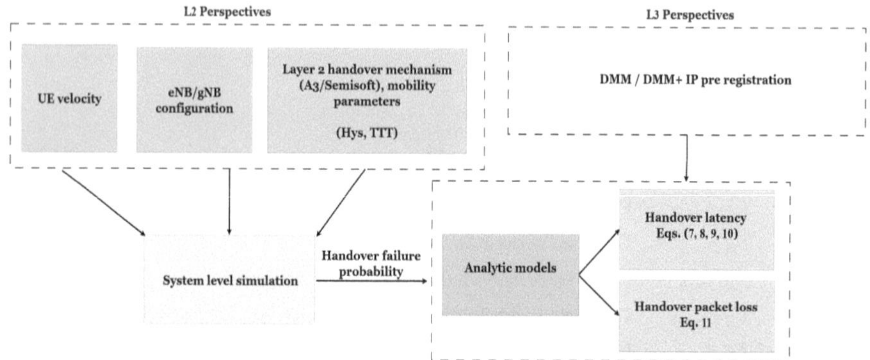

Fig. 3. Schematic representation of the proposed semi-analytic model.

Here T_{A3cond} denotes the TTT for the A3 event, T_{HOreq} is the time to send the handover request, T_{HOack} is the time for the gNB to acknowledge the handover request, T_{HOcmd} is the time for the eNB to send the handover command, T_{RRC} denotes the time for the RRC signalling exchange, $T_{RRCcomp}$ is the time required to receive the RRC reconfiguration complete message, T_{HOcomp} is the time required to confirm handover complete, T_{RLS} is the time for the radio link switch and T_{linkup} is the time required to establish the radio link with gNB.

The L3 handover latency comprises of IP registration and CoA configuration (t_{15} to t_{11} in Fig. 2). Accordingly, the L3 handover latency T_{L3} is computed as:

$$T_{L3} = T_{IPreg} + T_{CoAconfig} + T_{CoAack}, \qquad (3)$$

where T_{IPreg} denotes the time to send the IP registration request to the AMF, $T_{CoAconfig}$ is the time required for the CoA configuration, T_{CoAack} is the time to receive the CoA acknowledgement.

Further, the DMM-specific procedures for path switch involve binding information exchange and path switching (t_{22}-t_{16} in Fig. 2). Accordingly, the delay associated with DMM signalling can be computed as:

$$T_{DMM} = T_{LBU} + T_{LBA} + T_{RS} + T_{route} \qquad (4)$$
$$+ T_{resreq} + T_{rescomp} + T_{Dcommstart},$$

where T_{LBU} denotes the time to send Local binding update, T_{LBA} is the time required to receive Local binding acknowledgment at the AMF, T_{RS} is the time required for route solicitation, T_{route} is the time required for route solicitation and advertisement, T_{resreq} is the time required for resource request, $T_{rescomp}$ is the time required for resource allocation and $T_{Dcommstart}$ is the time required for the data communication to be started.

Hence, the total handover latency (T_{HO}) comprising all L2 and L3 delay components can be expressed as follows.

$$
\begin{aligned}
T_{HO} = {} & T_{L2} + T_{L3} + T_{DMM} \\
= {} & T_{A3cond} + T_{HOreq} + T_{HOack} + T_{HOcmd} \\
& + T_{RRC} + T_{RRCcomp} + T_{HOcomp} + T_{linkup} \\
& + T_{IPreg} + T_{CoAconfig} + T_{CoAack} \\
& + T_{LBU} + T_{LBA} + T_{RS} + T_{route} \\
& + T_{resreq} + T_{rescomp} + T_{Dcommstart}.
\end{aligned}
\tag{5}
$$

DMM+A3: In case of successful handover, the total handover latency is T_{HO}. In case of handover failure (at L2), the entire process need to be repeated. Hence, the expected handover latency for DMM+A3 can be computed as:

$$
L_1 = (1 - p) \times T_{HO} + p \times (T_{L2} + T_{HO}).
\tag{6}
$$

DMM with IP Pre-registration + A3: In this handover option, delay associated with IP address configuration is eliminated. In case of successful handover, the handover latency is computed as: $T_{L2} + T_{DMM}$. In case of handover failure, the entire process need to be repeated. Hence, the expected handover latency for this DMM based handover option can be computed as:

$$
L_2 = (1 - p) \times (T_{L2} + T_{DMM}) + p \times (2 \times T_{L2} + T_{DMM}).
\tag{7}
$$

DMM + Semisoft: In this option, delay associated with L2 handover is not present. Accordingly, the total handover latency in case of successful handover is computed as: $T_{L3} + T_{DMM}$. In case of handover failure, an extra T_{L2} component is added with the handover latency. Hence, the expected handover latency can be computed as:

$$
L_3 = (1 - p) \times (T_{L3} + T_{DMM}) + p \times (T_{L2} + T_{L3} + T_{DMM}).
\tag{8}
$$

DMM with IP Preregistration + Semisoft: In this handover option, T_{L2} and T_{L3} are eliminated. Similar to the previous cases, the expected handover latency can be computed as:

$$
L_4 = (1 - p) \times T_{DMM} + p \times (T_{L2} + T_{DMM}).
\tag{9}
$$

4.2   Modelling Handover Packet Loss

Handover packet loss is defined as the expected number of packets lost in downlink during handover duration. Accordingly, expected number of packet loss is computed as:

$$PL^{(\cdot)} = \lambda \times L_{(\cdot)} \times P_d, \qquad (10)$$

here (.) is the indicator of handover option.

5   Results and Discussions

In this section, we evaluate different DMM based handover solutions in terms of handover latency and packet loss. First, we compute handover failure probability (p) for LTE-A $\to$ NR and NR $\to$ LTE-A handovers using system level simulation. Then the value of p is used to compute handover latency and packet loss from Eqs. (6), (7), (8), (9) and (10). Considered parameter values are adopted from [14,16–18]: $T_{A3cond} = 2$ ms, $T_{HOreq} = 2$ ms, $T_{HOack} = 2$ ms, $T_{HOcmd} = 2$ ms, $T_{RRC} = 2$ ms, $T_{RRCcomp} = 2$ ms, $T_{HOcomp} = 2$ ms, $T_{linkup} = 2$ ms, $T_{RLS} = 2$ ms, $T_{IPreg} = 3$ ms, $T_{CoAconfig} = 4$ ms, $T_{CoAack} = 2$ ms, $T_{LBU} = 2$ ms, $T_{LBA} = 2$ ms, $T_{RS} = 1$ ms, $T_{route} = 2$ ms, $T_{resreq} = 2$ ms, $T_{rescomp} = 1$ ms, $T_{Dcommstart} = 1$ ms, $\lambda = 0.7$ packets/ms and $P_d = 64$ Kbytes.

5.1   Computing p

Our simulation scenario consists of one eNB located at (0,0) and 6 gNBs deployed randomly within 500×500 square meter area. The eNB operates at a frequency of 2 GHz and the total bandwidth is set to 5 MHz. The gNBs operate at a frequency of 2.12 GHz and the total bandwidth is set to 10 MHz. 10 UEs are moving randomly within the coverage region of the eNB and gNBs. The velocity of the UE varies from 8 m per second to 17 m per second with a step of 3 m per second. In each iteration, UEs' movement trajectory is determined using a uniform random angle of $\pm\pi/4$ radians. The gain for the direct link between the UE and the serving base station is modeled using Rayleigh fading. Total transmitting powers of LTE-A and NR are set to 46 dBm and 20 dBm respectively. For A3 handover, hysteresis values range from 10 to 13 dB, whereas TTT values range from 160 to 2560 ms. Simulation results have been obtained based on 10000 independent run of the simulator. Handover failure is recorded if radio link failure is detected during the TTT time interval.

Figure 4 depicts the effect of UE velocity on handover failure probability. The result show that handover failure monotonically increases with increasing velocity. This is because, due to high velocity, the RSRP from the serving base station degrades drastically leading to radio link failure during TTT time, which in turn causes handover failure.

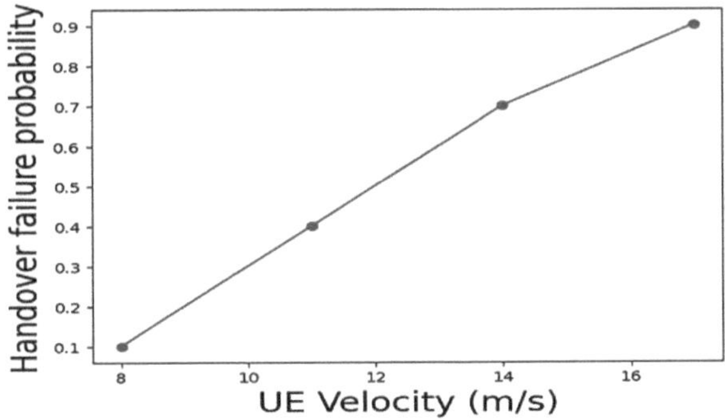

Fig. 4. UE velocity vs. handover failure probability.

5.2 Computing Handover Latency and Handover Packet Loss

Figure 5 depicts the effect of UE velocity on handover latency for all possible DMM based handover options. It may be observed that DMM + A3 exhibits the highest latency among other DMM based handover options. DMM with IP pre-registration + A3 significantly reduces latency by configuring IP address prior to handover. DMM + semisoft further lowers latency by maintaining simultaneous links with current and target access networks and thereby eliminating the L2 handover latency. Finally, DMM with IP pre-registration + semisoft demonstrates the lowest latency among all handover options. This is because, combining pre-assigned IP addresses with the absence of L2 delay minimizes the handover latency significantly. Moreover, it is observed that handover latency monotonically increases with the increasing UE velocity. This is because, higher UE velocity causes higher handover failure which in turn increase handover latency.

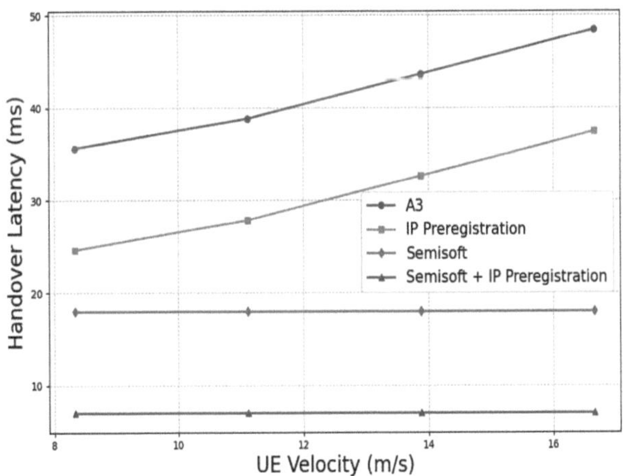

Fig. 5. UE velocity vs. handover latency.

Figure 6 depicts the effect of UE velocity on handover packet loss. Assuming infinite traffic for enhanced mobile broadband (eMBB) services with packet arrival rate of 0.7 packets/ms, the handover packet loss shows an increasing trend with UE velocity. This is because of the increasing trend of handover latency with UE velocity. Result show that DMM + A3 consistently suffers from highest packet loss across all UE velocities. This can be attributed to its sequential approach (L3 followed by L2), which increases the likelihood of packet drops during the extended transition period. DMM with IP pre-registration + A3 outperforms the DMM + A3 option because preregistering IP eliminates the IP configuration delay, leading to fewer disruptions in data transmission. DMM + semisoft achieves further packet loss reduction by eliminating L2 handovers delay. Finally, DMM with IP preregistration + semisoft show the lowest packet loss across all handover options, highlighting its effectiveness towards serving uRLLc. **Using this option, the upper bound on handover packet loss for uRLLc services is 1.54 (attained at UE velocity 16.8 m/s) assuming that the uRLLc users generate small bursts of data packets according to the FTP3 model [15] with the mean arrival rate of 2.12 packets/10 ms.**

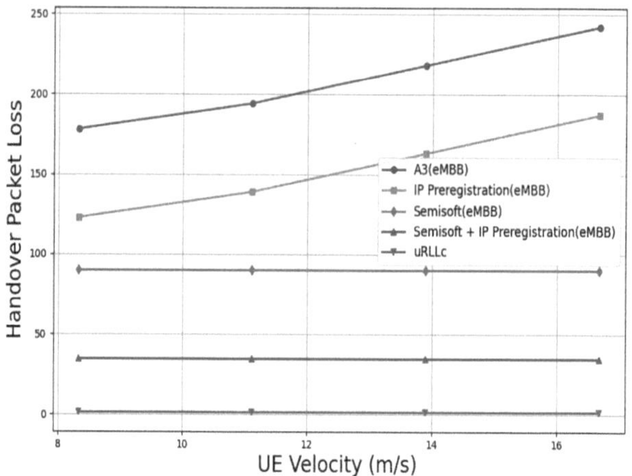

Fig. 6. UE velocity vs. handover packet loss.

It may be observed that DMM with IP preregistration+ A3 demonstrates substantial performance gain (22.73%-30.90% with a mean of 26.80%) as compared to DMM+A3 in terms of handover latency. By eliminating the delay for IP configuration phase, DMM with IP preregistration + A3 significantly reduces handover latency. DMM + semisoft achieve more significant performance gains (49.44% to 62.81% with a mean of 56.15%) by eliminating L2 handover latency.

The most notable performance gains are observed with the DMM with IP preregistration + semisoft approach, consistently achieving

performance gain between **80.34%** and **85.54%** with a mean gain of **82.95%**, making it particularly suitable for uRLLc applications.

6   Conclusion and Future Research Scope

This work presents a semi-analytic evaluation of different DMM-based handover solutions namely DMM + A3, DMM with IP preregistration + A3 handover, DMM + semisoft and DMM with IP preregistration + semisoft, in terms of handover latency and handover packet loss. Our analysis show that DMM with IP preregistration + semisoft can reduce the handover latency up to 7 ms, whereas the minimum L2 handover latency in NR system is known to be 50 ms. DMM with semisoft handover at L2 and IP preregistration at L3 can reduce the handover latency up-to 7 ms and therefore reducing the packet loss per handover upto 1.5 packets for uRLLc services in HetNet scenario. From the analysis we conclude that DMM with IP preregistration + semisoft is the best option for uRLLc among other DMM based handover solutions. Our future research scope includes the following:

- Comparing different software defined networking (SDN) based mobility management techniques with DMM based approaches through analytic and simulation results.
- Measuring ping-pong rates for different DMM based mobility management solutions.
- Developing a new DMM based cross-layer mobility management protocol to minimize handover latency in heterogeneous network scenario.

Acknowledgement. We would like to thank 5G lab of HCLTech (India) for taking part in extensive discussion and pointing out the criticality of uRLLc services. Krati Rastogi would like to thank Souvik Deb (PhD student, ISI) for his suggestions towards developing the mathematical framework.

References

1. Ali, R., Zikria, Y.B., Bashir, A.K., Garg, S., Kim, H.S.: URLLC for 5G and beyond: requirements, enabling incumbent technologies and network intelligence. IEEE Access **9**, 67064–67095 (2021). https://doi.org/10.1109/ACCESS.2021.3073806
2. Park, H.-S., Lee, Y., Kim, T.-J., Kim, B.-C., Lee, J.-Y.: Handover mechanism in NR for ultra-reliable low-latency communications. IEEE Netw. **32**(2), 41–47 (2018). https://doi.org/10.1109/MNET.2018.1700235.
3. Hong, G., Yang, B., Su, W., Wen, Q., Hou, X., Li, H.: Decentralized vehicular mobility management study for 5g identifier/locator split networks. Wirel. Commun. Mob. Comput. 1–14 (2022). https://doi.org/10.1155/2022/6300715.
4. Ullah, Y., Roslee, M.B., Mitani, S.M., Khan, S.A., Jusoh, M.H.: A survey on handover and mobility management in 5g HetNets: current state. Challenges Future Dir. Sensors **23**(5081), (2023). https://doi.org/10.3390/s23115081.

5. Giust, F., Bernardos, C., de la Oliva, A.: Analytic evaluation and experimental validation of a network-based IPv6 distributed mobility management solution. IEEE Trans. Mob. Comput. **13**(11), 2484–2497 (2014). https://doi.org/10.1109/TMC.2014.2307304

6. Karmakar, R., Kaddoum, G., Chattopadhyay, S.: Mobility management in 5g and beyond: a novel smart handover with adaptive time-to-trigger and hysteresis margin. IEEE Trans. Mob. Comput. **22**(10), 5995–6010 (2023). https://doi.org/10.1109/TMC.2022.3188212.

7. Ghosh, S.K., Ghosh, S.C.: Analyzing handover performances of mobility management protocols in ultra-dense networks. J. Netw. Syst. Manage. **28**(4), 1427–1452 (2020). https://doi.org/10.1007/s10922-020-09544-x

8. Mahenthiran, M.P., Muruganadam, D.: Handoff performance analysis of PMIPv6-based distributed mobility management protocol-urban scenario. Concurrency Comput. Pract. Exper. **36**(11), e8010 (2024). https://doi.org/10.1002/cpe.8010

9. Lee, H., Son, H., Lee, S.: Semisoft handover gain analysis over OFDM-based broadband systems. IEEE Trans. Veh. Technol. **58**(3), 1443–1453 (2009). https://doi.org/10.1109/TVT.2008.927041

10. Khan, A., Ahmad, S., Ali, I., Hayat, B., Tian, Y., Liu, W.: Dynamic mobility and handover management in software-defined networking-based fifth-generation heterogeneous networks. Int. J. Network Mgmt. e2268 (2024). https://doi.org/10.1002/nem.2268.

11. Bellaj, M., Naja, N., Jamali, A.: Distributed mobility management support for low-latency data delivery in named data networking for UAVs. Future Internet. **16**(2), 57 (2024). https://doi.org/10.3390/fi16020057

12. Park, H.-S., Lee, Y., Kim, T.-J., Kim, B.-C., Lee, J.-Y.: ZEUS: handover algorithm for 5g to achieve zero handover failure. ETRI J. **44**, 361–378 (2022). https://doi.org/10.4218/etrij.2020-0356

13. Deb, S., Rathod, M., Balamurugan, R., Ghosh, S.K., Singh, R.K., Sanyal, S.: Performance evaluation of conditional handover in 5G systems under fading scenario (2024). arXiv preprint arXiv:2403.04379

14. Ouali, K., Kassar, M., Sethom, K.: Handover performance analysis for managing D2D mobility in 5g cellular networks. IET Commun. **12**(15), 1925–1936 (2018). https://doi.org/10.1049/iet-com.2018.5561

15. Korrai, P., Lagunas, E., Sharma, S.K., Chatzinotas, S., Bandi, A., Ottersten, B.: A RAN resource slicing mechanism for multiplexing of eMBB and URLLC services in OFDMA based 5g wireless networks. IEEE Access **8**, 45674–45688 (2020)

16. Ouali, K., Kassar, M., Sethom, K.: Handover performance analysis for managing D2D mobility in 5G cellular networks. IET Commun. **12**(12), 1925–1936 (2018). https://doi.org/10.1049/iet-com.2018.5561

17. Ali-Ahmad, H., Ouzzif, M., Bertin, P., Lagrange, X.: Performance analysis on network-based distributed mobility management. Wireless Pers. Commun. **74**(4), 1245–1263 (2014). https://doi.org/10.1007/s11277-013-1575-0

18. Han, D., Shin, S., Cho, H., Chung, J.-M., Ok, D., Hwang, I.: Measurement and stochastic modeling of handover delay and interruption time of smartphone real-time applications on LTE networks. IEEE Commun. Mag. **53**(3), 173–181 (2015). https://doi.org/10.1109/MCOM.2015.7060501

An Anomaly Causal Analysis Method in Complex 5G Network Environments

Zhijian Xu, Zhiwei Zhang$^{(\boxtimes)}$, Guiyuan Tang, Yingyu Chen, and Yuzi Wang

School of Computer Science and Technology, Xidian University, Xi'an 710071, China
{xuzhijian,tanggy}@stu.xidian.edu.cn, zwzhang@xidian.edu.cn

Abstract. The complexity of services and multi-layered data in 5G networks is severely affecting the accuracy of existing anomaly detection techniques in identifying the root causes of anomalies. In this paper, we propose an anomaly analysis method based on Bayesian causal model, aiming at identifying root causes by uncovering causal links across multiple layers. Experimental results demonstrate that the proposed method outperforms traditional machine learning methods across multiple evaluation metrics, which makes it effective for anomaly detection in 5G network environments.

Keywords: Cause Analysis · 5G Networks · Anomaly Detection · Intelligent network operation

1 Introduction

Anomaly detection plays a critical role in ensuring the performance and managing anomalies in 5G networks, particularly in application domains such as autonomous driving, cloud computing, and big data [9]. It effectively prevents malicious intrusions and system failures, ensuring the continuity and security of key services [2,6,8].

In complex 5G networks, anomalies or attacks are not confined to a single layer but often exhibit causal dependencies across multiple network layers. However, most existing machine learning (ML)-based anomaly detection methods rely on single-layer or single-source data correlation analysis [5,10], which fails to fully capture the true causal chains between features and anomalies, thus limiting detection accuracy [3,4]. Causal analysis provides deeper insights into event chains, enabling more accurate diagnosis of network anomalies. However, the inherent complexity of 5G networks and the multi-source nature of data present significant challenges for applying causal analysis to such environments [7].

We propose a multi-source causal model for anomaly analysis. The model effectively explores the causal chains between multi-source features and anomalies, accurately identifying the root causes of anomalies. Our main contributions are as follows:

© ICST Institute for Computer Sciences, Social Informatics and Telecommunications Engineering 2026
Published by Springer Nature Switzerland AG 2026. All Rights Reserved
S. Li et al. (Eds.): BROADNETS 2024, LNICST 674, pp. 177–182, 2026.
https://doi.org/10.1007/978-3-032-14350-1_13

– We develop a Bayesian causal model to address the complexity of multi-source 5G network environments.
– We overcome the limitations of traditional ML methods by leveraging causal analysis to reveal the true causal relationships between multi-source features and anomalies.

2 Problem Formulation

We consider a real-world 5G network road test scenario, where data is collected from multiple layers of the 5G network, including network performance metrics, signal strength, and spatial positioning. The main anomaly observed in this setting is a slowdown in user downlink speed [9].

In the mathematical formulation, the feature variables representing network state observations are denoted by X_i, while the root causes of anomalies are represented by R_i. The sets $\mathcal{X}$ and $\mathcal{R}$ refer to the collections of random variables for features and root causes, respectively. These realizations, $x_i \in \mathbb{R}^d$ and $r_i \in \{0,1\}^m$, represent the feature values and the anomaly causes, where d is the feature dimension and m is the dimension of the root causes. In our anomaly detection framework, the system state is described by a set of observable variables $X = \{X_1, X_2, \ldots, X_d\}$, where each X_i is a time-series variable with a temporal dimension T. When the system encounters faults due to one or more anomalies from the set $R = \{R_1, R_2, \ldots, R_m\}$, a subset of X exhibits abnormal behavior. Our primary goal is to infer the root causes of these anomalies $r = \{r_1, r_2, \ldots, r_m\}$, given the observed features $x = \{x_1, x_2, \ldots, x_d\}$.

To improve the model's performance, feature engineering is conducted on the dataset. In analyzing the correlation matrix heatmap of the training data, the Spearman rank correlation coefficient is employed to handle the correlations among ordinal variables [1]. As shown in Fig. 1, the analysis reveals a high positive correlation among features within the same group (e.g., $Feature_Y$ and $Feature_X$). Based on these observations, we combine these grouped features with spatial features to create distance features ($Feature_{dis}$) and interference features ($Feature_{if}$). This transformation mitigates model overfitting and reduces redundancy in the training data, ensuring better generalization performance.

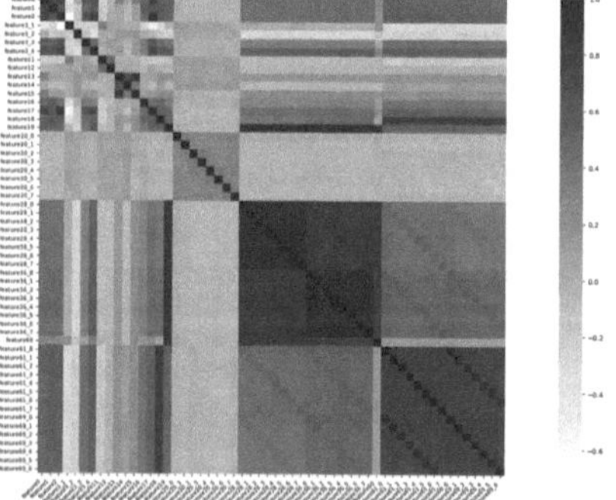

Fig. 1.   Spearman   Correlation Heatmap of Features

3   Proposed Solution

The primary objective of the model design is to handle the complexity of multi-source data in 5G environments. The process begins with feature engineering as described in Sect. 2, where multi-source 5G data is preprocessed. Causal structure learning is then performed using intervention techniques for each identified anomaly cause. After constructing the Bayesian network, the model is trained and validated using probabilistic relationships. Finally, anomaly prediction and causal effect estimation are conducted to assess the model's performance.

Algorithm 1 presents the detailed steps for constructing a Bayesian causal model tailored for the AIOps system. This algorithm takes raw 5G network data as input and outputs detected anomalies and their root causes. The feature engineering process occurs in lines 2–3, where raw data is transformed into structured data, and $root_n$ causes are extracted, which $n = 3$. Line 2 specifically focuses on combining features to reduce overfitting and data redundancy. In lines 5–7, for each root cause, the algorithm applies do-intervention techniques to learn causal structures [11], which form the foundation for constructing the Bayesian network. The dataset is then split into 80:20 ratios for training and validation in line 9. In line 10, the Conditional Probability Table (CPT) is fitted, establishing the probabilistic relationships between features and anomalies. Line 11 predicts anomalies on the test data, while line 12 estimates causal effects. The model's performance is evaluated using the metrics defined in Sect. 4.

Algorithm 1. Bayesian Causal Model for 5G Anomaly Detection

1: **Begin:**
2: data, roots ← featureEngineering(raw_data)   ▷ Extract structured data and root causes
3: roots ← [root1, root2, root3]
4: processedData ← preprocess(data)
5: **for** each root ∈ roots **do**
6:       model ← learn(processedData, root, do-intervention)
7:       bn ← BayesianNetwork(model)
8: **end for**
9: train, test ← split(processedData, 0.8)
10: CPT ← fit(train, bn)
11: predictions ← predict(test, CPT)
12: effect ← estimate(model)
13: **End**

The implementation of the Bayesian causal model involves the following four major steps:

Step 1. Structure Learning: The NoTears algorithm is employed to construct the model structure from the preprocessed data. This algorithm optimizes the learning process to identify causal relationships between network attributes, providing a robust foundation for subsequent inference.

Step 2. Structure Review: As structure learning is an NP-hard problem, adjustments are made through do-intervention before evaluating the model with test data. These adjustments include setting edge weight thresholds and modifying causal paths by adding, deleting, or reversing edges to ensure path accuracy. For example, Fig. 2 areveals complex structural relationships with certain root nodes displaying reverse causality. After applying do-intervention adjustments, the final causal graph is shown in Fig. 2 b.

Step 3. Likelihood Estimation: During model construction, data is first discretized to reduce the complexity of categorical combinations. CPTs are then built for each attribute state. As illustrated in Table 1, the first column displays $P\{r_2 = 0|f_1\} = 0.91964$, $P\{r_2 = 1|f_1\} = 0.08035$,which $f_1 = \{feature_{13} = 0, feature_{15} = 0, feature_{X,if} = 0, feature_{Y,id} = 0, feature_{Y,mean} = 0\}$. These probabilities reflect the direct causes of the anomaly. The CPTs for other attributes follow a similar structure and are used for predictions on test data.

Step 4. Prediction and Inference: The trained model is applied to predict anomalies, and the performance is evaluated using the metrics defined in Sect. 4. The results, summarized in Table 2, demonstrate the effectiveness of the proposed model across various scenarios.

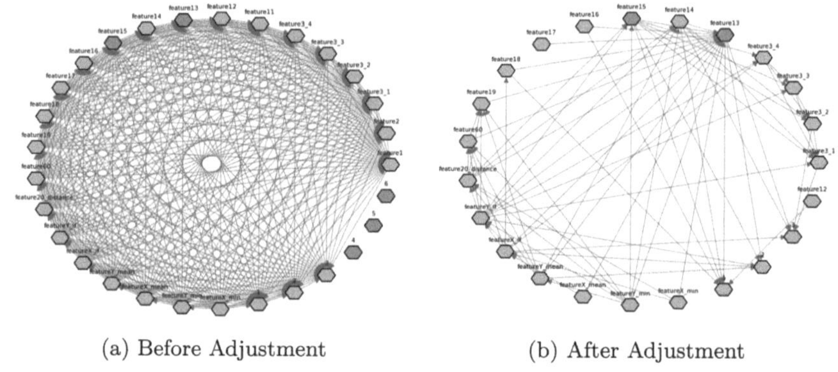

(a) Before Adjustment   (b) After Adjustment

Fig. 2. 5G Network Structural Relationships.

4   Evaluation

All experiments were conducted on a Windows 11 machine with an Intel 13th Gen Core i9-13900K CPU and NVIDIA GeForce RTX 4090 GPU, using Jupyter as the development environment for model implementation and evaluation.

The performance of the proposed model is evaluated using standard metrics, including Accuracy, Precision, Recall, and F1-score. These metrics are defined as follows:

Table 1. CPT for Anomaly Root

$feature_{13}$	0	0	0	0	...1	1	1	1
$feature_{15}$	0	0	0	0	...1	1	1	1
$feature_{X,if}$	0	0	0	0	...1	1	1	1
$feature_{Y,if}$	0	0	1	1	...0	0	1	1
$feature_{Y,mean}$	0	1	0	1	...0	1	0	1
$P(r_2 = 0)$	0.91964	0.97142	0.9	0.98550	...0.99609	0.99411	0.88235	0.99404
$P(r_2 = 1)$	0.08035	0.02857	0.1	0.01449	...0.00390	0.00588	0.11764	0.00595

- **Accuracy**: The ratio of correctly predicted instances to the total instances.
- **Precision**: The proportion of true positives among all predicted positives, indicating the accuracy of positive predictions.
- **Recall**: The proportion of true positives among all actual positives, measuring the ability to identify relevant cases.
- **F1-score**: The harmonic mean of Precision and Recall.

Table 2 presents the performance comparison of various algorithms. The results show that KNN achieved an accuracy of 91.79%, and SVM 95.31%, both struggling with small anomaly classes due to sensitivity to data imbalance. MLP performed poorly, with an accuracy of only 69.68%, likely due to its limited ability to model complex data.

Table 2. Algorithm Performance on 5G Dataset

Algorithm	Accuracy	Precision	F1-score
Ours	**97.724%**	**97.679%**	**97.690%**
Random Forest	96.482%	94.294%	94.904%
CatBoost	97.487%	96.973%	96.307%
KNN(k=5)	91.792%	84.925%	86.597%
SVM	95.310%	90.881%	90.470%
MLP	69.682%	57.641%	66.698%

Random Forest reached an accuracy of 96.48%, while CatBoost performed better at 97.49%, especially excelling in handling non-linear feature relationships. The proposed Bayesian causal model outperformed all others, achieving an accuracy of 97.72%, with both precision and F1-score exceeding 97%.

5   Conclusion

This paper presents a Bayesian causal model for anomaly detection in 5G networks. Experimental results demonstrate that the model performs exceptionally well across all metrics, significantly improving the accuracy and efficiency of anomaly diagnosis. Unlike traditional correlation-based methods, this approach uncovers true causal relationships between feature changes and anomalies. The model shows strong innovation and adaptability in causal inference and performance optimization. Future work will focus on reducing computational complexity and extending the model to handle unknown anomalies, improving robustness and scalability.

Acknowledgments. This work was supported by the National Key R & D Program of China (Grant No. 2023YFB3107500), the Major Research plan of the National Natural Science Foundation of China (Grant No. 92267204), Shandong Provincial Natural Science Foundation (ZR2021LZH006).

References

1. Chen, H., Covert, I.C., Lundberg, S.M., Lee, S.I.: Algorithms to estimate shapley value feature attributions. Nat. Mach. Intell. **5**(6), 590–601 (2023)
2. Cheng, Z., et al.: Kairos: Practical intrusion detection and investigation using whole-system provenance. In: 2024 IEEE Symposium on Security and Privacy (SP), pp. 3533–3551 (2024). https://doi.org/10.1109/SP54263.2024.00005
3. Fu, C., Li, Q., Xu, K., Wu, J.: Point cloud analysis for ml-based malicious traffic detection: Reducing majorities of false positive alarms. In: CCS, pp. 1005–1019 (2023)
4. Horchulhack, P., Viegas, E.K., Santin, A.O.: Toward feasible machine learning model updates in network-based intrusion detection. Comput. Netw. **202**, 108618 (2022)
5. Jing, Y., Zhang, Z., Hu, T., et al.: Sustainable intrusion detection with new attack classification in private clouds. J. Netw. Netw. Appl. **1**(4), 150–159 (2022). https://doi.org/10.33969/J-NaNA.2021.010402
6. Rahman, A.u., et al.: Network anomaly detection in 5g networks. MMEP **9**(2) (2022)
7. Vowels, M.J., Camgoz, N.C., Bowden, R.: D'ya like dags? a survey on structure learning and causal discovery. ACM Comput. Surv. **55**(4), 1–36 (2022)
8. Xu, Z., Zhang, Z., Tang, G., Shi, Z., Shen, Y., Xi, N.: Multidimensional intrinsic identity construction and dynamic seamless authentication schemes in iot environments. In: Algorithms and Architectures for Parallel Processing, pp. 134–153. , Springer Nature Singapore, Singapore (2025). https://doi.org/10.1007/978-981-96-1545-2_9
9. Zhang, T., et al.: Root cause analysis for wireless network fault localization. In: ICASSP, pp. 9301–9305 (2022)
10. Zhang, Z., Tang, G., Ren, B., Li, H., Shen, Y.: Tv-ads: a smarter attack detection scheme based on traffic visualization of wireless network event cell. J. Internet Technol. **25**(2), 301–311 (2024)
11. Zheng, X., Dan, C., Aragam, B., Ravikumar, P., Xing, E.: Learning sparse nonparametric dags. In: AISTATS, pp. 3414–3425 (2020)

Pixel-Level Privacy Preserving in DICOM Anonymisation

Jinxiang Dai[✉] and Hongping Li

School of Computer Science and Engineering, University of Electronic Science and
Technology of China, Chengdu 611731, China
jinxiang_dai_ue@163.com

Abstract. DICOM (Digital Imaging and Communications in Medicine)
is a standard format for medical images, often containing sensitive
patient information. To protect patient privacy, anonymizing DICOM
files before sharing or storage is essential, this work introduces a novel
DICOM medical image anonymization approach that employs Optical
Character Recognition (OCR) to identify personally identifiable information (PII) within both tags and textual content embedded within
images. By employing Named Entity Recognition (NER) techniques, the
system accurately detects PII in textual data. The proposed method
operates independently of metadata, enabling the anonymization of sensitive information in both tags and pixel-level image content. This approach can help efficient and automated anonymization of medical image
files, significantly enhancing patient privacy.

Keywords: DICOM · Healthcare Data Analysis · Privacy enhancing

1 Introduction

Digital Imaging and Communications in Medicine (DICOM) is a widely used
international standard in the medical field. DICOM-compliant medical images
contain not only patients' medical health information but also their personal
privacy information [3]. During the transmission and storage of medical images,
failure to anonymize the data can lead to privacy breaches, resulting in significant economic losses [2]. Additionally, regulations such as the Health Insurance
Portability and Accountability Act (HIPAA) and the General Data Protection
Regulation (GDPR) explicitly mandate the protection of personal health information [11].

In the research of privacy protection for medical imaging, anonymization is
a commonly used method. However, during the process of anonymizing medical images, there arises the issue of privacy information handling choices [9].
Depending on the specific application scenarios of the images, different types
of privacy information may need to be selectively processed. Furthermore, in
cases where PII is embedded in the images, the identification, localization, and
anonymization of PII present significant challenges in the field of research.

S. Li et al. (Eds.): BROADNETS 2024, LNICST 674, pp. 183–192, 2026.
https://doi.org/10.1007/978-3-032-14350-1_14

To protect personal privacy information in medical imaging, this work develops a comprehensive and efficient medical image anonymization system [1]. It supports the anonymization of both DICOM format images and pixel-based images. Compared to traditional methods and tools, this research offers the following features:

1. Adopting deep learning methods to achieve efficient and high-precision image text recognition, with enhanced accuracy and robustness through advanced image preprocessing techniques.
2. A general-purpose PII detection method is proposed, based on Named Entity Recognition (NER) technology for the identification and localization of PII. It is applicable to the anonymization of pure image-based medical images in pixcel level and does not rely on any metadata references.
3. Providing comprehensive anonymization, capable of handling PII in both DICOM format medical images and pure image-based medical images.

By utilizing appropriate methods, healthcare organizations can effectively anonymize DICOM files, protecting patient privacy while enabling data sharing and research.

2   Related Works

2.1   DICOM Privacy and Anonymization

Since the release of the DICOM standard, concerns over privacy breaches have gained significant attention. Researchers have begun to focus on the desensitization of PII within DICOM metadata and have developed numerous tools for modifying PII in DICOM files [6,10].

While existing tools are effective in anonymizing metadata (tags), they fall short in handling PII embedded in pixel data. To address this, [8] modified an open-source DICOM anonymization tool to comply with DICOM Supplement 142 standards and introduced a threshold-redaction algorithm to tackle the challenges of removing embedded textual PHI from low-resolution medical images. This approach supplements or replaces OCR technology. Although the prototype demonstrates strong performance in anonymizing radiotherapy EMRs, it faces limitations in OCR technology and software integration, particularly when dealing with low-resolution images and coordinating multiple software systems.

In another approach, [7] developed a CNN-based pipeline for automatic de-identification of sensitive information in ultrasound medical images, achieving a de-identification rate of 89.2%. While this method effectively supports secure image sharing, misidentification still occurs with low-resolution text and complex backgrounds.

To further improve efficiency in large image datasets, Macdonal *et al.* proposed combining metadata de-identification with targeted OCR, successfully removing PHI from DICOM images with high accuracy and low false detection rates [5] . However, their method's reliance on full processing and a small whitelist strategy for metadata de-identification can lead to misidentification, and the dependency on metadata for pixel-based PHI detection limits its applicability to images without metadata.

2.2   Literature Review and Research Innovation

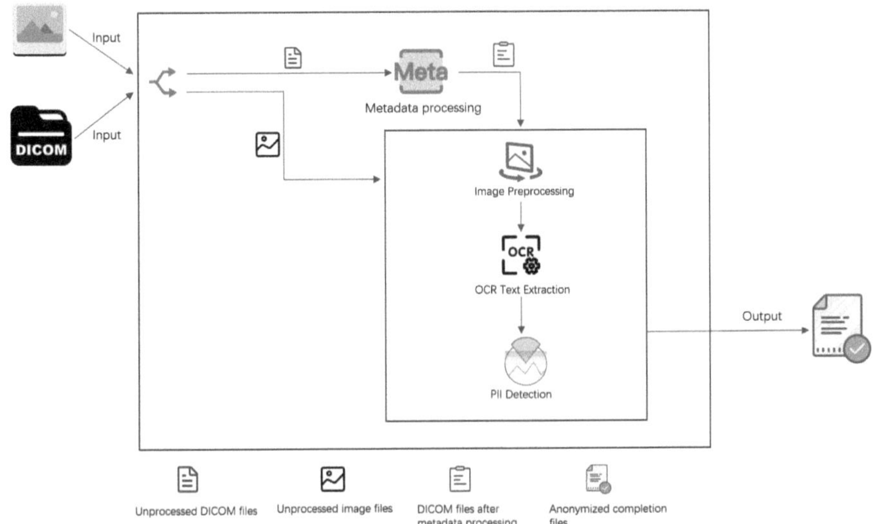

Fig. 1. System framework diagram.

Previous studies on metadata de-identification either apply full anonymization or follow specific standards, lacking flexibility. Additionally, in pixel-based de-identification, challenges arise in recognizing PII in low-quality images, and PII detection in pixel data often depends on metadata support.

To address the issues identified in previous studies, this work proposes a novel medical image anonymization method. For metadata de-identification, the proposed approach adopts the minimization principle for privacy data selection, enabling flexible and effective anonymization by expanding the data scope based on different anonymization goals. In pixel-based anonymization, a series of image pre-processing techniques are introduced to enhance recognition accuracy in low-quality images. Additionally, NER technology is employed to detect PII without relying on metadata, allowing the method to be applied to images that lack metadata.

3   Method and Experiment

This work involves the design and implementation of a multi-format medical image anonymization solution that supports input files in both DICOM standard format and image formats. The anonymization process is divided into phases: Phase One focuses on processing the PII in the metadata header of DICOM files, while Phase Two addresses the anonymization of image information. In Phase Two, we employ a text recognition model with higher accuracy and enhance the image resolution. By NER technology, we perform PII detection on the identified text, achieving efficient, precise, and comprehensive anonymization. The system framework is illustrated in Fig. 1.

Figure 2 presents the workflow of the present study. The DICOM medical image anonymization solution is as follows: Input the DICOM file or pixel image file to be processed. Depending on the format of the input file, different processing methods will be applied: 1. For DICOM format files, first address the PII in the DICOM metadata, followed by the PII in the pixel data; 2. For pixel image files, perform pixel-level anonymization directly. Finally, generate the anonymized output file.

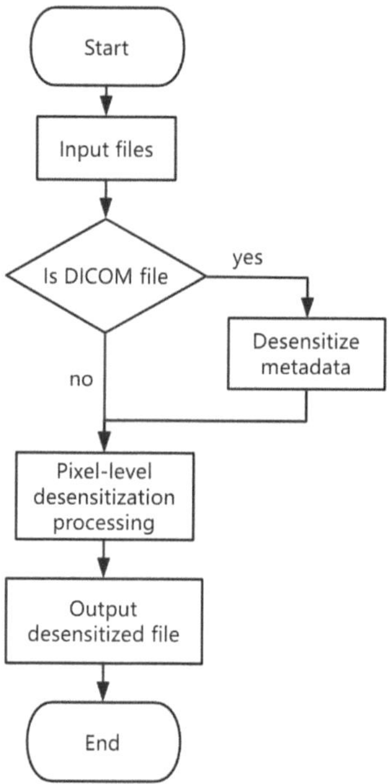

Fig. 2. Working flow.

In this processing workflow, the key components are the anonymization of metadata PII and pixel-level anonymization. The following sections will provide a detailed introduction to each of these aspects.

3.1   Anonymization of Metadata PII

DICOM format files generally adhere to the DICOM standard for organizing data within the file. A DICOM file consists of File Metadata and the Dataset. The File Metadata contains descriptive information about the DICOM file and its related metadata, while the Dataset contains all information and data related to the medical images. This section is organized in a label-value pair format, represented by "data elements." The dataset consists of data elements, which include five components: label, value representation, value length, and value field.

When processing PII in the metadata, the data is retrieved using the corresponding label and handled in a format that adheres to the DICOM standard. This work introduces the Privacy Data Minimization Principle, which defines a core set of privacy data to ensure the maximum anonymization of patient identity. Based on this core set, additional privacy data can be selected for de-identification depending on the specific application purpose. The core privacy data consists of four components: patient, study, series, and image, including clear PII such as patient name, ID, birth date, gender, phone number, and age. In practice, additional anonymization is applied to information such as image acquisition time and institution name, which may also contain personal data.

3.2   Pixel-Level Anonymization

Image Preprocessing In this processing stage, the image undergoes preprocessing to enhance OCR accuracy. The preprocessing steps include image resolution enhancement, noise reduction, and edge handling.

1) **Image Resolution Enhancement** Image resolution is crucial for the efficiency and accuracy of OCR text recognition. Low-resolution images can lead to issues such as missed or incorrect text, while improving image resolution can significantly reduce such errors. In this work, we leverage OpenCVs image enhancement functionality to improve image resolution using Super-Resolution (SR) techniques, thereby enhancing the performance of OCR recognition.

   OpenCV provides several image processing algorithms, with convolutional neural networks (CNNs) being particularly effective for enhancing image details. FSRCNN (Fast Super-Resolution Convolutional Neural Network), as an efficient super-resolution model, directly processes low-resolution images to generate high-resolution outputs, significantly improving image clarity and information content. FSRCNN not only enhances visual quality but also improves the accuracy of OCR recognition, ensuring more precise text extraction in subsequent processing.

   For the selection of the super-resolution model, we compared EDSR, SRCNN, and FSRCNN. Ultimately, FSRCNN was chosen due to its balance of high processing efficiency and excellent image reconstruction quality, making it particularly suitable for OCR tasks in medical image processing.

2) **Noise Reduction** Medical images are typically grayscale, where reducing image noise improves text-background contrast, facilitating more accurate

OCR recognition. We use Gaussian filtering to diminish noise while preserving text edges.

3) **Edge Handling** In medical images, text edges may overlap with the image boundaries, causing OCR errors. Adding a border around the image mitigates this issue by preventing text edges from aligning with image boundaries.

OCR Text Extraction. After the preprocessing stage, the enhanced image is used as input for the OCR process. In this work, we selected the PP-OCRv3 recognition system for text extraction. PP-OCR is an ultra-lightweight OCR system that employs techniques such as Collaborative Mutual Learning (CML), CopyPaste, Lightweight CPU Network (PP-LCNet), Unified-Deep Mutual Learning (U-DML), and Enhanced CTCLoss to achieve efficient text detection and recognition [4]. During operation, the image is input into the model, which extracts all identifiable text information along with its positional data.

PII Detection. Formatted PII can be easily and quickly detected using regular expressions. However, non-formatted information, such as names and organization names, cannot be identified through simple expression matching. To enable the detection of PII even in the absence of metadata, this work introduces NER technology for identifying unstructured information, utilizing the Presidio framework. Presidio is an open-source tool developed by Microsoft for recognizing and protecting PII. It integrates multiple technologies and models for efficient PII identification and processing.

Anonymization of Identified PII. After identifying the PII and its location in the image, anonymization is applied to all detected PII. Since the PII exists in pixel form within the image, direct masking of the text areas containing PII is considered. This masking modifies the pixel information, ensuring that the anonymization is irreversible. Additionally, due to image enhancement during preprocessing, the size of the enhanced image may differ from the original. Therefore, the PII coordinates need to be mapped accordingly. Algorithm 1 outlines the coordinate transformation process.

After obtaining the correct coordinates, the PII areas in the original image are masked, and the anonymized image is generated. The resulting image can either be saved as a new file or the anonymized data can be written back into the DICOM file.

Algorithm 1. Coordinate Transformation Algorithm

Data: coordinates array *coords*, scale factor f, and border width w
Result: transformed coordinate $(x_1, y_1), (x_2, y_2)$

1 **for** $i \leftarrow 1$ **to** 2 **do**
2   **if** $i = 2$ **then**
3 | $x_i \leftarrow (coords[i].x/f) - w$ $y_i \leftarrow (coords[i].y/f + f - 1) - w$
4   **end**
5   **else**
6 | $x_i \leftarrow (coords[i].x/f) - w$ $y_i \leftarrow (coords[i].y/f) - w$
7   **end**
8 **end**

3.3 Results

In the experimental validation phase of this system, the dataset selected is the Pseudo-PHI-DICOM-Data from The Cancer Imaging Archive (TCIA), a large archive of medical images that provides access to a variety of imaging datasets for research purposes. This specific dataset contains DICOM files with personally identifiable information (PII) embedded within the image data, making it suitable for validating the processing of both metadata and pixel image components of the system.

There are two types of input for the experiments: one is DICOM format files that embed PII in the image data, and the other is medical images exported from MicroDicom software. Figure 3 shows a comparison of the anonymization process for pixel image formats, with the left side displaying the image before processing and the right side showing the image after anonymization. The comparison

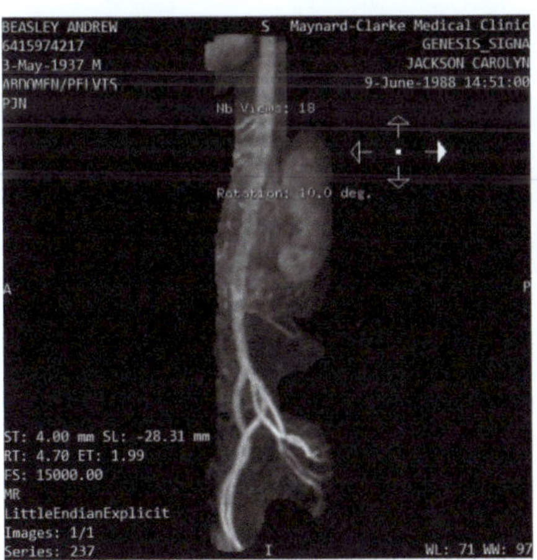

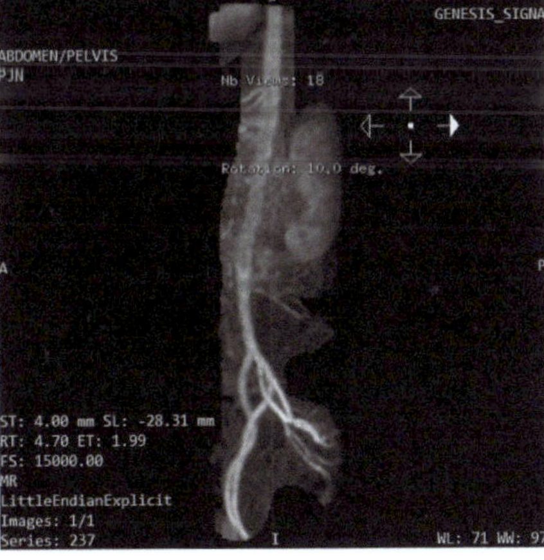

Fig. 3. Comparison of the anonymization process for pixel image formats.

highlights that PII information such as the patients name, ID, date of birth, and gender has been anonymized. Additionally, the institution name, names of relevant doctors, and the date of capture have also been anonymized, while the anonymization process does not affect the medically relevant areas of the images.

Figure 4 illustrates the anonymization process for DICOM format files. The comparison shows that during the anonymization, both the personally identifiable information (PII) in the metadata and the PII embedded within the images are effectively anonymized.

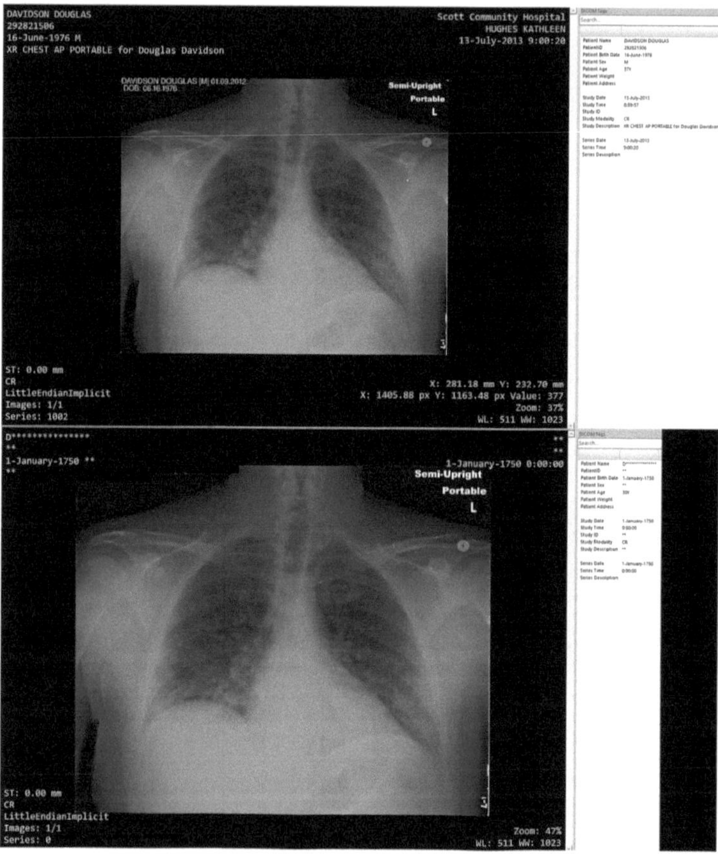

Fig. 4. DICOM file anonymization comparison. The image is opened using MicroDicom software, which simultaneously displays both the image and the associated metadata. The upper portion shows the interface before anonymization, while the lower portion shows the interface after anonymization.

4   Conclusion

To achieve the de-identification of medical images under the DICOM standard, this work proposes a comprehensive DICOM format medical image de-identification solution. This solution accepts various formats, including DICOM and pixel images, enabling the anonymization of PII in both the metadata and the images of DICOM files. The approach demonstrates excellent de-identification effectiveness on the Pseudo-PHI-DICOM-Data dataset. Developed using open-source tools, it performs well, is easy to deploy, and possesses significant industrial value.

However, the solution has limitations: PII recognition relies heavily on the dataset of the NER model, leading to lower generalizability, and it lacks the capability to intelligently select different PII for anonymization based on specific use cases.

In summary, the proposed DICOM medical image de-identification solution not only effectively protects patient privacy but also provides a solid foundation for the secure sharing of medical image data. Despite certain limitations, its strong performance and ease of deployment highlight its significant potential for industrial applications, making it a promising tool for advancing healthcare informatics.

References

1. Hafsa, L., Kozeta, S.: Preserving privacy in medical images while still enabling ai-driven research: a comprehensive review. In: 2024 13th Mediterranean Conference on Embedded Computing (MECO), pp. 1–5. IEEE (2024)
2. Jesus, R., Frias, J., Gouveia, P., Santinha, J., Silva, L.B., Costa, C.: In: Dicom gateway anonymizer: a cloud architecture for a scalable research pacs, In: 2024 IEEE Symposium on Computers and Communications (ISCC), pp. 1–6. IEEE (2024)
3. Larobina, M.: Thirty years of the dicom standard. Tomography **9**(5), 1829–1838 (2023). https://doi.org/10.3390/tomography9050145
4. Li, C., et al.: Pp-ocrv3: more attempts for the improvement of ultra lightweight OCR system. arXiv preprint arXiv:2206.03001 (2022)
5. Macdonald, J.A., et al.: A method for efficient de-identification of DICOM metadata and burned-in pixel text. J. Imaging Inf. Med., 1–7 (2024)
6. Mason, D.: Su-e-t-33: pydicom: an open source dicom library. Med. Phys. **38**(6Part10), 3493–3493 (2011)
7. Monteiro, E., Costa, C., Oliveira, J.L.: A de-identification pipeline for ultrasound medical images in dicom format. J. Med. Syst. **41**(5), 89 (2017)
8. Newhauser, W., et al.: Anonymization of dicom electronic medical records for radiation therapy. Comput. Biol. Med. **53**, 134–140 (2014). https://doi.org/10.1016/j.compbiomed.2014.07.010, https://www.sciencedirect.com/science/article/pii/S0010482514001759
9. Rempe, M., Heine, L., Seibold, C., Hörst, F., Kleesiek, J.: De-identification of medical imaging data: a comprehensive tool for ensuring patient privacy. arXiv preprint arXiv:2410.12402 (2024)

10. Rodríguez González, D., et al.: An open source toolkit for medical imaging de-identification. European Radiol. **20**, 1896–1904 (2010)
11. Sun, P., Wan, Y., Wu, Z., Fang, Z., Li, Q.: A survey on privacy and security issues in IOT-based environments: technologies, protection measures and future directions. Comput. Secur. **148**, 104097 (2025)

Author Index

MIX
Papier aus verantwortungsvollen Quellen
Paper from responsible sources
FSC® C105338

If you have any concerns about our products,
you can contact us on
ProductSafety@springernature.com

In case Publisher is established outside the EU,
the EU authorized representative is:
Springer Nature Customer Service Center GmbH
Europaplatz 3, 69115 Heidelberg, Germany

Printed by Libri Plureos GmbH
in Hamburg, Germany